Strategic Marketing: Planning and Control

Strategic Marketing:
Planning and Control

Third edition

Graeme Drummond

John Ensor

Ruth Ashford

AMSTERDAM • BOSTON • HEIDELBERG • LONDON • NEW YORK • OXFORD
PARIS • SAN DIEGO • SAN FRANCISCO • SINGAPORE • SYDNEY • TOKYO
Butterworth-Heinemann is an imprint of Elsevier

Butterworth-Heinemann is an imprint of Elsevier
Linacre House, Jordan Hill, Oxford OX2 8DP
30 Corporate Drive, Suite 400, Burlington, MA 01803, USA

First edition 1999
Second edition 2001

Copyright © 1999, 2001, 2008
Published by Elsevier Ltd. All rights reserved.

British Library Cataloguing-in-Publication Data
A catalogue record for this book is available from the British Library

Library of Congress Cataloging-in-Publication Data
A catalog record for this book is available from the Library of Congress

ISBN: 978-07506-8271-8

For information on all Butterworth-Heinemann publications
visit our web site at books.elsevier.com

Typeset by Charon Tec Ltd (A Macmillan Company), Chennai, India
www.charontec.com

Printed and bound in Slovenia

Working together to grow
libraries in developing countries

www.elsevier.com | www.bookaid.org | www.sabre.org

ELSEVIER   BOOK AID
             International   Sabre Foundation

Contents

Preface

The aim of this text is to enable the reader to develop a sound theoretical and practical understanding of marketing, planning and control. Although primarily written for those studying for the Chartered Institute of Marketing Professional Diploma and Postgraduate Diploma professional marketing qualifications, this text is equally useful for industry practitioners. This is not an introductory text to the subject of marketing planning, but builds on the existing knowledge that students and practitioners already hold about the principles of the subject. The aim has been to provide a clear, concise guide to the tools, techniques and concepts necessary to undertake strategic marketing decisions.

The text also covers contemporary issues by exploring current developments in marketing theory and practice including:

- Customer relationship management
- Ethics and strategic marketing decision making
- The concept of a market-led orientation
- A resource/asset-based approach to internal analysis and planning

Innovation is a theme throughout the text, reflecting the growing importance of this issue, both in terms of its academic profile and current business practice. There is also an emphasis on developing a view of the future through various forecasting techniques.

This new edition also includes three new chapters which relate to CRM, ethics and problem-based learning approaches. Throughout this new edition new illustrative examples have been included to reinforce the material covered in each chapter.

An instructor's manual is available to academic staff adopting this text. This contains expanded versions of selected illustrative examples featured in the main text, new cases and a pack of lecture material.

■ Information for students studying for the CIM qualifications

The Chartered Institute of Marketing has continued to offer the Professional Diploma in Marketing for a number of years (QCA level 6). The CIM also still offers Postgraduate Diploma in Marketing (QCA level 7) which was launched in 2004.

The Marketing Planning syllabus, which is part of the Professional Diploma stage is divided into four major areas:

1 The marketing plan in its organisational and wider marketing context
2 Marketing planning and budgeting
3 The extended marketing mix and related tools
4 Marketing in different contexts

The CIM has designed their syllabus around the statements of marketing practice, which were developed by the Standard Setting Body for marketing under the direction of the Chartered Institute of Marketing. These statements identify the practical tasks that marketers undertake within their marketing career. These standards are available on the CIM website (www.cim.co.uk).

This textbook includes important strategic theory, some of which is not specifically included within the Marketing Planning syllabus, however, this does add further understanding for the student and thus goes beyond this syllabus. Also it is not the intention of this text to cover the theory relating to the marketing mix elements, as this is available in most fundamental marketing texts. However, the Marketing Planning syllabus requires candidates to be able to discuss the operationalisation of their marketing planning decisions using the marketing mix and so students should ensure that they have this knowledge also.

■ Links with other papers

The Marketing Planning syllabus was developed to provide the key skills and knowledge required by an operational marketing manager. This module replaced the 'Marketing Operations' module in the old CIM Advanced Certificate. It aims to prepare marketers for practice at management level and does consider operational issues as well as strategic marketing decisions. The general basis of this module is the marketing planning function and the implications for the operational decisions. However, as many organisations today are small- or medium-sized businesses, the marketing planning process is undertaken at a lower level of management than in larger multi-national organisations as cited in many other text books.

Therefore, the Marketing Planning module acts as a central base for the other CIM modules to build upon at the Professional Diploma (QCA level 6) and also is very much required for Postgraduate Diploma (QCA level 7) underpinning theory for this higher level of study.

This text will provide students with an understanding of the nature of strategic marketing decisions and the marketing decision process. This text covers key elements of the syllabus (such as forecasting, control mechanisms and budgeting) which are not covered well in other text books on the market and so is of major benefit to all students studying for this examination. Indeed, these are the areas of the syllabus which tend not to be taught well and consequently students do not perform well in response to questions in this area. Therefore, this text offers a useful and directed aid to this section of the Marketing Planning syllabus both for lecturers, students and practitioners.

The Marketing Research and Information module, which is another of the CIM modules within the Professional Diploma, includes the management of information and this is important to understand in relation to inform the marketing planning. This unit offers knowledge to operationalise the concepts discussed in this text.

The CIM Integrated Marketing Communications module within the Professional Diploma offers understanding of customer dynamics, which again offers information to make marketing planning decisions discussed in this text.

The final CIM Professional Diploma module, Marketing Management in Practice, requires students to operationalise and illustrate their skills and their knowledge of marketing planning processes as discussed in this text. Therefore, this text can add value to the reading for this syllabus also.

The CIM offer two assessment routes for the Professional Diploma syllabus, which are by examination or assignment. Any CIM centre at which students are studying will be able to inform them of the assessment route, which will be offered at that centre.

■ The CIM examination route

The examination paper for the Marketing Planning module is in two parts. Part A is a mini case study with three or four compulsory questions and this is worth 50 per cent of the examination. Each element of the syllabus will be tested in some way in Part A. Part B of the paper is made up of four questions, of which candidates are required to answer two and each question is worth 25 per cent of the paper.

Part A is normally a mini case study (similar to the ones found in Chapter 15 of this text) but it could also be an abstract of an article. Normally it will be up to one or one and a half sides of A4. Students will be asked to analyse the material, make comments upon it and propose further actions. Therefore, it will be expected that candidates can illustrate their knowledge and understanding of appropriate theory and apply their knowledge to the case study. Normally the answers will be required in report format.

Part B will contain four questions from across the syllabus, and will normally have two parts of one question. Students should be aware that in some questions two areas of the syllabus will be tested. These questions will require students to understand marketing theories and concepts, and show that they can apply them to a given situation. Students will also need to demonstrate that they have an ability to critically appraise appropriate models and concepts. Again, answers will be required in report format.

For the Professional Diploma examination, the CIM examiners are looking for candidates to demonstrate interpretative skills, insight and originality in answering the questions. At the same time, it is expected that candidates will show a critical awareness and understanding of the relevant theoretical framework surrounding the issues being discussed. Therefore, candidates will be required to demonstrate in their examinations paper an understanding of the theory, application of the theory and they will be required to evaluate practice and theory.

To perform well on this paper the following characteristics should be observed and adhered to:

- Candidates need to concentrate on the specifics of the question which may be strategic or operational in nature.
- Candidates have to demonstrate that they have the knowledge and skills required to critically appraise and apply models and concepts, not merely describe them.
- Candidates have to illustrate their answers, wherever possible, with relevant examples and provide the examiner with evidence that they have undertaken wider reading about the subject.
- Candidates need to ensure that they concentrate on the specifics of the question set, rather than answering in a generalised way, and that they answer all elements of the question (which have now been increased due to the new syllabus requirements).
- Candidates should ensure that they answer the question in the format requested. If the question asks for a report format they need to ensure that this is provided. Generally candidates should try to give well-presented answers. Where possible candidates should use diagrams as this helps them to use their time more efficiently.

In order for candidates to do well on this paper they need to be fully prepared. The best preparation would include:

- Practice on selected questions from either past examinations or the CIM specimen papers.
- Reading the examiners' reports and specimen answers that are available for each past paper.
- Reading as widely as possible, not only textbooks but also the marketing and business press on a regular basis. *Note:* suggestions for further reading will be found at the end of each chapter in this text.

The CIM assignment route

The CIM offer an assignment route for all modules within the Professional Diploma qualification. Therefore, certain CIM study centres may now offer the assignment route as an alternative to the examination route.

The assignment route requires candidates to complete coursework instead of sitting an examination for the Marketing Planning module. The Chartered Institute of Marketing devises the coursework and assessment criteria and these are then delivered at the study centres which have been given CIM approval to run this type of assessment rather than the examination.

This route comprises:

- *Core section*: This attracts a 50 per cent weighting and is often about the creation of an effective marketing plan. The word count for this would be 3000 words.
- *Elective section*: This is worth 25 per cent weighting and requires two pieces of work (where the candidate can choose 2 out of 4 areas). Examples of such areas are: the role of environmental analysis; a report on the potential for a new Internet-based service; a report on the extended marketing mix in not-for-profit organisations; an external analysis of an organisation of choice. Each assignment would be 1500 words.

CIM has to approve each study centre before this route can be offered to students. Therefore, CIM has written guidelines for study centres offering this route.

Whatever assessment route candidates undertake, they should always ensure that:

- They focus upon the application of models in a variety of markets and industry sectors, for example the service sector, small business sector or business to business sector.
- Wherever possible, they make use of their own business experience and other illustrative sources to provide relevant examples. Regular reading of the business press is useful in order to identify illustrative examples.
- They make themselves aware of the broader implications of marketing planning decisions. In particular, as well as understanding the benefits of planning and control techniques, they should be aware of the draw-backs, in terms of costs, and other resource implications.

Dr Ruth Ashford
Chartered Institute of Marketing Chief Examiner

■■Acknowledgements■ ■

The authors and publisher wish to thank the following for permission to use copyright material:

The Free Press/a division of Simon & Schuster, Inc., for Figures 8.2 and 8.7 adapted from Michael E. Porter, *Competitive Strategy: Techniques for Analysing Industries and Competitors*, Figure 1.3, p. 12, Figure 2.2, p. 37. Copyright © 1980 by Michael E. Porter.

Harvard Business Review for Figure 13.1 adapted from Thomas V. Bonoma, 'Making Your Marketing Strategy Work', Harvard Business Review, **62**(2), March/April 1984, p. 72. Copyright © 1984 by the President and Fellows of Harvard College.

The Controller of Her Majesty's Stationery Office for Figure 4.8 data from 'New Earnings Survey', Office for National Statistics. Crown copyright © 1991.

Pearson Education for Figures 8.9 and 8.10 from Kotler, Armstrong, Saunders and Wong, *Principles of Marketing*, 2nd European edition, Prentice Hall (1999), Figure 12.6, p. 531 and Figure 12.5, p. 527; and for Figures 1.2, 5.2, 7.1 and 7.2 from Johnson, G. and Scholes, K., *Exploring Corporate Strategy*, 5th edition/Prentice Hall (1999).

Penguin Books Ltd for adapted material from Hugh Davidson, *Even More Offensive Marketing*, Penguin Books (1997), Table 120, p. 285. Copyright © Hugh Davidson, 1997.

John Wiley & Sons Ltd for Figure 5.9 adapted from J. R. Montnari and J. S. Bracker, article in *Strategic Management Journal*, **7**(3), 1986. Copyright © 1986 John Wiley & Sons Ltd.

John Wiley, Inc. for Figure 14.7 from Watson, *Strategic Benchmarking* (1993), p. 4.

Whilst every effort has been made to contact copyright holders, the publisher would like to hear from anyone whose copyright has unwittingly been infringed.

CHAPTER 1

The strategic perspective

Increasingly competitive market conditions require strategic responses. Strategic decisions define core competencies and integrate activities. Strategic management recognises the importance of implementation and managing change. Essentially, strategic marketing management and subsequent marketing strategies, contribute to overall business goals through a three stage process: analysis, formulation and implementation.

■ Introduction

The concept of marketing is inherently simple – business success through a process of understanding and meeting customer needs. Few would argue with this basic principle, and even the most inexperienced of business managers would intuitively see the sense in this. Given this basic simplicity, why do we need something as complicated, and time consuming, as a marketing strategy?

While basic business principles may be simple common sense, achievement involves many complex, interdependent or even conflicting tasks. Increasingly, such tasks are undertaken against a backdrop of constant change, intense competition and limited resources. To further enhance the challenge, managers are often at the mercy of incomplete data and unexpected events, often being left to 'second guess' customer and competitor reactions. It is to this end, marketing strategy has become a vital component of success. A well considered, effectively implemented, marketing strategy should go some way to alleviating the aforementioned problems and reduce the complexity of business tasks. Strategy should restore simplicity to the art of management. In essence, it is a series of tools and techniques that guide (hopefully) the organisation to the marketing panacea – success through a process of understanding and meeting customer needs.

The modern business world now recognises the importance of strategic issues and the contribution of strategic management to business success. While this has many benefits it also brings many problems. It could be argued that 'strategy' (or 'strategic') is the most overused/misused phrase in business today. Everybody seems to have a 'strategy' for everything. By attaching the term 'strategy' to an activity, it somehow becomes more important – more grand – but in reality very little actually gets done! To illustrate this, the authors recall the recent experience of sitting through a seemingly endless meeting, listening to people jabber on-and-on about their 'strategy' or the need for a strategic view. Finally, someone said something sensible; '... *there's too much strategy and not enough people doing things!*'. This blunt comment is memorable for two reasons. Firstly, it ended a tedious meeting. Secondly, and more importantly, it illustrated a key point: strategy must lead to action, not be a substitute for it. Ultimately, all organisations need '... people doing things'. The goal of strategy is to ensure that they are doing the right things. These actions need to be co-ordinated, efficiently executed and focused on meeting customer need.

Essentially, strategy is a three stage process involving analysis, formulation and implementation. During the analysis phase management needs to look both internally and externally. Understanding the wider business environment is fundamental. It is then necessary to formulate plans appropriate to current and future circumstances. Finally, implementation needs to make sure our plans are put into practice. Managers must ensure that due care and attention are paid to each of these stages. In this way, strategy avoids being little more than rhetoric and starts to become a practical reality of business life.

■ What is strategy?

Over the years, many definitions of 'strategy' have been developed and close examination of such definitions tends to converge on the following – strategy is concerned with making major decisions affecting the long-term direction of the business. Major business decisions are by their very nature strategic, and tend to focus on:

● *Business definition*: A strategic fundamental is defining the business we are in. Organisations need to anticipate and adapt to change by keeping in touch with the *external competitive environment*. Business leaders need to define the *scope* (or range) of the organisation's activities and determine the markets in which the organisation will compete. We are defining the boundaries of activity and ensuring management face up to the challenges of change.

● *Core competencies*: The organisation must be competitive now and in the future. Therefore, strategic decisions need to define the basis of *sustainable competitive advantage(s)*. What skills and resources are needed in order to prosper within our defined markets and how can they be used to optimum advantage? It is essential that this is considered over the long-term and aims to *match* organisational capability with desired goals and the external environment. This process often has *major resource implications*, both in terms of investment and rationalisation.

● *Integrative*: Strategy has a wide ranging impact and therefore affects all functional areas within the organisation. Effective strategy is able to *co-ordinate* the different functions/activities within the organisation in order to achieve common goals. By taking a 'whole-organisation's' view of the corporation, managers should be better able to target resources, eliminate waste and generate synergy. *Synergy* occurs when the combined effect of functions/activities is greater than their individual contribution. It is vital that business leaders articulate a common *vision* and sense of purpose, in order to achieve an integrative approach.

● *Consistency of approach*: Strategy should provide a consistency of approach, and offer a focus to the organisation. Tactical activities may change and be adapted readily in response to market conditions, but strategic direction should remain constant. Additionally, strategic management can provide common tools and analytical techniques enabling the assessment and control of complex issues, situations and functional areas.

The process aims to specify corporate objectives and establish ways of achieving such objectives. The intent is to react to, and of course influence, the competitive environment to the advantage of the organisation. Any such advantage must be sustained over the long-term, but be flexible enough to adapt and develop as required.

Note, strategy and a *corporate/strategic plan* are not one and the same. Strategy defines the general concepts of future competitive advantage and reflects intent, whereas a strategic plan specifies the selection, sequence, resources, timing and specific objectives required to achieve the strategy.

Figure 1.1 summarises the above issues. Note: issues of strategy, tactics and corporate planning are further developed in Chapter 11.

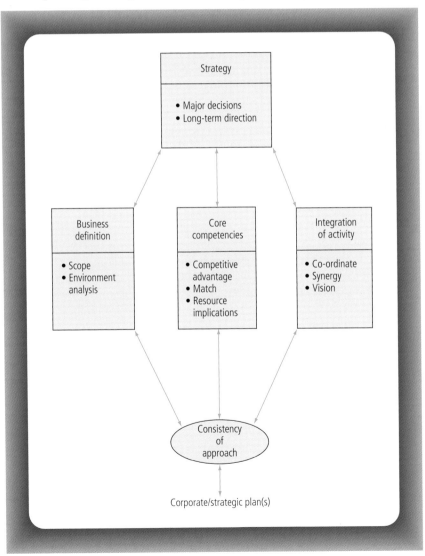

Figure 1.1
The basics of strategy

■ Towards strategic management

Over a period of some 30 years, we have seen the concept of strategy evolve. Aaker (1995) provides a historical perspective showing how this evolution has progressed and acknowledges that strategic activity has been described over the years as:

- *Budgeting*: Early strategic activity was concerned with budgetary and control mechanisms. Structured methods of allocating, monitoring and investigating variances from budget provided a means of managing complex processes. The process was often based on past trends and assumed incremental development.
- *Long-range planning*: Here greater emphasis was placed on forecasting. Planning systems and processes tended to extrapolate current trends (with varying degrees of sophistication) and predict factors such as sales, profits and cost. Management could use such forecasts as a basis for decision making.
- *Strategic planning*: The 1970/1980s was the era of strategic planning, with emphasis placed on: (i) specifying the overall direction and (ii) centralised control of planning activities. While still based around forecasting and extrapolation of past trends, far greater attention was paid to understanding the business environment. Managers hoped to be able to anticipate events through a detailed analysis of cause-and-effect relationships. Planning systems aimed to provide data and logic as a means of decision support. While promoting more awareness of strategic issues in terms of the external environment, the process still tended to focus on the preparation of corporate-wide plans. This was often achieved in a highly bureaucratic, centralised fashion.
- *Strategic management*: We are currently in the age of strategic management. Strategic management concerns both the formulation of strategy and how such strategy is put into practice. While still undertaking analysis and forecasting, far greater prominence is placed on implementation. The concern is with managing change and transforming the organisation within an increasingly turbulent business environment.

Johnson and Scholes (1999) provide a useful model (see Figure 1.2) summarising the main elements of strategic management. Strategic problems can be viewed as having three distinct components. Firstly analysis, we need to understand the business environment and the resource capabilities of the organisation. This needs to be considered in the context of the organisation's culture and the aspirations and expectations of the stakeholders. Note, 'stakeholders' are taken to be anyone with a stake in the organisation (e.g. customers, employees, suppliers, etc.). Secondly, managers need to make strategic choices. This is achieved via a process of identifying, evaluating and selecting options. The organisation needs to define: (i) what is the basis of our strategy – so-called 'generic' strategy, (ii) what product/market areas will we operate in and (iii) developing specific strategies to achieve corporate goals. Finally, the issue of implementation must be considered.

There is the need to plan actions, allocate resources and, where appropriate restructure, to achieve strategic change.

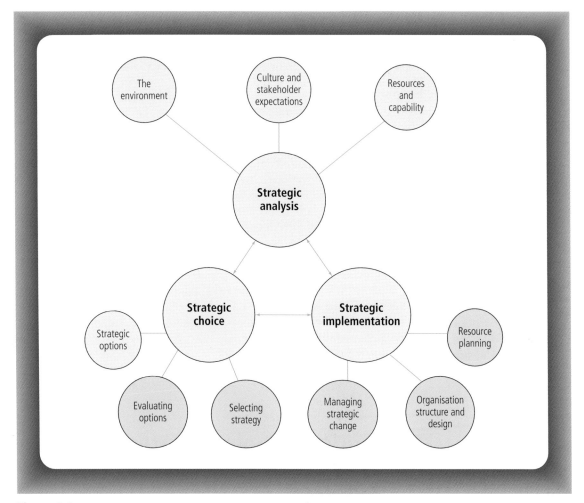

Figure 1.2
Elements of strategic management (*Source*: Johnson and Scholes, 1999).

It is important to remember that strategic management is not the orderly, logical sequence of events/activities that managers wish for. Practical reality means processes are interlinked and overlapping. For example, strategic analysis does not stop (or at least should not stop) when other stages take place. Analysis is an on-going activity. Equally, creativity, vision and leadership are required to turn analysis into successful strategy. Given the volatility in today's business world, a contingency approach may be required. This provides flexibility by developing contingencies for a range of future scenarios.

Porter (1998) provides an interesting perspective and views of strategy in terms of: (i) developing a unique position by choosing to perform differently from the opposition, (ii) making 'trade-offs' with other possible competitive positions, in order to protect your competitive advantage, (iii) combining activities to fit into, and reinforce, an overall competitive position and (iv) ensuring operational effectiveness when executing activities.

Illustrative Example 1.1

DSL International launches 'TechGuys'

DSL International owns leading electrical retailers such as Currys, Dixons and PC World. The company now hopes to expand its service operations in the UK through the launch of 'TechGuys'. This service aims to provide rapid technical support to the increasingly IT-dependent UK consumer. Services include installation, upgrades and maintenance of computers and audio-visual devices regardless of where they were purchased. Chief Executive John Clare states that '... *calling out an engineer to help connect a laptop to the Internet will become as commonplace as using plumbers and electricians*' (Cavazza, 2006). Support will be available on-site, call centre or over the Internet. DSL feels demand for such services will grow rapidly and will be bolstered by the forthcoming switch to digital TV in the UK. The 'TechGuys' concept will be implemented through a number of stand-alone shops and TechGuy service points in existing PC World stores. DSL will invest £50 million in the venture and hopes to develop the initiative in other European markets. Research undertaken by the firm shows that almost 80 per cent of adults need technical support in relation to everyday technology

Consider Figure 1.2 *'Elements of Strategic Management'*, how does this development fit in with this model?

■ Change – shaping strategy

Change is an accepted consequence of modern life. Indeed, the phrase – *'change is the only certainty'* – has become something of a business mantra. All organisations are subject to increasing levels of change. We can view change in terms of cyclical change and evolutionary change. Cyclical change involves variation that is repetitive and often predictable (e.g. seasonal variation in demand or fluctuation in economy circumstances). Evolutionary change involves a more fundamental shift. It may mean sudden innovation or a gradual 'creeping' process. Either way, the result can have drastic consequences for strategic development.

Given that strategic management is concerned with moving the organisation to some future desired state, which has been defined in terms of a corporate vision and corporate-wide issues, it is important to see the concept of 'change' as an integral part of strategy. We can examine this in terms of the following questions: (i) What drives change? (ii) How does change impact on our markets/business environment? (iii) What is the result of change on the organisation's strategy? Figure 1.3 summarises the following:

● *Drivers of change*
  Consistently, current products and methods of operating rapidly being displaced by a combination of competitors' actions and shifting customer needs. This discontinuity is being driven by the following factors: *Political, Economic, Social* (e.g. demographics) and *Technological*. A so-called *'PEST'* analysis (see later) provides a useful analytical framework with which to study the business environment.

● *Impact of change*
  Quite simply, change means we need to re-define our markets. While fast growth is still possible within certain 'sun-rise' industries, many industries have to accept the days of incremental annual growth are over. Variation in consumer habits and demographic patterns mean traditional markets are becoming more challenging. Change is accompanied by intense competition, which the phenomenon of business globalisation can only intensify. Increasingly, we see shorter product life cycles and increasing difficulty in predicting the future.

● *Result of change*
  There are two main outcomes. Firstly, change creates opportunity. Organisations that are flexible and in touch with customer needs are likely not just to survive, but prosper. Secondly, past actions, strategies and methods offer no guarantee of future success. There is a need to guard against complacency and ensure that the strategic thrust of the organisation does not drift from the true needs of the market place (beware strategic drift).

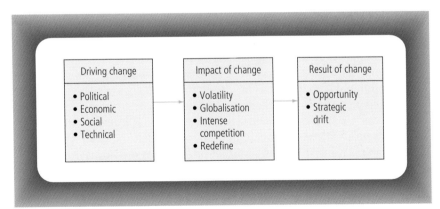

Figure 1.3
Strategy and change

■ Balanced scorecard approach

As change pervades all aspects of business strategy, it is important to set appropriate measures of business success. Rather than relying on a few narrow financial measures, a system is needed which provides an overall view of business success. To this end, Kaplan and Norton (1992) advocate using a *'balanced scorecard'* approach. This involves taking both financial/non-financial measures and examines the benefits delivered to all the organisation's stakeholders. A balanced scorecard approach involves four sets of measures:

1 *Financial measures*: Here we examine how we are perceived by investors and shareholders.
2 *Customers*: How do our customers view us?
3 *Internal activities*: By examining the key areas of activity which deliver customer satisfaction, we can identify where the organisation must outdo it's competitors.
4 *Innovation and learning*: To survive and prosper, all organisations need to improve and adapt. Any business activity can be viewed as a learning experience with the goal of continuously creating value.

Performance indicators are established within each of these areas. These become an objective basis with which to evaluate and formulate strategy. A winning strategy should address the above and offer a range of initiatives for the future.

■ The role of marketing within strategy

As noted earlier, all organisations need to make strategic decisions relating to their external environment. Strategy must address issues such as customers, competitors and market trends. It needs to be proactive as opposed to simply reacting to events. In this way, strategy can detect and influence changes in the business environment. By its nature, marketing defines how the organisation interacts with its market place. Consequently, all strategic planning, to a greater or lesser degree, requires an element of marketing. Only in this way can organisations become strategically responsive to customer need and commercial pressures. Indeed, it is possible to view marketing as more than a functional activity. It can be adopted as a business philosophy. Here the organisation adopts a marketing orientation – *success by a process of understanding and meeting customer need.* Basically, the company's orientation defines it's fundamental business philosophy, highlighting what is perceived as the primary route to success. Market orientations are now widely established within the business world (and often seen as the 'holy grail' of marketers) but other business orientations are equally common.

● *Production orientation*: Here business success is attributed to efficient production. The emphasis is on mass production, economy of scale and cost control. Management's key concern is with achieving volume and meeting production schedules. This philosophy has its place, but risks limiting operations to low added-value assembly work.
● *Product orientation*: The belief is that product innovation and design will have buyers beating a path to our door. Management's perception is that our products are so good they will, in effect, sell themselves.

Little, or no effect, is put into establishing what the customer actually wants – a dangerous route! Naturally, product innovation is important but it needs to appeal to the market place, otherwise it risks being innovation for the sake of innovation.

- *Sales orientation*: This views sales volume as the key determinant of success. The focus is on aggressive selling that persuades the customer to buy. Given that the process is driven by sales targets, a short-term perspective dominates, with little regard to building longer-term relationships. Often, this follows on from a production orientation, as management tries to create a demand for unwanted products.
- *Market orientation*: As previously stated, success is derived from understanding and meeting customer needs. This process starts with the customer and uses actual customer demand as a means to focus resources. In simple terms, we provide what the market wants. Additionally, the importance of building long-term relationships with customers is recognised. We seek to build loyalty and consistently offer superior value. An awareness of competitors' proficiency and strategy is required in order to optimise this process.

It is not our intention to decry production, product innovation or selling – indeed they are vital. However, the truly 'world-class' organisation understands how to marshal these factors into a coherent market-led orientation. Creating such focus will facilitate the sustainable competitive advantage required to prosper.

How do we go about achieving a market orientation? The answer to this question can be summarised as follows:

1 *Customer focused*
   Understand your customer base and be responsive to their needs. Treat loyal customers as assets and strive to build on-going and long-term relationships. Regularly monitor levels of customer satisfaction and retention. Note, to achieve this we must: (i) define our markets, (ii) effectively segment/target customers and (iii) listen to customers.

2 *Competitor focused*
   In terms of competitors, be watchful and assess their objectives, strategies and capabilities. There is the need to 'benchmark' their products, processes and operations against our own.

3 *Integrate marketing into the business*
   Marketing should not be confined to the marketing department. Every function and person within the organisation has a role to play in creating value and achieving the goal of being a market-led organisation. This may require fundamental changes in culture and organisation structure.

4 *Strategic vision*
   Develop a long-term, market-orientated strategic vision by viewing marketing as more than a series of promotional tools and techniques. It must be on the agenda of senior management, who should develop and implement market-led strategy and define the future in terms of creating long-term value for stakeholders.

5 *Realistic expectations*

We cannot be all things to all people. Expectations have to be realistic and matched to capabilities, resources and external conditions. We may well need to make 'trade-offs' to ensure we focus on activities that add value.

■ What is marketing strategy?

In a strategic role, marketing aims to transform corporate objectives and business strategy into a competitive market position. Essentially, the concern is to differentiate our actives/products by meeting customer needs more effectively than competitors. Marketing strategy can by characterised by: (a) analysing the business environment and defining specific customer needs, (b) matching actives/products to customers segments and (c) implementing programmes that achieve a competitive position, superior to competitors. Therefore, marketing strategy addresses three elements – customers, competitors and internal corporate issues (see Figure 1.4).

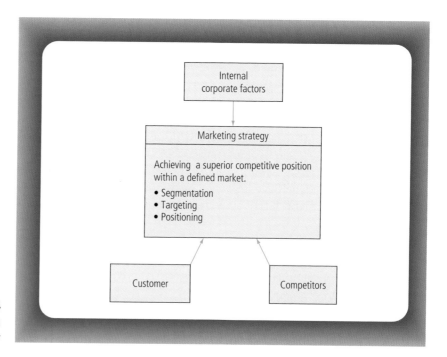

Figure 1.4
Basis of marketing strategy

Firstly, we consider customers. How is the market defined, what segments exist and who should we target? Secondly, how can we best establish a competitive position? A precursor to this is a detailed understanding of our competitors within targeted market segments. Finally, we need to match internal corporate capabilities with customer need. The successful achievement of these factors should enable the organisation to develop, and maintain, a strong market position.

Essentially, a marketing strategy aims to deliver the following:

1 *Segmentation*

This process breaks the market down into groups displaying common characteristics, behaviours and attitudes. Fundamentally, this process aims to understand need and forecast reaction and/or demand.

2 *Targeting*

This involves evaluating and selecting market segments. We aim to look for opportunities which are sustainable, where we can build long-term relationships with customers.

3 *Positioning*

As previously stated, we establish a distinctive superior position, relative to competitors. The competitive position adopted, should be based on matching product attributes to customer need.

It goes without saying that the three key constituents of marketing strategy – customers, competitors and internal corporate factors – are dynamic and constantly changing (summarised in section Change – shaping strategy). Therefore, organisations must develop and deploy processes, procedures and techniques that ensure market strategy is: (a) relative to the current/future business environment, (b) sustainable, (c) generating optimal benefits to both the organisation and customers and (d) correctly implemented. This is the process of *strategic marketing management*.

As a process, strategic marketing (and the subsequent structure of this book) has three distinct phases.

1 *Strategic analysis*

To move forward, we must first answer the question; where are we? This stage entails a detailed examination of the business environment, customers and an internal review of the organisation itself. Tools such as portfolio analysis and industry structure models help management to objectively assess the organisation's current position. Equally, it is important to develop some view regarding future trends. This is achieved through forecasting and defining assumptions about the future market trends.

Illustrative Example 1.2

Fairtrade – An independent consumer label

Marketers are critically aware of the importance of branding. A brand can be defined as:

A distinctive product offering created by the use of a name, symbol, design, packaging or some combination of these intended to differentiate it from its competitors (Jobber, 2004).

From a marketing perspective Fairtrade provides the consumer with a brand identity that independently guarantees labelled products will offer disadvantaged producers in the developing world a better deal. Products are licensed by the Fairtrade Foundation and require suppliers to meet Fairtrade standards in relation to factors such as sustainable production costs and social or economic developed.

(Continued)

Illustrative Example 1.2 (Continued)

Consider Figure 1.5 '*Strategic Marketing*', how does the Fairtrade initiative correspond to the factors listed under formulating strategy?

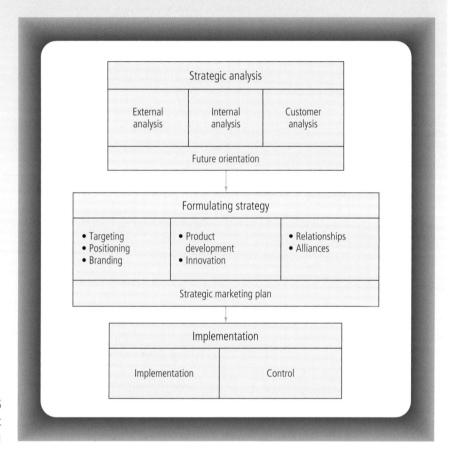

Figure 1.5
Strategic
marketing

2 *Formulating strategy*

Having analysed our situation, we then determine a way forward. Formulation involves defining strategic intent – what are our overall goals and objectives? Managers need to formulate a marketing strategy that generates competitive advantage and positions the organisation's products effectively. To be successful, this must be based on core competencies. During this stage, product development and innovation are strategic activities, offering the potential to enhance competitive position and further develop products and brands. Additionally, formulation emphasises the need to form relationships with customers and other businesses. Increasingly, we see organisations recognising that they cannot do everything themselves and look to form joint ventures and partnerships.

The formulation stage culminates with the development of a strategic marketing plan.

3 *Implementation*

Consideration needs to be given to implementing the strategy. Marketing managers will undertake programmes and action that deliver strategic objectives. Such actions, will often focus on individual elements of the marketing mix. Additionally, a process of monitoring and control needs to be put in place. This ensures compliance and aids decision making.

Figure 1.5 provides an overview of the process of strategic marketing management. Additionally, it provides a template to the structure of this text. The three components form a planning cycle (analysis, formulation and implementation) and are interactive in nature, with information being fed-back to enable objectives and strategy to be reviewed and amended. Ultimately, the process will establish the organisation's marketing mix – products, price, promotion and place, which underpins and conveys our marketing strategy.

■ Summary

Today's business world recognises the importance of strategy and strategic management. Normally, any strategic process has three distinct stages – analysis, formulation of plans and implementation. Increasingly, the importance of implementation is recognised as an integral part of the strategic framework. Strategy aims to define core competencies, understand the external environment and offer an integrative, consistent approach to decision making.

Any strategy is significantly influenced by environmental change. Political, economic, social and technological factors drive change and impact on the organisation. This results in a volatile, intensely competitive market place. Organisations need to ensure that they fully embrace the opportunities change brings and guard against complacency and strategic drift. To this end, a 'balanced scorecard' approach is advocated, thus encouraging the organisation to address wider strategic issues.

Marketing has a role to play within the strategic process. Namely, marketing can be adopted as a business philosophy. This sees commercial success as stemming from a process of understanding and meeting customer needs.

Marketing strategy involves achieving a superior competitive position within a defined market. Essentially, it involves segmentation, targeting and positioning. This must address customers, competitors and internal corporate factors. Strategic marketing management is the process of ensuring our marketing strategy is relevant and sustainable.

■ References

Aaker, D., *Strategic Market Management*, 4th edn, Wiley, New York, 1995.

Cavazza, M., *Daily Mail*, 5th September, 2006.

Johnson, G. and Scholes, K., *Exploring Corporate Strategy*, 5th edn, Prentice Hall, London, 1999.

Kaplan, R. and Norton, D., The balanced scorecard: measures that drive performance, *Harvard Business Review*, **70**(1), 1992.

Jobber, D., *Principles and Practice of Marketing*, 4th edn, McGraw-Hill, London, 2004.

Porter, M., What is strategy? in Segal-Horn (ed.), *The Strategy Reader*, Published: Blackwell in association with The Open University, 1998.

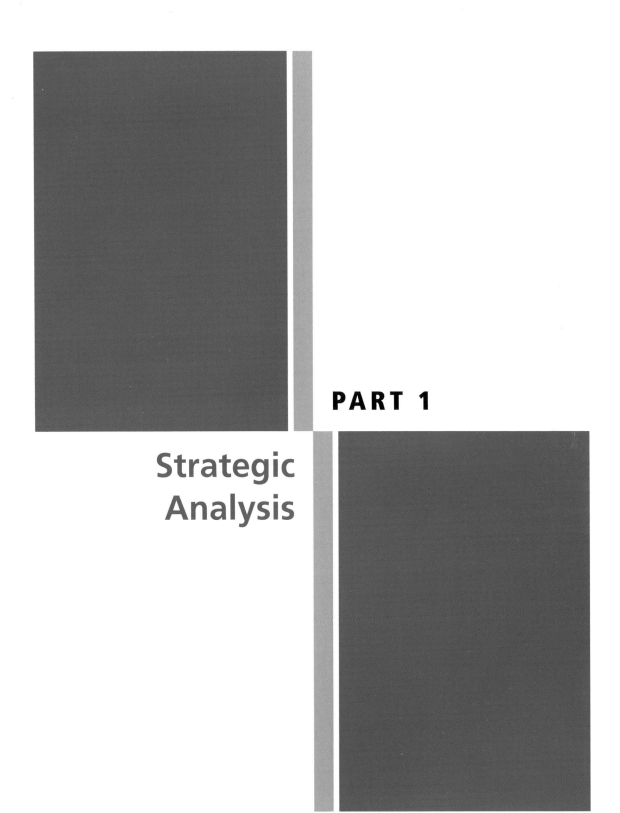

PART 1

Strategic
Analysis

- External analysis
- Customer intelligence
- Segmentation
- Internal analysis
- Developing a future orientation

Undertaking a strategic analysis is the foundation upon which strategic decisions are constructed. In this text strategic analysis is broken down into three constituent elements: external analysis, customer analysis and internal analysis. Undertaking the analysis is not however a linear process and there are areas of the analyses that overlap. The aim of the process is to develop a detailed and all embracing view of the company and its external environment to permit the organisation to formulate informed strategic decisions.

Chapter 2 explores the external analysis. This consists of an initial audit of the macro-environment. The organisation's micro-environment is then considered and an initial analysis of the company's competitive position is undertaken.

Chapter 3 explores the increasingly critical function of competitive intelligence and examines how organisations can employ such a practice to support and develop successful marketing strategies.

Chapter 4 examines the customer. Consumer behaviour is explored to illustrate what the effect of changes in the external environment can have on customers. Market segmentation techniques are then discussed.

Chapter 5 describes the process of internal analysis. This looks at the ways of identifying the organisation's assets and competencies.

These four chapters illustrate the groundwork that needs to be undertaken by an organisation before it can begin to form a view of the future.

Chapter 6 discusses different approaches that organisation's can take to develop a view of what developments may occur, and affect their activities, in the future. Part 1 also covers the process of matching the organisation's resources and competencies to attractive market opportunities that is at the heart of strategic choice (the topic of Part 2 of this book).

CHAPTER 2

External analysis

The external analysis is the first stage of the auditing process. It creates the information and analysis necessary for an organisation to begin to identify the key issues it will need to address in order to develop a successful strategy. The chapter explores the process of PEST analysis, industry analysis, competitor analysis and market analysis. The use of various approaches to facilitate this process, in particular the 'five forces' model and strategic groups, are covered.

■ Introduction

An analysis of the external environment is undertaken in order to discover the opportunities and threats that are evolving and that need to be addressed by the organisation. A study by Diffenbach (1983) identified a number of positive consequences that stem from carrying out organised environmental analysis (see Figure 2.1).

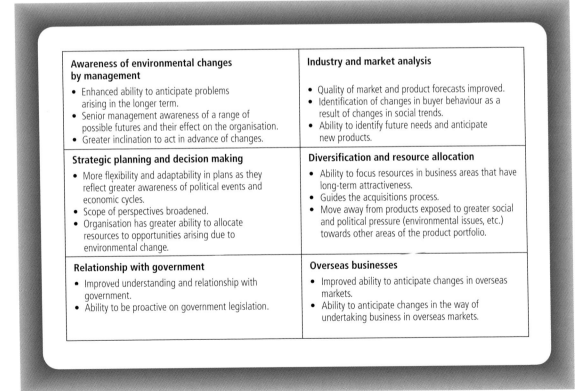

Awareness of environmental changes by management
- Enhanced ability to anticipate problems arising in the longer term.
- Senior management awareness of a range of possible futures and their effect on the organisation.
- Greater inclination to act in advance of changes.

Industry and market analysis
- Quality of market and product forecasts improved.
- Identification of changes in buyer behaviour as a result of changes in social trends.
- Ability to identify future needs and anticipate new products.

Strategic planning and decision making
- More flexibility and adaptability in plans as they reflect greater awareness of political events and economic cycles.
- Scope of perspectives broadened.
- Organisation has greater ability to allocate resources to opportunities arising due to environmental change.

Diversification and resource allocation
- Ability to focus resources in business areas that have long-term attractiveness.
- Guides the acquisitions process.
- Move away from products exposed to greater social and political pressure (environmental issues, etc.) towards other areas of the product portfolio.

Relationship with government
- Improved understanding and relationship with government.
- Ability to be proactive on government legislation.

Overseas businesses
- Improved ability to anticipate changes in overseas markets.
- Ability to anticipate changes in the way of undertaking business in overseas markets.

Figure 2.1
A selection of benefits derived from organised environmental analysis (*Source*: Adapted from Diffenbach, 1983)

An analysis of the external environment can be broken down into three key steps each becoming more specific to the organisation. The first step is an analysis of the macro-environmental influences that the organisation faces. This is followed by an examination of the competitive (micro) environment the organisation operates within. Finally a specific competitive analysis is undertaken.

■ Scanning

The environmental audit is reliant on the monitoring activity that is undertaken by the organisation. The process is normally referred to as scanning.

There are four forms of scanning according to Aguilar (1967). They are as follows:

1 *Undirected viewing*: This activity concerns the viewer exploring information in general without carrying a specific agenda. The viewer is exposed to a large amount of varied information but this is not an active search looking for particular issues, just a broad attempt to be aware of factors or areas that may have changed.
2 *Conditional viewing*: Again this is not an organised search but the viewer is sensitive to information that identifies changes in specific areas of activity.
3 *Informal search*: This is an organised but limited search for information to support a specific goal.
4 *Formal search*: This type of search is actively pursued and specifically designed to seek particular information.

There is of course an unlimited amount of information that can be scanned. Any organisation can only scan a certain amount of this information. A balance has to be struck between the resources allocated to this activity and the potential benefits. More information also does not lead to better decision making. Understanding the dynamics of the environment is the critical aspect to this activity, not the volume of information reviewed (see the section on Market sensing in Chapter 6).

Managers search for information in five broad areas (Aguilar, 1967) (see Figure 2.2):

1 Market intelligence
2 Technical intelligence
3 Acquisition intelligence
4 Broad issues
5 Other intelligence

Note: Aguilar uses the word tidings rather than intelligence.

The study showed that 58 per cent of managers saw market intelligence as the most important area for obtaining external information, three times more important than the next most significant area, technical intelligence

Area of external information	Category	General content
Market intelligence	• Market potential • Structural change • Competitors and industry • Pricing • Sales negotiations • Customers	→ Capacity, consumption, imports, exports → Mergers, acquisitions, new entries → Competitor information, industry policy → Effective and proposed prices → Information on specific current or potential sales → Current or potential customers, markets and problems
Technical intelligence	• New product, processes and technology • Product problems • Costs • Licensing and patents	→ Technical information relatively new or unknown to enterprise → Involving current products → For processing, operations, etc. for suppliers, customers and competitors → Products and processes
Acquisition intelligence	• Leads for mergers, joint ventures, or acquisitions	→ Information concerning possibilities for the organisation
Intelligence on broad issues	• General conditions • Government actions and policies	→ General information on political, demographic, etc. → Decisions affecting the industry
Other intelligence	• Suppliers and raw materials • Resources available • Miscellaneous	→ Purchasing information → Availability of people, land, other resources → Any other information

Figure 2.2
Critical areas of external information (*Source*: Adapted from Aguilar, 1967)

at 18 per cent. The importance placed on market intelligence was true across all functional areas. The most significant categories of information within this area were market potential, accounting for 30 per cent alone and structural change, accounting for 10 per cent. The only other category that reached double figures was for the category of new products, process and technology under technical intelligence.

One crucial aspect of this activity, especially where it underpins futures forecasting, is to detect weak signals. That is, identifying fragments of information that indicate significant changes, but whose potential impact has generally not been perceived. This is obviously difficult especially as many organisations fail to recognise major signals in the environment.

■ Macro-environmental analysis

The macro-environment audit examines the broad range of environmental issues that may affect the organisation. This will include the political/legal issues, economic factors, social/cultural issues and technological developments. This is normally referred to as a PEST (Political, Economic, Social and Technological) analysis, although some writers use the alternative acronym of STEP analysis (see Figure 2.3). The aim of this analysis is to identify the critical issues in the external environment that may affect the organisation. Before moving on to judge the impact they may have on the organisation.

Political/legal issues	Economic factors
• Taxation policy • Monopoly controls • Environmental protection measures • Employment law • Environmental legislation • Foreign trade agreements • Stability of the governmental system	• Interest rates • Inflation rates • Money supply • Business cycles • Unemployment • GNP trends
Social/cultural issues	Technological factors
• Age profiles • Social mobility • Changes in lifestyles • Family structures • Levels of education • Work behaviour • Leisure activities • Distribution of income • Patterns of ownership • Attitudes and values	• Focus of government research • Rate of technology transfer • Materials • Developing technological processes

Figure 2.3
The PEST analysis of influences in the external environment

Political/legal issues

There is a range of political organisations that have to be considered when looking at influences in this area of the audit. The structure of a political system defines the centres of political influence. A state with a federal political structure will differ from a unitary political system. In the UK there is a parliament for Scotland and an assembly for Wales. There are however be a number of decision areas that are still be the responsibility of the Westminster parliament. At the same time there is also an increasing range of decisions taking place both politically and legally within the framework of the European Union. Political pressure groups such as Greenpeace can also affect the political agenda. Therefore when considering this area of the environment a much wider view has to be taken than just the domestic national government or the legal process.

Economic factors

Similarly, economic factors have to be viewed from a wider perspective than the organisation's domestic economy. In the global economy, domestic economic conditions are heavily influenced by events in other areas of the world. Economics is concerned with the allocation of resources. Therefore issues such as conservation of natural resources, costs of pollution, energy consumption and the whole area of the management of natural resources should be considered under this heading.

Social/cultural issues

Demographic changes are important and can be used as lead indicators in certain areas, such as health care and education. However other critical areas such as social/cultural values and beliefs that are central to changes in consumer behaviour are harder to predict and can be subject to more dramatic shifts.

Technological developments

There is a great danger in using a particular technology to define an industry. In a situation where technological developments are fast moving it is critical to understand the fundamental consumer needs which the organisation's technology are currently serving. Identifying new technology's that can service that consumer's needs more completely or economically is the critical part of this area of the analysis.

Illustrative Example 2.1

On-line clothing sales

The on-line sales of clothing and shoes in the UK rose by 44 per cent in 2007 to reach £1.4 billion. This represents a five-fold increase in on-line sales since 2001. Next Directory is the biggest single operator in this sector of the clothing market. Research has shown that the biggest reason for purchasing on-line was to avoid having to search for the right size on the clothes rack

(Continued)

Illustrative Example 2.1 (Continued)

in traditional retail stores. A secondary factor was to avoid the high street retail experience. One on-line retailer is reported as saying sales in this sector have been growing at 50 per cent a year over the last few years. This is in line with Internet retail sales generally which rose 50 per cent in the 10 weeks leading up to Christmas 2006 to hit sales of £7.5 billion against £5 billion in 2005. Internet sales in November 2006 reached £3.2 billion the first time monthly sales had broken through the £3 billion barrier. Despite the general evidence of high growth in Internet sales and the specific evidence of growth in the on-line clothing market a number of fashion retailers currently have no on-line clothing operation these include Zara, Selfridges, Matalan, Bhs and Primark.

The central role of this PEST analysis is to identify the key factors that are likely to drive change in the environment. Then the aim is to establish how these key factors will affect the industry in general and the organisation in particular.

■ Industry analysis

An organisation has to understand the nature of the relationship within its industry, in order to allow the enterprise to develop strategies to gain advantage of the current relationships.

A useful framework, that can be utilised when undertaking this analysis, is Porter's 'five forces' model of establishing industry attractiveness for a business (see Figure 2.4). This analysis should be conducted at the level of the individual strategic business unit (SBU) rather than at the level of the organisation as a whole, otherwise the range of relationships facing a company with several divisions, causes the analysis to loose focus. Porter identified five factors that affect the level of competition and therefore profitability within an industry:

1 *Suppliers*: The power of suppliers is liable to be strong where:
   - Control over supplies is concentrated into the hands of a few players.
   - Costs of switching to a new source of supply are high.
   - If the supplier has a strong brand.
   - The supplier is in an industry with a large number of smaller disparate customers.
2 *Buyers*: The power of buyers is liable to be strong where:
   - A few buyers control a large percentage of a volume market. For example grocery and electrical goods retailers in the UK dominate the market and are in a very strong position versus their suppliers as a result.
   - There are a large number of small suppliers. In the meat industry in the UK there are a large number of small farmers supplying a retail sector dominated by a small number of large supermarkets.
   - The costs of switching to a new supplier are low.
   - The supplier's product is relatively undifferentiated, effectively lowering barriers to alternative sources of supply.

3 *Potential entrants*: The threat of potential entrants will be determined by a number of barriers to entry that may exist in any given industry:
  ● The capital investment necessary to enter the industry can be very high in areas such as electrical power generation or chemical production.
  ● A well-entrenched competitor who moved into the industry early may have established cost advantages irrespective of the size of their operation. They have had time to establish crucial aspects of their operation such as effective sources of supply, the best locations, and customer franchises.
  ● Achieving economies of scale in production, distribution or marketing can be a necessity in certain industries.
  ● Gaining access to appropriate distribution channels can be difficult. Peugeot/Citroen bought Chrysler's entire UK operations in order to gain an effective dealership network in Britain.
  ● Government legislation and policies such as patent protection, trade relations with other states and state owned monopolies can all act to restrict the entry of competitors.
  ● The prospect of a well-established company's hostile reactions to a new competitor's entry to the market may be enough to act as a deterrent.

4 *Substitutes*: Substitution can arise in a number of ways:
  ● A new product or service may eradicate the need for a previous process. Insurance services delivered directly by producers over the phone or Internet are substitutes for the services of the independent insurance broker.
  ● A new product replaces an existing product or service. Cassette tapes replaced vinyl records, only to be replaced by compact discs.
  ● All products and services, to some extent, suffer from generic substitution. Consumers may choose to substitute buying a car in order to purchase an expensive holiday instead.

5 *Competitive rivalry*: The intensity of competition in the industry will be determined by a range of factors:
  ● The stage of the industry life cycle will have an effect. Natural growth reaches a plateau once an industry reaches maturity; the only way a organisation can continue to grow in the industry is to take market share off its rivals.
  ● The relative size of competitors is an important factor. In an industry where rivals are of similar size, competition is likely to be intense as they each strive for a dominant position. Industries that already have a clear dominant player tend to be less competitive.
  ● In industries that suffer from high-fixed costs, companies will try to gain as much volume throughput as possible, this may create competition based on price discounting.
  ● There may be barriers that prevent companies withdrawing from an industry. This may be plant and machinery that is specialist in nature and therefore cannot be transferred to other uses. The workforce may have non-transferable specialist skills. If the industry is in maturity, moving towards decline, and rivals cannot easily leave the industry then competition inevitably will increase.

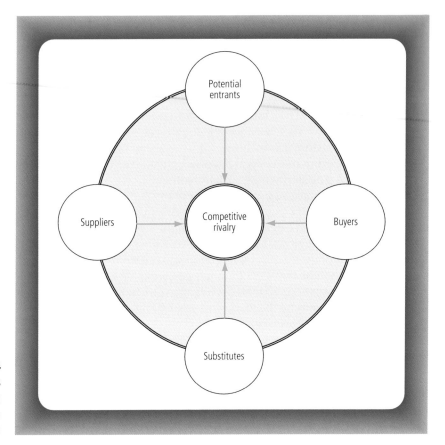

Figure 2.4
The five forces
model (*Source*:
Adapted from
Porter, 1980)

This model allows an organisation to identify the major forces that are present in the industry sector. This can be related to the critical factors that were identified by the PEST analysis. Several issues then need to be considered:

- What is the likelihood that the nature of the relationships identified by the 'five forces' model will change given the trends in the external environment? Are there ways of benefiting from these potential changes?
- What actions can the organisation undertake that will improve its position against the current forces in the industry? Can the company increase its power, relative to suppliers or buyers? Can actions be taken to reduce competitive rivalry, or are there ways of building barriers to dissuade companies from considering entering the industry? Are there ways of making substitute products less attractive?
- The organisation will also need to consider their competitors. Given the forces in the industry, what is the relative position of the organisation's rivals. Do conditions favour one particular operator? Could conditions

change in favour of one particular competitor? Consideration of relative competitive position of rivals is an important aspect of an audit and needs now to be considered in more detail.

■ Competitor analysis

The 'five forces' analysis has examined the overall industry and is a starting point in assessing a company's competitive position. This is likely to be a rather broad definition of an industry and contains a number of companies that would not be direct competitors. Toyota's is likely to have a number of natural direct competitors, Aston Martin is not likely to be one of them, although both companies are in the car industry. Toyota's scale is global and manufacture cars across the full range, Aston Martin is a specialist, low-volume prestige sports car manufacturer. Companies that are direct competitors in terms of products and customer profiles are seen as being in a strategic group. The car industry would be made up of a number of strategic groups.

Strategic groups

Strategic groups are made up of organisations within the same industry that are pursuing equivalent strategies targeting groups of customers that have similar profiles. Aston Martin's strategic group is likely to contain Ferrari, Lotus, Lamborghini, etc. All these companies are following similar strategies and facing similar strategic questions. They are also aiming at very similar market segments. In the airline industry there are at least three strategic groups. One group consists of airlines with regional operations who offer scheduled flights and compete on cost. There is a group of major airlines who have global operations and offer scheduled flights with quality environments and service. The third group offer charter services to a range of holiday destinations (see Figure 2.5).

There is a range of attributes that can be used to identify strategic groups. Some examples are as follows:

- Size of the company
- Assets and skills
- Scope of the operation
- Breadth of the product range
- Choice of distribution channel
- Relative product quality
- Brand image

For many companies analysing every competitor in its generic industry, would be a difficult task in terms of management time and company resources. Defining an organisation's strategic group allows a company to concentrate its analysis on its direct competitors and to examine them in more detail.

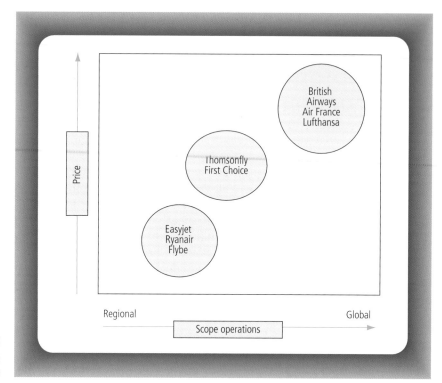

Figure 2.5
Strategic groups in
airline industry

Tools which are used to analyse the internal environment, such as the value chain, can of course be used to analyse competitors (see Chapter 8). For each competitor in their strategic group an organisation needs, as far as possible, to establish the following:

- *Competitors objectives*: Competitors objectives can be identified by analysing three important factors. They are as follows:
  1 Whether the competitor's current performance is likely to be fulfilling their objectives. If not the competitor may initiate a change of strategy.
  2 How likely the competitor is to commit further investment to the business. Financial objectives may indicate this. Investment is more likely from companies that have objectives, which are long term in nature, such as market share and sales growth, rather than organisations under pressure to produce short-term profitability. This also reveals potential trade-offs the competitor may be willing to take. If short-term profitability is the key objective then the rival is likely to be willing to loose market share in the short term in order to achieve its profitability targets.
  3 The likely future direction of the competitor's strategy. The organisation may have non-financial objectives, such as gaining technology leadership.

- *Competitor's current and past strategies*: There are three areas that should be explored in order to establish a competitor's current activities. They are as follows:

  1 Identification of the current markets, or market segments, within which the competitor currently operates. This will indicate the scope of the business.

  2 Identification of the way the competitor has chosen to compete in those markets. Is it based on quality of service, brand image or on price? This may be an indication of whether a low cost or differentiation strategy is being pursued (see Chapter 8).

  3 Comparison between the current strategy and past strategies can be instructive. Firstly it can illustrate the direction the competitor is moving, in terms of product and market development, over time. It can also highlight strategies that the organisation has tried in the past and have failed. The competitor is unlikely to attempt these approaches again without considerable reservations.

- *Competitor's capabilities*: An analysis of a competitor's assets and competencies allow a judgement to be made about how well equipped they are to address the market, given the dynamics in the industry and the trends in the external environment. In order to evaluate a competitor's potential challenge to an organisation a number of areas need to be examined (Lehman and Weiner, 1991):

  - *Management capabilities*: The background and previous approaches of leading managers in a competitor company can give clues as to their likely future strategy. The level of centralisation or de-centralisation of management decisions will also affect decision making. Recruitment and promotion policies, along with the remuneration and rewards scheme, all give an indication as to the culture and style of the management team.

  - *Marketing capabilities*: An analysis of the competitor's actions, with the marketing mix, uncovers the areas where their marketing skills are high and also areas of vulnerability. There are a number of questions that can be asked: How good is the competitor's product line? Do they have a strong brand image? Is their advertising effective? How good are their distribution channels? How strong is their relationship with customers?

  - *Innovation capabilities*: Evaluating a competitor's ability to innovate allows an organisation to judge how likely the rival is to introduce new products and services or even new technology. Assessing the quality of a competitor's technical staff, its technical facilities and their level of investment in research and development will all help indicate their likely potential in this area.

  - *Production capabilities*: The configuration of a competitor's production infrastructure can highlight areas that may place them at an advantage or conversely point out areas that are problematic to a competitor. Such factors could be geographic spread of plant, level of vertical integration or level of capacity utilisation. Low-capacity utilisation can increase fixed costs, per unit of manufacture. On the other hand, it offers a competitor production capacity for new products. The flexibility of production staff is also an important issue to identify. In the service sector, capacity and staff flexibility are just as important. Factors such as the ability to pull in additional staff on a temporary basis gives a service company an important capability.

- *Financial capabilities*: The ability to finance developments is a critical area. Competitors that have strong cash flows, or are a division of a major group, may have the ability to finance investment not available to other competitors.

- *Competitors future strategies and reactions*: One of the aims of the competitor analysis so far has been to gather information on rivals to establish their likely future strategy. Equally important is to evaluate competitor's likely reactions to any strategic moves the organisation might instigate. The reactions of organisations can be categorised into four types of response (Kotler et al., 1996):

  1 *Certain retaliation*: The competitor is guaranteed to react in an aggressive manner to any challenge. Market leaders, in particular, are likely to react in this manner against any threat to their dominant position. Companies that have an aggressive culture may also fall into this category.

  2 *Failure to react*: Competitors can be lulled into a false sense of security in an industry that, over a long period of time, has seen very little change. In this situation companies can be extremely slow to react to a competitive move. The classic example is British motorcycle companies failing to react to the entry of Japanese manufacturers into the lower end of the market.

  3 *Specific reactions*: Some competitors may react, but only to competitive moves in certain areas. For instance they may always react to any price reductions, or sales promotions, as they believe these will have an important impact on their business. But they may fail to respond to a competitor's increase in advertising expenditure. The more visible the competitor's move the more likely a competitor is to respond. Actions that are less visible such as support material for the sales force or dealerships are less likely to face a response.

  4 *Inconsistent reactions*: These companies' reactions are simply not predictable. They react aggressively on occasion but at other times ignore similar competitive challenges.

Illustrative Example 2.2

Second Life

Second Life is a player controlled computer environment where individuals create 'avatars' – digital cartoon like images – of themselves and inhabit a cyber space world. Around three million people have experienced Second Life and 350 000 visit it regularly. Individuals can manufacture virtual products, offer services, trade, buy real-estate, all in the world's currency

(Continued)

Illustrative Example 2.2 (Continued)

Linden dollars. It is already possible to exchange Linden dollars into US dollars at a rate of l$275 to the US$1 and they are about to become convertible into Euros. More than $600 000 changes hands between Second Life avatars every day. The world has already created one US Dollar millionaire who made their money through buying blocks of land and building housing to sell to other avatars. Now commercial companies are beginning to see the potential of this virtual and other virtual realms and a number of companies have set up operations in Second Life including IBM, Nike, Adidas and Sony. The Chief Executive of IBM, Sam Palmisano, has even held a virtual company meeting in Second Life. The company felt the meeting was more interactive than holding a meeting through a conference call or video link. Mr Palmisano is quoted as saying that 3-D worlds such as Second Life are the next phase in the Internet's evolution believing it could have the same impact as the first stage of web revolution.

■ Problems in identifying competitors

Analysing members of a strategic group provides crucial information on which to base strategic decisions. However there are risks in the process of identifying an organisation's competitors and a number of errors should be avoided:

● Overlooking smaller competitors by placing too much emphasising on large visible competitors.
● Focusing on established competitors and ignoring potential new entrants.
● Concentrating on current domestic competitors and disregarding international competitors who could possibily enter the market.

The competitive analysis has allowed the organisation to establish its relative position versus its competitors on a range of important criteria. However the organisation has to judge itself and its competitors against the market it is operating within. At this stage in the external analysis it is useful to establish a range of information about the market. The customer and market segmentation would also be considered under a market analysis and this will be explored in detail in Chapter 4.

■ The market analysis

A market analysis will be made up of a range of factors relevant to the particular situation under review, but would normally include the following areas:

● *Actual and potential market size*: Estimating the total sales in the market allows the organisation to evaluate the realism of particular market share objectives. Identifying the key sub-markets of this market, and potential areas of growth, is crucial to developing a marketing strategy, as is establishing if any areas are in decline.

- *Trends*: Analysing general trends in the market identifies the changes that have actually taken place. This can help to uncover the reasons for these changes and expose the critical drivers underlying a market.
- *Customers*: The analysis needs to identify who the customer is and what criteria they use to judge a product offering. Information on where, when and how customers purchase the product, or service, allows an organisation to begin to understand the needs of the customer (Chapter 4 will look at consumer behaviour in more detail). Identifying changing trends in consumer behaviour may begin to signal potential market developments and opportunities (see Chapter 6).
- *Customer segments*: Identifying current market segments and establishing the benefits each group requires allows an organisation to detect if it has the capability to serve particular consumer's needs.
- *Distribution channels*: Identifying the changes of importance between channels of distribution, based on growth, cost or effectiveness, permits a company to evaluate its current arrangements. Establishing the key decision makers in a channel of distribution also helps to inform strategic decisions.

■ Summary

The external auditing process creates the information and analysis necessary for an organisation to begin to identify the key issues it will have to address in order to develop a successful strategy. The PEST analysis uncovered the critical areas in the external environment that the organisation needed to consider. The industry analysis revealed the structure and strengths of players in the industry that any strategy will be required to address. The competitor analysis disclosed the relative position of the direct competitors in the strategic group. Finally the market analysis began to explore current trends and areas of growth. More importantly it began to build a picture of the consumer.

The external analysis is the initial step in the process of establishing the key issues facing an organisation. The next stage is to examine the consumer, before establishing methods for segmenting markets.

■ References

Aguilar, J. A., *Scanning the Business Environment*, Macmillan, New York, 1967.

Diffenbach, J., Corporate environmental analysis in large US Corporations, *Long Range Planning*, **16**(3), 1983, 107–116.

Kotler, P., Armstrong, G., Saunders, J. and Wong, V., *Principles of Marketing: The European Edition*, Prentice Hall, Hemel Hempstead, 1996.

Lehman, D. R. and Weiner, R. S., *Analysis for Marketing Planning*, 2nd edn, Irwin, Homewood, Illinois, 1991.
Porter, M. E., *Competitive Strategy*, Free Press, New York, 1980, p. 4.

■ Further reading

Aaker, D., *Strategic Market Management*, 4th edn, Chapters 4–7, Wiley, New York, 1995.
Davidson, H., *Even More Offensive Marketing*, Chapter 5, Penguin Books, London, 1997.
Mudie, P., *Marketing: An Analytical Perspective*, Chapter 2, Prentice Hall, Hemel Hempstead, 1997.

CHAPTER 3

Competitive intelligence

Business success is as much determined by the actions of competitors, as the actions of the organisation itself. For example, the success of Coca-Cola is partly determined by the actions of Pepsi-Cola. This chapter explores the increasingly vital practice of competitive intelligence and examines how organisations can use such a function to support/develop successful marketing strategies. Gathering, analysing and disseminating intelligence relating to competitors' strategies, goals, procedures and products greatly underpins competitiveness.

■ What is competitive intelligence?

Competitive intelligence (CI) has something of an image problem. The term conjures up an image of elicit activities involving private detectives, telephoto lenses and hidden microphones. While such images are not completely unappealing, they are far removed from the truth. Put simply, CI is a structured, ethical and legal process designed to gather, analyse and distribute data/information relating to current and potential, competitors. The key to successful CI is the ability to turn basic raw data into actionable intelligence. Actionable intelligence involves providing decision makers with timely, appropriate information which facilitates action. Additionally, CI stresses the need to protect business activities against competitors' intelligence gathering operations.

The need for CI has always been recognised. Indeed, Sun Tzu's 'The Art of War', written in China over 2000 years ago, makes many references to CI.

> Know the enemy and know yourself, in a hundred battles you will never be defeated.
>
> (Sun Tzu 'The Art of War' 400 BC)

Such reference is equally applicable to today's business world. Given the established business trends of: (a) globalisation (b) rapid technological development and (c) merger and acquisition, CI is likely to be a strategic priority for most organisations. Currently management information tends to fall into two main categories. Firstly, reporting and control information. This monitors what has happened internally within any given period. Secondly, information relating to key performance indicators providing measures of success/failure relative to pre-set benchmarks (e.g. accounting ratios, profit and loss accounts, etc.). Such data is of course necessary, but managers increasingly need to be forward looking. CI serves this purpose.

Illustrative Example 3.1

Competitious social networking for CI

The next generation of CI vehicles may deploy social network as a powerful analytical tool.

Competitious, an innovative web-based service, offers clients the opportunity to collaboratively share and manage competitive knowledge. Co-founders Kris Rasmussen and Andrew Holt aim to provide tools which allow organisations to collectively build an on-going knowledge base about competitive companies or products. The effective use of such information allows users to identify threats, find opportunities and plan future strategy. The concept can be thought of as a social networking specifically focusing on the client's completive business environment.

Source: www.competitious.com, Accessed 5/2/07.

CI can provide a number of useful functions within any organisation. These can be summarised as follows:

- *Anticipating competitors' activities*: The most obvious advantage of CI is in provision of system(s) to consider the likely action of specific competitors. The various strengths and weaknesses of the opposition can be considered and frameworks established to anticipate and pre-empt competitor initiatives. Early warning of competitors' actions enables the organisation to judge the seriousness of a threat and develop appropriate responses. The process may also uncover potential competitors who are about to target your existing customer base or industry activities.

- *Analysing industry trends*: By examining the actions of groups of competitors within specific segments and/or market leaders it is possible to proactively establish growing trends. If management can spot the convergence of technologies and operating procedures, it is possible to 'steal a march' on competitors.

- *Learning and innovation*: The CI process offers tremendous opportunities to learn. CI forces managers to have an external focus. By constantly reviewing the opposition, we are better able to develop, adapt and innovate our own product offerings. For example, the process of reverse engineering – involving detailed examination of competitors' products – can provide a valuable insight into improving our own products. Scenario planning exercises, which anticipate competitors' actions, can enhance the organisations' understanding of the competitive environment.

- *Improved communication*: Key principles of CI are: (a) the delivery of concise, timely information to decision makers and (b) the ability to share information across functional boundaries and provide wider access to knowledge. These general concepts do much to enhance overall corporate communication and promote teamwork. Correctly applied CI concept enable staff to overcome many problems associated with information overload.

The reality is that most organisations have some form of CI. For example they conduct benchmarking exercises, commission market research or monitor competitors' prices. CI offers the opportunity to bring together the various stands of information which already exist into one cohesive, practical system.

■ The CI cycle

Kahaner (1997) develops the concept of CI cycle (see Figure 3.1). This basic concept is derived from government agency intelligence gathering operations (e.g. CIA).

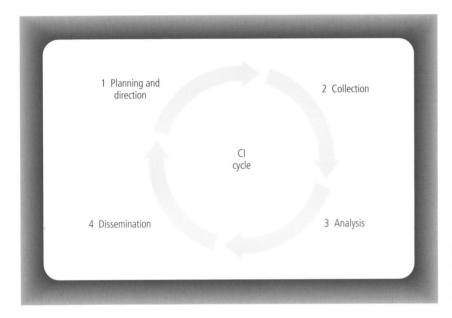

1 Planning and direction

2 Collection

CI cycle

4 Dissemination

3 Analysis

Figure 3.1
CI cycle
(*Source:* Adapted from Kahaner, 1997)

Planning and directing

The cycle begins with establishing intelligence requirements. It is important to prioritise information needs and set appropriate time-scales/reporting periods. This phase requires a detailed understanding of what business decisions are being taken and how information will be used. When prioritising information it is important to differentiate between 'targeted intelligence' – collected to achieve a specific objective – and 'awareness intelligence' – collecting general information which will be 'filtered' in order to build a general picture of the competitive environment. Targeted intelligence is used to resolve specific problems, while awareness intelligence is designed to monitor the competitive environment on an on-going basis. The planning process is concerned with obtaining the correct balance between the two.

Collection

Based on established intelligence requirements, a collection strategy is now developed. Pollard (1999) advocates translating key intelligence requirements into more specific key intelligence questions and then identifying and monitoring intelligence indicators. These intelligence indicators are identifiable signals that are likely to precede particular competitor actions (Table 3.1).

Common sources of competitive information are considered later in this chapter.

Table 3.1 Example of intelligence indicators	
Key intelligence question(s)	**Intelligence indicators**
Is the competitor about to initiate a customer loyalty scheme?	Actively recruiting customer service staff
	Buying media advertising space

Analysis

Analysis is concerned with converting raw data into useful information. The process involves classification, evaluation, collation and synthesis. Once information has been processed informed judgements relating to competitors' intent can be established. The classification stage may involve tagging data as: (a) primary – facts directly from the source (e.g. interviews, annual reports, promotional material, etc.) and (b) secondary – reported by third parties (e.g. newspaper comment, books, and analyst's reports). Data can then be prioritised in terms of importance. When necessary, triangulation can be used to confirm findings. This involves cross checking an item against a number of sources. The CIA (1999) offers the following guidelines relating to classification of data/information:

● *Fact*: Verified information, something known to exist or have happened.
● *Information*: The content of reports, research and analytical reflection on an intelligence issue that helps analysts evaluate the likelihood that something is factual and thereby reduces uncertainty.
● *Direct information*: Information which can, as a rule, be considered factual, because of the nature of the sources, the sources direct access to the information, and readily verifiable content.
● *Indirect information*: Information which may or may not be factual, the doubt reflects some combination of sources questionable reliability, lack of direct access to information and complex content.
● *Sourcing*: Depicting the manner, or method, in which the information was obtained, in order to assist in evaluating the likely factual content.

History teaches us the importance of evaluation and classification. Most military, political and commercial intelligence failure has not been due to inadequate information collection, but due to poor evaluation of available information.

Many analytical tools/techniques exist to facilitate management decision making and such techniques provide vehicles for forecasting/speculating competitive intent. Common techniques included are as follows:

- *SWOT/portfolio analysis*: The classic SWOT or portfolio analysis (e.g. Boston Matrix, Ansoff Matrix, etc. see later chapters) are applied to the competitor(s) in question.
- *Behavioural traits*: While not an absolute indicator of future action, it is true to say that organisational leaders tend to repeat past successful behaviour and avoid previous mistakes. Therefore, to some degree, future behaviour is likely to be predictable. Understanding the behaviour and reactions of rival corporate leaders to given sets of circumstances can be highly revealing of future intent.
- *War gaming*: In-house teams take on the simulated role of competitors for a workshop exercise. The team is provided with actual data and asked to simulate the strategies/actions they believe the competitor is most likely to follow. Their responses are then analysed in a de-brief session. Numerous advantages stem from this process, such as; identifying competitors' weaknesses, enhancing teamwork and identifying information 'gaps' relating to knowledge of competitors.
- *Synthesis reports*: Information from numerous sources is collated under common key themes. It is possible to electronically scan large amounts of text for key words (e.g. brand names, patent applications, etc.) and selectively extract/flag information. Techniques such as word and pattern analysis can identify underlying themes and trends.
- *Mission statement Analysis*: The main aim of analysis is to predict what a competitor will do. Therefore it is possible to analyse competitors' mission statements in order to establish their goals, values and generic strategies. Analysing how mission states have changed or been interpreted over time is highly insightful. Rumours of likely activity can be checked against a rival stated mission. Does the rumour seem to equate with overall corporate aims?

Dissemination

CI needs to be tailored to meet user needs. Effective dissemination is based on clarity, simplicity and appropriateness to need. CI should (if merited) form the basis of competitive action plans. A useful test is to consider what are the implications of the intelligence not being passed on? If there are no real implications, it is questionable whether it is necessary. Research shows that many CI projects fail during this phase. Therefore, presentation of CI is critical. Pollard (1999) recommends developing structured templates for reports, as follows: (i) information – bullet points, graphics, etc. (ii) analysis – interpretation of information (iii) implication – what could happen and (iv) actions.

■ Sources of competitive information

As outlined above data/information can be classified in a number of ways and the source is important in establishing its reliability.

Competitive information comes from three general areas. Firstly, *'public domain'* information – information available to anyone. Most industries are heavily regulated and any publicly listed company has legal obligations to make certain information available. Additional promotional materials, product advertising, annual reports and recruitment activities are, by nature, publicly available. Secondly, *'internal'* information. It is often surprising just how much information organisations already hold on competitors. The problem is one of analysis and dissemination. The sales force and customer service staff are a primary source of CI. They are well positioned to 'pick-up' CI from customers, suppliers and industry contacts. Organisations need to establish mechanisms, such as internal networks, to facilitate this process. It is also possible to set up internal systems to monitor competitors (e.g. monitoring competitor's prices on a weekly basis). Finally, *'third party'* information – specific sources not directly connected to the competitor (e.g. market research agencies, media/journalists, credit rating organisations and consumer groups). Many electronic sources exist, providing powerful search engines enabling detailed inquires to be made. The Internet provides a vast array of free and fee paying information services. Some commonly used Internet sites are listed in Table 3.2. However, the problem is often dealing with the sheer volume of information Internet searches generate.

Table 3.2 Common Internet sources

Search engines	Financial/business information
www.google.co.uk www.yahoo.com	www.FT.com www.thisismoney.com www.realnames.com
Meta search engines	**Specialist search engines**
www.Askjeeves.com www.MetaCrawler.com	www.DejaNews.com www.Newsbot.com

Note: realnames.com has been established to alleviate the problem of matching company and products names to actual web addresses. Essentially, it operates as a specialist search engine.

■ Summary

CI provides an increasingly vital function, which underpins marketing strategy. The process provides numerous benefits including anticipating competitors' actions, improved teamwork and promoting learning and innovation within the organisation. CI is based on a four-stage cycle. The cycle starts with planning and direction then moves on to collection, analysis and dissemination. Internal and electronic data sources have greatly widened the availability of data/information.

■ References

Kahaner, L., *Competitive Intelligence*, Touchstone, New York, 1997.
Pollard, A., *Competitor Intelligence*, Financial Times Pitman Publishing, London, 1999.

■ Further reading

Pollard, A., *Competitor Intelligence*, Financial Times Pitman Publishing, London, 1999.
Taylor, J., Competitive intelligence: a status report on US business practices, *Journal of Marketing Management*, **8**(2), 1993.

CHAPTER 4

Segmentation

About this chapter

The segmentation process is a crucial aspect of strategic marketing. This chapter explores both consumer and organisational segmentation. Initially both consumer and organisational behaviour is summarised to illustrate the areas from which segmentation criteria have developed. A full analysis of segmentation is then undertaken, to provide the foundation of the targeting and positioning activities that will be addressed in Chapter 9.

■ Introduction

At a fundamental level an organisation's marketing objectives become a decision about which products or services they are going to deliver into which markets. It follows that decisions about the markets to be serviced are a critical step in strategy formulation. The segmentation process is therefore central to strategy and it can be broken into three distinct elements: segmentation, targeting and positioning. This chapter will examine the segmentation aspect of both consumer and organisational markets.

Successful segmentation relies on a clear understanding of the market. Knowledge of consumer behaviour is the crucial foundation on which that market understanding is built. This chapter will briefly summarise both consumer and organisational buyer behaviour as an introduction to market segmentation criteria.

■ Why segment?

There are a number of reasons organisations undertake segmentation (Doyle, 1994):

- *Meet consumer needs more precisely*: In a generic market customer's demands will differ, by developing a distinct marketing mix for each consumer segment an organisation can offer customers better solutions for their needs.
- *Increase profits*: Different consumer segments react in contrasting ways to prices, some are far less price sensitive than others. Segmentation allows an organisation to gain the best price it can in every segment, effectively raising the average price and increasing profitability.
- *Segment leadership*: In any particular market the brands that have dominant shares of the market will be highly profitable. Their market leadership gives them economies of scale, in marketing and production they will also have established access to distribution channels. Small companies or new entrants in a market are unlikely to be able to gain leadership; they can however take a dominant share of a particular market segment. This focus can allow them to develop a specialist

marketing mix to satisfy the needs of the consumers in that group while at the same time building a competitive cost position relative to other companies in that segment.

- *Retain customers*: Providing products or services aimed at different consumer segments allows an organisation to retain that customer's loyalty as their needs change. As an individual moves through life, their needs in financial services will change. For example, young single individuals may need a minimum of credit and banking facilities and car insurance, younger families, however, will need in addition life insurance policies and mortgages, in middle age these needs will turn to pension provision. If an organisation can provide all these services they may retain a customer who otherwise would transfer to another brand.

  An organisation may also be able to use segmentation as a way of moving a customer over time from entry level products or services to products at the premium end of the market.

- *Focus marketing communications*: Segmentation allows an organisation to identify media channels that can specifically reach the target groups. For example, young women interested in fashion are likely to read certain fashion magazines. Rather than spending money on mass-market media that reach far wider than the target group, organisations can target their money and effort by using media, focused directly on their potential consumer group.

■ The segmentation process

The segmentation process involves establishing criteria by which groups of consumers with similar needs can be identified. These criteria have to establish consumer groups that have the following characteristics:

- The consumers in the segment respond in the same way to a particular marketing mix.
- The consumers within the segment have to react in a clearly different way from other groups of consumers to the marketing mix on offer.
- The group has to be large enough to provide the return on investment necessary to the organisation.
- The criteria used to identify the segment have to be operational. Recently a small company in the magazine market identified a group of customers that had clear needs. Overseas nationals living in the UK wished to buy magazines from their home country. The organisation's proposed marketing offer was to import magazines from overseas and mail them out directly to the consumers' homes. This was a potential customer group that all responded in the same way to the proposed marketing mix. They clearly acted differently from other groups in the magazine market. This potential segment was large and potentially profitable however this was a difficult group to make operational. You cannot identify overseas nationals easily as no official organisation or

overseas institute will give you the names and addresses of overseas nationals. The only way of pursuing this opportunity was to persuade overseas nationals to identify themselves. This could have been accomplished by attracting consumers to respond to a promotional campaign, allowing the organisation to build a customer database. However, for a small organisation this was likely to be a costly operation and the idea was dropped in favour of other options.

Given the fact that segments need to demonstrate these four characteristics, the next step is to examine the variables that can be used to usefully segment a market (see section Consumer behaviour). Comprehension of consumer buyer behaviour theory is central to the successful development and application of segmentation criteria.

■ Consumer behaviour

Consumer buyer behaviour relates to the end customer, the individuals who purchase products and services for personnel consumption. This section of the chapter will summarise the main sources of influence on consumer buyer behaviour (see Figure 4.1), in order to illustrate the

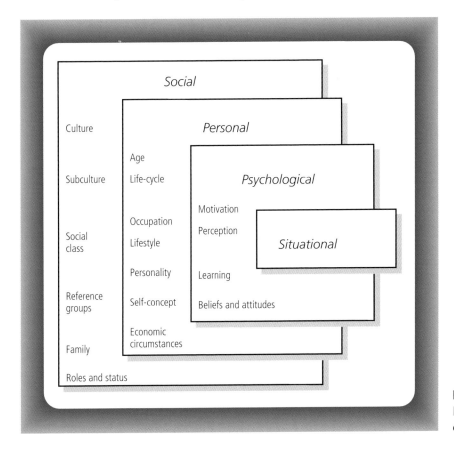

Figure 4.1
Influences on consumer behaviour

influences that affect consumer's purchasing decisions. These influences can be broken down into four major categories: social, personal, psychological and situational.

Social influences

There is a range of social influences on a consumers purchasing behaviour:

- *Culture*: Behaviour is largely learned so the traditions, values and attitudes of the society an individual is brought up in will influence their behaviour. Cultural norms form the codes that direct behaviour. Therefore in an informal culture such as the USA or the UK the use of first names in a formal business meeting may be acceptable. In other cultures, such as mainline China more formal behaviour would be the norm. Within a larger culture there are obviously some sub-cultures these may be based on religion, nationality, geographical areas or racial groups.
- *Social class*: An individual's social class has been seen as an important influence on consumer behaviour. With individuals in lower social groups generally been seen to be more culture bound. Social class groupings are heavily dependent upon societies' cultural background. Some societies are more hierarchical than others many have a few people in the top and bottom classes with the majority in the middle. However, some societies such as Scandinavia and Japan have much flatter structures (see Figure 4.2). Some societies are more open than others, that is, individuals can move from one class to another in an open society; in a closed society this is not possible.

In western societies social classification has been criticised as a predictor of purchasing behaviour. In the UK a household in the higher AB category, after paying for a mortgage and private school tuition for their children, may have less disposable income than a lower category C2 or D household. There can also be wide discrepancies in purchasing patterns within social groups. Individuals are also influenced by smaller social groups, such as friends, co-workers and family. These can be categorised into reference groups and family:

- *Reference groups*: Reference groups can be formal (be members of a professional association or society) or informal groupings (social friends, etc.). These reference groups influence an individual's attitude or behaviour. Individuals will tend to exhibit purchasing behaviour that is deemed to be acceptable by their reference group. Group norms and the role an individual plays within a group exert considerable influence on their behaviour. Recent research into the behaviour of first time mothers illustrated the power of reference groups in shaping their expectations of the quality of service they would experience during their stay in the maternity ward. For individuals from residential areas of lower economic status, doctors, mid-wives and information from ante-natal classes were less influential than friends with young

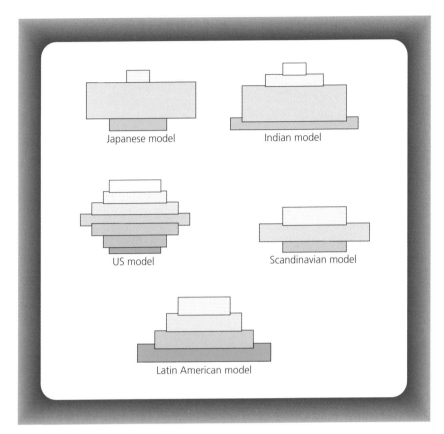

Japanese model

Indian model

US model

Scandinavian model

Latin American model

Figure 4.2
Examples of social
class profiles in
different cultures
(*Source*: De Mooij
and Keegan, 1991)

children – and more importantly than the individual's sisters and mother. These reference groups influenced their subsequent behaviour in terms of length of stay and treatment (Tinson, 1998). This also underlines the power of one key reference group, the family.

- *Family*: The family is a key group not only because it is a primary reference group but also because it is the group within which individual purchasing behaviour is socialised. Attitudes and beliefs in general and patterns of purchasing behaviour in particular are all learnt initially from the family into which an individual is born and raised (the family of orientation).

Once individual's start to have their own children they set up their own family unit (family of procreation). This developing family group also exerts an influence on the behaviour of individual's. There are moreover purchasing decisions that are taken by the household as a unit which reinforce the family as a key primary reference group.

Personal influences

An individual's personal attributes will have an influence on their purchasing behaviour. Factors such as the individual's age, occupation and financial situation, their personality, their family life cycle stage and their lifestyle in general will affect the pattern of their consumption decisions. These factors are commonly used as criteria to segment consumer markets and will be explored in greater detail in section Consumer behaviour of this chapter.

Psychological influences

Four key psychological factors: those of motivation, perception, learning, beliefs and attitudes are further influences on consumer behaviour.

- *Motivation*: Individuals have a range of needs from basic biological needs such as the need to satisfy hunger, thirst and physical distress to psychological needs like the need for social recognition, esteem or belonging. These needs may lie dormant at any particular time but once aroused to a high enough level of intensity they become a motivational force. A motive is a need that has reached a level that drives an individual to search for ways to alleviate its demands. There is a whole body of theory in this area that cannot be explored in this text (see further reading at the end of this chapter), however summarising two of the most influential theories is worthwhile to illustrate their influence on marketing practice:
    - *Freud's theory of motivation*: Freud proposed that individuals are motivated by unconscious psychological factors. Moreover as an individual grows up they conform to social norms which requires them to repress a range of desires and passions (urges). This theory would suggest that an individual's consciously stated reason for buying a product may hide a more fundamental unconscious motive. An individual proposing to purchase an executive car may claim that this decision is based on the need for quality and reliability, whereas the unconscious desire may be for status.
    - *Maslow's theory of motivation*: Maslow claimed that individuals have a hierarchy of needs. At the lowest level individuals are driven by basic physiological needs. When individuals are able to satisfy the needs at one level they will be motivated by the needs at the next level in the hierarchy (see Figure 4.3). The implication of the theory for marketers is that individuals will seek different products and services as they move up this hierarchy.

This theory is not universal and is biased towards Anglo-Saxon cultural values, in particular individualism and need for self-development. These needs would not have the same prominence in Japan or Germany were the need for personal security and conformity take a higher priority.

Motivation theories relate to consumer needs and satisfying consumer's needs is a central tenant of marketing. These motivation theories therefore have influenced approaches to market segmentation. It should be noted that although Freud and Maslow's theories have been very influential in management and marketing theory and practice, they have been challenged on the grounds that the research evidence to support their utility as a psychological theory of motivation is weak (Steers et al., 1996).

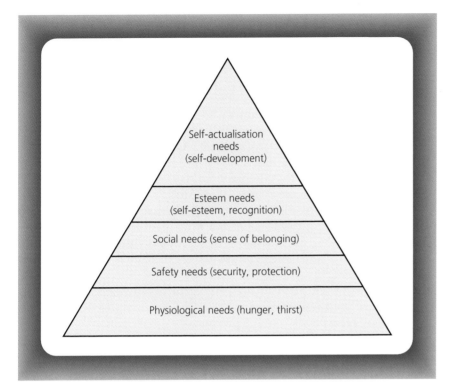

Figure 4.3
Maslow's hierarchy
of needs (*Source*:
Adapted from
Maslow, 1970)

However, they are useful for marketers as they help to categorise consumers into groups based on needs.

● *Perception*: The way an individual perceives an external stimulus will influence their reaction. Individuals can have different perceptions of the same stimulus due to the process of selective attention, selective distortion and selective retention:
  – *Selective attention*: Individuals cannot observe all the potential stimuli in the external environment. Selective attention refers to the tendency of individuals to screen out the majority of stimulants to which they are exposed.
  – *Selective distortion*: Individuals process information within the confines of their current set of attitudes and beliefs. The tendency to adjust perceptions to conform to their current mindset is called selective distortion.
  – *Selective retention*: Individuals do not remember everything they perceive. Information that reinforces their attitudes and beliefs is more likely to be retained.

Perceptual behaviour is relevant to the segmentation process because of its links with learning, attitudes and beliefs.

● *Learning, attitudes and beliefs*: Learning relates to any change in the content of an individuals long-term memory and is associated with how information is processed (covered under perception). There are various ways in which learning can take place including conditioning, social learning theory and cognitive learning theory:

– *Conditioning learning theories*: Propose that reinforcement is necessary for individuals to develop attitudes and beliefs. Therefore if an individual's experience of a particular product is positive this will reinforce their positive attitudes and beliefs about the brand. If the experience is negative it is unlikely the consumer will buy the product again. The negative attitude that has been formed to the product could also affect the individual's attitude to other products and services offered by the company or linked to the brand.

– *Social learning theories*: Suggest that learning can take place without direct personal reinforcement. Individuals may remember the slogan associated with a brand name and form an attitude about its attributes without any direct reinforcement. An individual may learn from observing the behaviour of others and the recognition or rewards they receive.

– *Cognitive learning theory*: In high involvement purchases an individual may use their own powers of cognitive reasoning to develop their attitudes and beliefs about a product.

Forming attitudes and beliefs about products effectively creates a position for the product or brand relative to other products and brands in the mind of the consumer. This lies at the heart of product positioning which is central to the successful implementation of segmentation strategy (see Chapter 9).

The buying situation

The buying process (see Figure 4.4) an individual goes through when making purchasing decisions is affected by the particular situational factors surrounding the activity.

High involvement purchases refer to situations where both the information search and the use of referent group consultation and post purchase evaluation is extensive and occurs when the following factors are involved:

● *Self-image*: The purchase has a major effect on an individual's self-image such as the purchase of a car.

● *Perceived risk*: The impact of a mistaken purchase would have a dramatic effect on the consumer. Expensive purchases would fall into this category, any mistake could have a major effect on an individuals financial position.

● *Social factors*: An individual's level of social acceptance may depend on the right purchasing decision.

● *Hedonic factors*: The purchase is concerned with products or services that are linked to providing personal pleasure.

Consumer behaviour theory is a complex area and only a brief overview has been provided here. Consumer behaviour is central to the segmentation, targeting and positioning process, in particular, in establishing useful segmentation criteria.

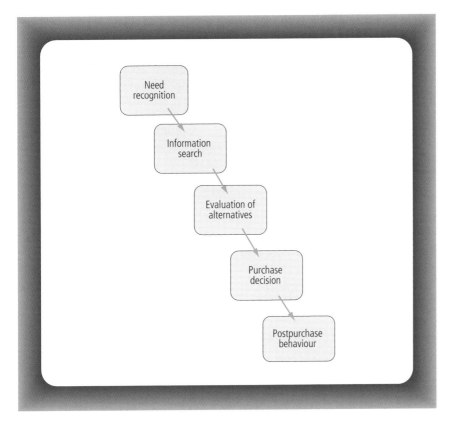

Figure 4.4
The buying process

■ Consumer segmentation criteria

Segmentation criteria can be divided into three main categories:

1 *Profile variables*: Are used to characterise the consumer but in terms that are not expressly linked to, or predictive of, an individual's behaviour in the specific market.
2 *Behavioural variables*: Relate to the behaviour of the consumer. Thus behavioural factors such as benefits sought, usage, and the purchase occasion all come under this category.
3 *Psychographic variables*: Identify individual's attitudes, opinions and interests to build up a lifestyle profile that includes the consumer's consumption patterns. Thus these profiles are inextricably associated with specific purchasing behaviour.

Segmentation is a creative process and can be conducted using a range of different variables each bringing a particular perspective to the dynamics of the market. The air travel market could be segmented according to the benefits sought (value or status), or usage occasion (business or holiday), or stage in the family lifecycle (young and single or middle aged, married with kids). On occasion it may be relevant to use a single variable to segment a market, more often than not they will be used in combination. For instance, a potential market segment in the air travel market could be middle-aged consumers with children who seek status benefits for business travel. Innovative combinations of variables from across the range can uncover new market segments, even in supposedly traditional markets.

There is no hierarchy to these variables. Marketers can use any variable as a starting point (first order variables), and then add further variables (second order variables) to give the grouping a clearer definition. Thus a segment of consumers seeking physical fitness may initially be determined using benefit segmentation. Profile variables may then be added such as age, gender, geodemographics, etc., in order to more clearly identify the consumer to allow the company to develop specific media communication and distribution plans.

■ Profile variables

There is a range of demographic, socio-economic and geographic segmentation variables in this category.

Demographic segmentation

The key demographic variables consist of age, gender and the family life cycle:

- *Age*: Consumer's purchasing decisions will change with age. Older people are likely to be looking for different benefits from a holiday than younger people. However, age by itself may not be a sophisticated enough variable to help identify a consumer segment. Using the age range of 25–35-year-old individuals to identify a consumer group results in a rather unclear grouping; 25–35-year-old women will have different needs from 25- to 35-year-old men in certain markets. A 30-year-old women who is single and has a professional job, is likely to have different needs to a 30-year-old women who is married with three children and has chosen not to work outside the home. Both will have different needs to a 30-year-old unemployed woman who is single with a child.

  There is also the issue of psychological age to be considered when using this variable. That is consumers may perceive themselves to be in a different age group to their true chronological age. Therefore a product or service aimed at 35-year-olds may attract older customers who still see themselves in this age range.

Age alone, therefore, has limitations as a method of breaking a market down into useful segments.

- *Gender*: Sex, as a variable, has similar limitations to age. Clearly there are differences between consumer groups based on gender. However this variable by itself only narrows the market down by 50 per cent. There are still major differences within the gender category. Younger women may have different needs to older woman. Cadbury's, when designing a box of chocolates called Inspirations, which was aimed at the female market, found that older women did not like the contemporary design used on a prototype, however younger women like the modern packaging (Ensor and Laing, 1993).

Obviously age and gender variables can be used together to help define a segment. Therefore we can define segments in terms of 25–35-year-old females, or 55–65-year-old males. However, this still gives us quite broad customer groupings that do not take into consideration wider factors that may affect consumers in these particular age and sex groupings. One way of attempting to overcome these deficiencies is to look at consumer life cycles.

● *Life cycle segmentation*: The essence of the family life cycle is that consumers are likely to go through one of the alternative routes in the life cycle (see Figure 4.5). The classic route would be for a consumer to

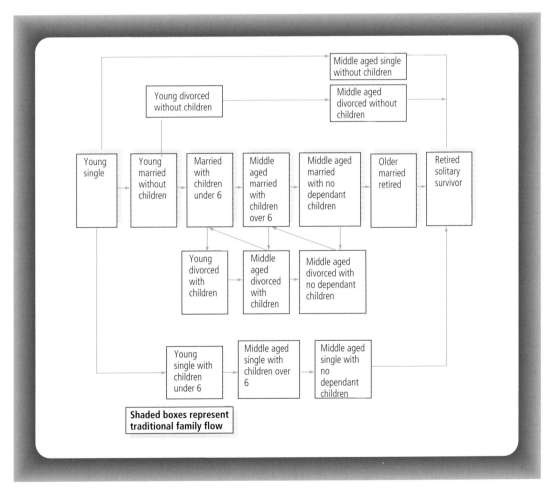

Figure 4.5
A contemporary family life cycle (*Source*: Adapted from Murphy and Staples, 1979)

move from being young and single to young married without children, to young married with children, to middle aged married with children, to middle aged married without dependent children, to older married, ending up finally as older unmarried.

At each stage a consumer's needs and disposable income will change. Someone who is young and single has very few commitments so although their income in real terms may be low, they have high disposable income. Once an individual is married with children, commitments have increased. They are likely to have to move into the housing market, plus they are now buying products for young babies and children. The couple may well start to take out savings and insurance policies to protect their children's future. In middle age they will begin to be more interested in pension arrangements. Quite obviously, as an individual moves through these stages, their propensity to buy certain types of products will change. This approach is therefore useful in identifying these consumer groupings. In western cultures there has been speculation that the family as a unit is of decreasing importance, however there is contradictory evidence on this issue. In 1985 a *Family Policy Studies Centre* report (cited in Rice, 1993) looking at the UK claimed that:

● Nine out of ten people will marry at some time in their lives.
● Nine out of ten married couples will have children.
● Two in every three marriages are likely to be ended by death rather than divorce.
● Eight out of ten people live in households headed by a married couple.

However, there was one key change from earlier studies. This was a growing trend for individuals to go through the cycle belonging to more than one family group, individuals were divorcing and remarrying. Therefore both parental figures in a family grouping may not be blood relatives of the children. Also the siblings may not be blood relatives. From a marketers point of view however it is the fact that family groupings are still a key feature in society that is important. These family life cycle stages are therefore still relevant for segmentation purposes.

Another trend that Lawson (1988) identified after analysing demographic trends in the UK was that the stages have altered in both length and importance.

Full nest stages, when children live with their parents, are shorter due to the fact that couples are having fewer children and that these children are being born closer together. This means that individuals spend more time in the bachelor and empty nest stages and there are more people in these groups.

As a result of this study, Lawson updated the family life cycle using the 1981 census, claiming this modernised version covers over 80% of the population (see Figure 4.6).

The 18.69 per cent of households excluded from this table are made up of young people living in joint households, households with residents other than family and households with more than one family.

Stage	Percentage of households
Bachelor	1.42
Newly married couples	3.11
Full nest 1 (with pre-school children)	11.91
Full nest 1 (lone parent)	1.26
Middle aged no children	1.19
Full nest 2 (school age children)	16.97
Full nest 2 (lone parent)	1.92
Launching families (with non-dependent children)	6.3
Launching families (one parent)	1.45
Empty nest 1 (childless, aged 45–54)	9.45
Empty nest 2 (retired)	9.51
Solitary survivor under 65	2.66
Solitary survivor retired	14.17
Total	**81.31**

Figure 4.6
The modernised family life cycle (*Source*: Lawson, 1988)

Illustrative Example 4.1

SKY TV

In 2004 7.4 million households had a contract with SKY for its subscription television channels, that was 43 per cent of the UK market. By 2010 SKY aimed to have increased that number to 10 million households. SKY's management believed that no household was beyond their reach. In order to achieve their aims SKY embarked on a comprehensive market research exercise to ascertain consumer perceptions of their product offering in order to develop targeted marketing campaigns to overcome consumer's reluctance to subscribe to their channels. An interesting feature in the profile of SKY subscribers that emerged was the fact that only 21 per cent of households that bought the Independent newspaper had a SKY contract. That was a lower percentage than for any other group of national newspaper readers.

Indeed households can be a useful way of looking at social grouping. Individuals sharing a flat have to take part in group decision making for products such as furniture, electrical appliances, etc. Lawson claims, when discussing the 18.69 per cent of the population that do not fit into the family life cycle, that households are likely to be a better unit with which to analyse consumer behaviour than the family.

Socio-economic segmentation

In socio-economic segmentation factors such as occupation, educational background, place of residence and income are used to classify individuals into larger 'social class' groupings.

In the UK JICNARS classification of social class has been a common tool to categorise an individual's social class (see Figure 4.7). JICNARS approach is heavily dependent upon income and occupation as the key factors which are used in determining its six major social groupings.

Social grade	Social status	Occupations	Examples	Approximate percentage of households
A	Upper middle class	Higher managerial/professional	Doctors, lawyers, professors, directors	3
B	Middle class	Intermediate managerial	Managers, teachers, computer programmers	10
C1	Lower middle	Junior managerial, supervisory, clerical administrative	Foreman, shop assistants, office workers	24
C2	Skilled working class	Skilled manual labour	Electricians, mechanics, plumbers and other crafts	30
D	Working class	Semi-skilled and unskilled manual labour	Machine operators, assembly workers	25
E	Subsistence	None	Pensioners, casual workers, unemployed, students	8

Figure 4.7
Jicnars social grade definitions

This is the traditional type of socio-economic classification system that has been used in the UK for censuses since 1911. The UK National Statistics Office, however, is planning to use a new categorisation system for the 2001 census (Rose and O'Reilly, 1999). This is as a result of the major shifts in make up of the UK population. Currently 60 per cent of the population are deemed to be middle class compared to 51 per cent in 1984. The new categories also take account of the increased role in the workplace of women who now occupy 18 per cent of all professional posts compared with 4 per cent in 1984. Women, under the new system, will be categorised in their own right rather than according to on their husband's occupation. The new classification was based on a survey of 65 000 people across 371 occupations (see Figure 4.8).

New social class	Occupations	Examples
1	Higher managerial and professional occupations	
1.1	Employers and managers in larger organisations	Bank managers, company directors, financial managers, senior local government officers
1.2	High professional	Doctors, lawyers, dentists, higher civil servants, academics, engineers, teachers, airline pilots, social workers, librarians, personnel officers, computer analysts
2	Lower managerial and professional occupations	Police officers, fire-fighters, prison officers, nurses, physiotherapists, journalists, actors and musicians
3	Intermediate occupations	Secretaries/PA's airline flight attendants, driving instructors, computer operators, clerical workers, computer engineers, dental technicians, precision instrument makers
4	Small employers and own account workers	
5	Lower supervisory, craft and related occupations	Electricians, TV engineers, car mechanics, train drivers, printers
6	Semi-routine occupations	Drivers, hairdressers, bricklayers, plasterers, welders, cooks, shop assistants, garage forecourt attendants, supermarket check-out operators
7	Routine occupations	Car park attendants, cleaners, road workers, refuse collectors, labourers, road sweepers

Figure 4.8
New classes for 2001 UK census (*Source*: Adapted from Rose and O'Reilly, 1999)

Despite this new classification there are still several problems with socio-economic approaches to segmentation for marketing managers:

● Social class isn't an accurate gauge of disposable income. An electrician or a plumber who would be classified as social class C2 may well have a higher income than a junior manager who would be classified as social class C1.

● In western societies there has been a major trend towards women working. Social classification has used the head of household's occupation to define social class; if both adults are working, defining the head of household becomes more difficult. Earlier in this chapter we have also seen that family structures themselves have become more complicated in the west. The new classification does attempt to address this issue but 'How does the new classification help to predict family purchasing behaviour?' Individuals from the same household may be in two completely different social classes.

- The variety and the changing nature of people's occupations make it increasingly difficult to apply social class categories consistently.

Most importantly in today's society social class is a less important predictor of behaviour than other methods of segmentation. For instance, an individual whatever their social class who is interested in sport is more likely to buy products and services in the sporting area than an individual in the same social class who is not interested in sport. It may, therefore, be more important for marketers to identify individuals who share a common interest (i.e. sport) rather than identify social class groupings.

Illustrative Example 4.2

Divine Chocolate Ltd

In 2006 the UK consumer spent £290 million on Fairtrade products, an increase of 46 per cent on sales in 2005 which were themselves 40 per cent up on the year before. In 2007 more than 2500 products that carry the Fairtrade logo are on offer in the UK market. The market for Fairtrade chocolate and cocoa products has also seen a huge growth in sales over the last 5 years. It is a market segment within which Divine Chocolate Ltd has become a major player developing its own Devine brand label. Divine Chocolate Ltd also supplies the Co-op with its own brand chocolate and much of the company's success is due to this relationship. The company's sales were £9 million in 2006 and this represents a very small percentage of the overall market chocolate market in the UK. However, Divine Chocolate Ltd by focusing on this specialist market is able to operate in a high growth segment with limited direct competition. This is also against the background of an overall chocolate market that is maturing and showing signs of much lower levels of growth.

In October 2006 Divine Chocolate Ltd extended its operations by setting up a new American operation based in Washington aimed at bringing Fairtrade chocolate to the US consumer.

Geographic segmentation

- *Geographic*: This variable was used more extensively in the past. There used to be clear consumer patterns in product areas such as food and alcohol across Europe, or even within a market such as the UK. Although some of these patterns still show through, mass communication and wider access to travel has tended to erode these regional differences. In the UK, individuals are eating a much more cosmopolitan diet than 30 years ago. Pizzas and pasta dishes are common in many homes. Where geographic variables are used, they tend to be used to reflect some wider cultural differences between markets. However geographic variables can be useful if they are used in conjunction with other factors.
- *Geodemographics*: Geodemographic segmentation combines information on household location with certain demographic and socio-economic data.

This approach relies on information that is gathered in census returns. In the UK the census information on family size, household size, occupation and ethnic origin can be used to group residential housing into geographic areas that display similar profiles. There are several geodemographic forms of classification, one of the best known in the UK is ACORN (A Classification Of Residential Neighbourhoods). The ACORN classification identifies six major categories (one group is unclassified) that can be further subdivided in seventeen groups (see Figure 4.9).

Categories	Population (%)	Groups	Population (%)
A – Thriving	19.8	1. Wealthy achievers, suburban areas	15.1
		2. Affluent greys, rural communities	2.3
		3. Prosperous pensioners, retirement areas	2.3
B – Expanding	11.6	4. Affluent executives, family areas	3.7
		5. Well-off workers, family areas	7.8
C – Rising	7.5	6. Affluent urbanites, town and city areas	2.2
		7. Prosperous professional, metropolitan areas	2.1
		8. Better-off executives, inner city areas	3.2
D – Settling	24.1	9. Comfortable middle agers, mature home owning areas	13.4
		10. Skilled workers, home owning areas	10.7
E – Aspiring	13.7	11. New home owners, mature communities	9.8
		12. White collar workers, better-off multi-ethnic areas	4.0
F – Striving	22.8	13. Older people, less prosperous areas	3.6
		14. Council estate residents, better-off homes	11.6
		15. Council estate residents, high unemployment	2.7
		16. Council estate residents, greatest hardship	2.8
		17. People in multi-ethnic, low income areas	2.1
Unclassified	0.5		0.5

Figure 4.9
The ACORN consumer targeting classification (*Source*: CACI Limited, 2004; © 2004; ACORN is a registered trademark of CACI limited)

These seventeen groups can be further subdivided into fifty-four neighbourhood types. For instance, ACORN category C (Rising), group 7 (Prosperous Professionals, Metropolitan Areas) is made up of two neighbourhood types. One of these is neighbourhood type 19 that is categorised as 'Apartments, Young Professional Singles and Couples'. These types of neighbourhood areas are heavily concentrated in London. Outside London these neighbourhoods are found in such places as Edinburgh, St Albans and Cambridge.

These neighbourhood areas allow specific patterns of consumption to be identified. For instance, ACORN type 5 'Mature, Well-off Suburbs' is a subgroup of category A, group 1 is 'Wealthy Achievers, Suburban Areas'. This group is made up of mature suburbs found all over the UK, particularly in Surrey, Hertfordshire, South Glamorgan and Outer London. Individuals in this group buy above average levels of fresh and dried pasta, ground coffee, fresh fish and fruit. Ownership of most financial products in this group is above the national average except for personal pensions. This type of detailed profile allows for highly sophisticated targeting.

This segmentation approach can be used to aid decision making in a variety of areas:

- Identifying favourable retail locations for a specific retail format.
- The specific mix of products and services delivered in a particular retail location.
- Decisions on direct mail campaigns.
- The boundaries of specific sales territories.
- Location of poster sites.
- Selection of media.

There are criticisms of this approach. It is claimed that all these geodemographic systems contain inaccuracies because of the difficulties in lining up the census enumeration districts with postal codes. There are also problems in reflecting the changes in housing that takes place between each census.

The geodemographic systems referred to so far are used at a relatively local level. There have been developments to try and use this approach at a much larger regional level. Geodemographic techniques have been used on a European scale to identify consumers who have common characteristics but may live in different countries. Using demographic (age), economic (income), cultural (language) and geographic (longitude and latitude) factors, six Euro-consumer segments can be identified (see Figure 4.10).

This approach illustrates the point that consumers in different countries can share similar characteristics. For instance, the consumers in segment 4 show more similarities to each other than to other consumers from their own country. This is the first step at European segmentation; it may well lead to the identification of sub-segments within these larger groups and to the ability for marketers to target relatively large geodemographic segments that transcend national boundaries.

■ Behavioural variables

The segmentation approaches that have been discussed so far are all using characteristics of the consumer as a way of identifying clear groupings.

Segment	Geographical boundaries	Description	Population (million)
1	UK and Ireland	Average age and income profile; English as a common language	60.3
2	Central Germany, central and northern France, southern Belgium, and Luxembourg	High proportion of older people and low proportion of middle aged; average income; German and French languages	54.5
3	Portugal and Spain	Young population; below average income; Portuguese and Spanish languages	50.4
4	Southeastern France, Southern Germany, Northern Italy	High proportion of middle-aged people; above average income; French, German and Italian languages.	71.5
5	Southern Italy and Greece	Young population; below average income; Italian and Greek languages	31.2
6	Northern Germany, the Netherlands, northern Belgium, Denmark, Sweden, Finland, Norway, Iceland and Switzerland	High proportion of middle-aged people; very high income; multilingual; German, French Italian and Scandinavian languages	57.6

Note: Norway, Iceland and Switzerland are not currently in the European Union.

Figure 4.10
Euro-consumer segments using geodemographic segmentation (*Source*: Adapted from Vandermerwe and L'Huillier, 1989)

However identifying consumer behaviour rather than their personal attributes can be a more effective way of identifying market segments.

The main behavioural variables in this category are benefits, usage and purchase occasion.

Benefit segmentation

Benefit segmentation uses the underlying reasons why an individual purchases a particular product or service, rather than trying to identify an individual's particular personal attributes.

Benefit segmentation is based on the concept that the key reason a consumer buys the product or service is for the benefit that product or service gives them. Identifying groups of consumers that are seeking a common benefit in a particular market allows a producer to develop specific products or service offering. An example of benefit segmentation would be in the management education market. A survey in the USA found that there were several benefit segments in the market for MBA qualifications (see Figure 4.11).

Quality seekers wish to have the highest-quality education available. They believe a top ranked education will benefit them during their entire business life, and will lead to job advancement or a career change.

Speciality seekers wish to have a specialised education and to become experts in their areas of particular interest. Concentrated courses tend to fit their needs, and they will search for institutions that offer them.

Career changers are seeking new jobs or employers and believe an MBA qualification will open up opportunities for career advancement and mobility. They have several years work experience and feel that they are in a career cul-de-sac.

Knowledge seekers wish to learn and feel increased knowledge will lead to power. They believe that an MBA will be an asset not only in their career but also in all aspects of their life.

Status seekers feel an MBA will lead to increased income and prestige.

Degree seekers believe that a first degree is no longer sufficient and that an MBA is needed in order to be competitive in the contemporary job market. These individuals tend to be active, self-oriented and independent.

Professional advancers are striving to climb the corporate ladder. They are looking for professional advancement, higher salaries and job flexibility. They are upwardly mobile, serious, future orientated and wish to build a career within the current corporate structures.

Avoiders look for MBA programmes that require the least effort to complete. They believe that all Business Schools will provide essentially the same education. Their motivation is 'other directed' and they will seek low cost, 'lower quality' programmes.

Convenience seekers will join MBA programmes that are located near their homes or place of work and which have simple entry procedures. They are interested in any Business School which provide these conveniences and are low cost.

Non-matriculators wish to undertake an MBA course without completing any formal application procedures. They are therefore attracted to a Business School that allows them to begin an MBA programme without any formal application.

Figure 4.11
MBA benefit segments (*Source*: Based on Miaoulis G. and Kalfus, 1983)

The advantage of benefit segmentation is that it is a market-orientated approach, which by seeking to identify consumers' needs allow organisations to set about satisfying them.

Usage segmentation

The characteristics and patterns of consumer usage is the essence of this segmentation approach. Consumers will generally fall into categories of heavy users, medium users, occasional users and non-users of a particular product or service. Identifying heavy users can be useful as they are likely to consume a larger percentage of an organisation's sales than other groups, as the Pareto effect would suggest (see Figure 4.12). This can lead to the identification of new segmentation opportunities for an organisation.

For example, Mangers re-launched their cleaning product Sugar Soap which was a universal non-silica-based household cleaner by identifying

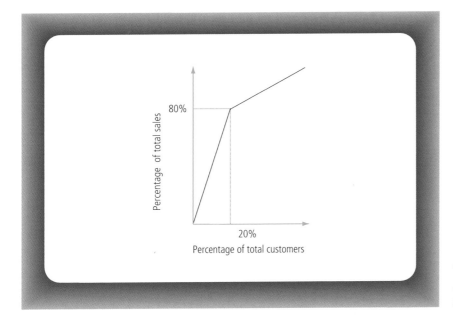

Figure 4.12
The Pareto effect also known as the 80/20 rule

that the heavy users of this product were professional household painters and decorators. In fact the reason this group were heavy users of the product was because it could be used to clean surfaces that needed to be painted and because it was a non-silica-based cleaner they could paint straight onto the surface. Once managers had identified this group of heavy users they re-launched the product to the 'Do It Yourself' market for individuals wishing to decorate their own houses.

Airlines use frequent flyers programmes to retain the heavy user of their services. Many other companies in other sectors use incentives to retain this important customer grouping.

Banks and building societies may wish to have charging scales on their accounts that give incentives for heavy users while at the same time increasing relative charges for light users as they are relatively more expansive to manage.

- *Purchase occasion*: Consumer groups can be identified on the basis of the type of occasion they buy a particular product or service. Some products may be bought as gifts, or for specific formal social occasions such as weddings or New Year celebrations. The convenience store concept is an example of occasion segmentation, where individuals can make purchases at a time and place that it is agreeable to them.

■ Psychographic variables

The techniques that have been discussed so far have used either consumer characteristics or behavioural variables as the basis for identifying consumer groupings. Psychographics is a more recent approach that attempts to identify segments based on lifestyle characteristics, attitudes and personality. Rather than concentrating on single factors such as age, sex, marital status it attempts to build a broader picture of consumers' lifestyles based on their activities, interests and opinions. Asking a series of questions about consumers' activities, interests and opinions as well as questions about product and service usage identifies these lifestyles (see Figure 4.13).

Activities	Interests	Opinions	Demographics
Work	Family	Themselves	Age
Hobbies	Home	Socialissues	Education
Social events	Job	Politics	Income
Vacation	Community	Business	Occupation
Entertainment	Recreation	Economics	Family size
Club membership	Fashion	Education	Dwelling
Community	Food	Products	Geography
Shopping	Media	Future	City size
Sports	Achievements	Culture	Stage in life cycle

Figure 4.13
Questions posed in
Lifestyle studies
(*Source*: Plummer,
1974)

Several models have been developed using this approach. These models do have broad similarities. There is a range of these models available, two will be discussed in more detail.

The VALs framework

The model was developed in the USA by asking 2713 individuals 800 questions. The VALs framework identified nine lifestyle groups in the American population. The model also identifies three developmental stages that individuals may pass through. Normally individuals would move from one of the need-driven stages to either an outer- or an inner-directed stage. This is a hierarchical model and relatively few would reach the integrated stage (see Figure 4.14).

The framework is divided into a series of segments:

● The needs driven segment identified by this model have relatively little purchasing power and are therefore of marginal interest to profit-making organisations. This is a declining group in western societies.
● The outer-directed groups are more affluent and are interested in status products that other individuals will notice. They are therefore interested in brand names such as Rolex and Cartier.
● Inner directed individuals in contrast are more concerned with their individual needs rather than external values. This is an important sector,

Developmental stage	Grouping (% of US population)
Need driven	*Survivors:* This is a disadvantaged group who are likely to be withdrawn, despairing and depressed (4%) *Sustainers* are another disadvantaged group, but they are working hard to escape poverty (7%)
Outer-directed	*Belongers* are characterised as being conventional, nostalgic, reluctant to try new ideas and generally conservative (33%) *Emulators* are upwardly mobile, ambitious and status conscious (10%) *Achievers:* This group enjoys life and make things happen (23%)
Inner-directed	*'I-am-me'* tend to be young, self-engrossed and act on whims (5%) *Experientials* wish to enjoy as wide a range of life experiences as possible (7%) *Societally conscious* have a clear sense of social responsibility and wish to improve society (9%)
Nirvana	*Integrateds* are completely mature psychologically and combine the positive elements of outer-and inner-directedness (2%)

Figure 4.14
The VALs framework developed by Arnold Mitchell at the Stanford Research Institute

as they tend to be trend-setters. This group is also the fastest growing group in western societies.
- Very few individuals reach the integrated group.

The Monitor framework

This framework was developed by the Taylor Nelson research agency. The model similarly divides consumers into three main groups each with its own sub-groups (see Figure 4.15).

The advantages of this lifestyle approach are:

- It takes into account factors other than status and class.
- Purchasing patterns are encompassed in the lifestyle profile.
- Well-defined communication channels may emerge as part of the lifestyle.
- Brand personalities can be built to appeal to specific lifestyles.

These models allow a more rounded view of consumer groups to emerge. Identifying the lifestyle of potential consumer segments allows the marketer to develop sophisticated marketing mixes that tie in with a particular lifestyle group. The lifestyle profile may highlight the type of retail outlets that the consumer group is attracted to, or the publications they are more likely to read. Thus allowing managerial decisions to be made about the distribution and promotional aspects of the mix.

Groups	Sub-groups (% of UK population)
Sustenance-driven are concerned about material security	*Aimless*: This group includes the young unemployed and elderly drifters (5%)
	Survivors working class people who retain traditional attitudes (16%)
	Belongers this sub-group straddles the sustenance driven and outer-directed groups. They are a conservative family-orientated group (The sub-group is 18% of the UK population in total; 9% in the sustenance driven group.)
Outer-directed	*Belongers* (9%), this half of the sub-group are still conservative and family orientated but are also status driven.
	Conspicuous consumers are driven by a desire for status (19%)
Inner-directed	*Social resisters,* this group are caring and tend to hold doctrinaire attitudes (11%).
	Experimentalists are individualistic and are interested in the good life (14%)
	Self-explorers hold less doctrinaire attitudes than the social resistors and are less materialistic than the experimentalist sub-group (17%)

Figure 4.15
The Monitor framework developed by the Taylor Nelson research agency

Weaknesses with psychographical models are that they currently tend to reflect a western social hierarchy and culture. As a result these frameworks are not always easily transferred to different social settings. Cultural values may mean that aspirations are different than those represented by western values of individualism, self-development and status. These models also do not easily represent the flatter social class structures that occur in certain cultures such as Scandinavia.

Some critics of the approach would also argue that these broad lifestyle profiles are not accurate predictors of consumers purchasing behaviour in any particular market sector. An outer-directed individual who may, in general, buy status products may not buy branded goods in a market area where there is very little risk of damage to their self-image. The soap powder they buy is unlikely to be of major significance to the way they feel about themselves or about the way other people see them. However, the car they drive or the clothes they wear is likely to be a much more significant indicator of their status to both themselves and others.

Lifestyle segmentation has led to the proliferation of acronyms to describe consumer groupings (see Figure 4.16).

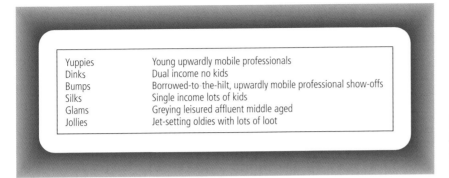

Yuppies	Young upwardly mobile professionals
Dinks	Dual income no kids
Bumps	Borrowed-to-the-hilt, upwardly mobile professional show-offs
Silks	Single income lots of kids
Glams	Greying leisured affluent middle aged
Jollies	Jet-setting oldies with lots of loot

Figure 4.16
Acronyms developed from lifestyle groupings

■ Organisational/industrial segmentation techniques

So far this chapter has concentrated on segmentation of consumer markets. Obviously many companies' main markets lie in the organisational or industrial sphere. In these markets, companies have to sell products and services directly to organisational purchasers. There are differences between the type of segmentation variables used in an organisational market and the ones that have so far been outlined for consumer markets. The difference in approach lies in the nature of organisational buyer behaviour.

■ Organisational buyer behaviour

Organisation's purchase decisions are likely to be more complex because of the number of individuals and groups involved in the purchase decision and the possibility of the actual product/service being more expensive and sophisticated. All the individuals that participate in the decision-making process will have interdependent goals and share common risks although they may face different systems of reward. What emerges is a decision-making unit (DMU) made up of all these individuals and groups. Individuals in the DMU will play one of six main roles:

1 *Initiator*: Identifies a problem that can be overcome by the purchase of a product or service. An individual in a retail company may, for instance, identify a problem in the merchandising function of the company that could be resolved by a new piece of software. (The merchandise function develops the buying plan for a retail company, monitors sales and product margins amongst other things.)

2 *User*: Will be the actual user of the product in the merchandising function of the company in this case. They may well be the initiators although this role may be someone outside the user group.

3 *Buyer*: Actually undertakes the negotiation with potential suppliers. The brief for the technical requirements of the software needed, however, is likely to come from one of the other areas of the DMU.

4 *Influencer*: Does not directly make the product or supplier choice but has a major impact on the decisions made. In this case an individual from the computer services unit in the organisation will lay down the technical requirements of the software based on the need for it to integrate with the current hardware system.

5 *Decider*: This is the individual who actually makes the decision to purchase. This individual may not have direct line management control of the merchandise or IT areas of the business but occupies this role because of the power and influence they have over the area being investigated. This is a crucial position in the DMU and yet it can be the most difficult to identify because several individuals may potentially play this role. In this case it may be the merchandise director, the finance director (many finance directors are responsible for the IT function) or the managing director.

6 *Gatekeeper*: Determines the flow of information within the DMU without being directly involved in the buying decision. They control whether a potential supplier gains access to other individuals in the DMU. The flow of promotion material and information about suppliers is also under their guidance. Secretaries are very obvious gatekeepers but any individual in the DMU can potentially play this role. A technical person may favour one particular supplier and only passes their promotional material to other members of the DMU.

The size of the DMU will depend in part on the type of purchase decision being undertaken. Where a simple low risk purchase is being made one or two individuals could undertake all the roles in the DMU. A high-risk expensive purchase may involve a large number of people from different functional areas in the company. Organisational purchases can be classified in terms of their level of risk as follows:

- *Routine order products*: These are used and ordered on a regular basis. The product or service are unlikely to pose any problems regarding their use or performance and are therefore low risk (e.g. office stationary).
- *Procedural problem products*: These products may involve some level of training in order for individuals to successfully adopt them. This will increase the risks associated with the successful introduction of the purchase to the company (e.g. personal computers or word processors).
- *Performance problem products*: The risks here lie with the question of whether the product can perform at the level required to meet the users' requirements. There may also be concerns about the product's ability to be compatible with the companies existing resources and current equipment (e.g. introducing new technology).
- *Political problem products*: Political problems could arise where a purchase takes away resources from another area within the organisation. A high investment in a product for one area of the business may mean that another area has to forgo investment. Political problems can also take place where it is planned that the same product will be used by several different units, each having their own requirements (e.g. a new information system).

Political pressures also build up in the DMU because individuals look for different attributes from a particular product. This is partly based on the operational needs of their department. Individuals also pursue their own self-interest and are motivated by the formal rewards available to them. Individuals in different areas of the company may be given incentives in different ways. Buyers may be evaluated and/or given incentives to save the organisation money. Production managers may be given quality and output targets. This can lead to strange effects. Bonoma (1982) talks of an organisation that reduced its list price to well under its competitors, but gave only small discounts off this list price. All the competitors charged higher prices but gave larger discounts. Even though the company had lower prices organisations favoured the competitors. The main reason for this turned out to be that the buyers were evaluated and given incentives based on the price concessions they were able to obtain during negotiations rather than on the end price paid.

Figure 4.17 shows how each unit may have its own set of rewards. These disparate incentives can also lead to conflict within the DMU. Buyers may feel they cannot save money because the production engineers are setting technical specifications on a product that are too high. Alternatively production engineers may not be able to reach their output targets because the buyer has bought a cheaper product from a supplier who has less dependable delivery times.

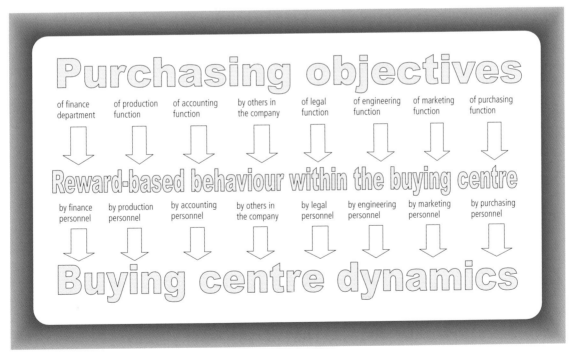

Figure 4.17
Rewards/incentives as a source of conflict in organisational DMUs (*Source*: Adapted from Morris, 1988)

This demonstrates that organisational buying decisions that are more complex than general consumer buyer behaviour. Frameworks have been developed to give a more comprehensive view of the complex factors involved. These also act as a foundation for developing meaningful segmentation criteria in organisational markets. The Webster–Wind and the Sheth frameworks both try to develop logical models of this process.

■ The Webster–Wind framework

This framework identifies four categories of variables that have an influence on organisational buying decisions (see Figure 4.18).

1 *Environmental*: Any aspect of the external environment that may affect the organisation buying behaviour is embraced under this heading. This includes political, economic, cultural, legal, technological and physical environments. Competitors marketing actions are also deemed to be in the external environment.
2 *Organisational*: There are several organisational factors that affect behaviour. The company's goals and objectives set parameters on activity. The organisation's structure and resources act as constraints on its culture in terms of the type of policies and procedures that are followed, these all affect buying behaviour.
3 *Interpersonal*: The relationship between the individuals in the buying centre are an important determinate of how decisions are reached. How coalitions are formed and where loyalties lie within an organisation will be dependent on these relationships.
4 *Individual*: Attitude to risk, creativity, competitiveness, style of problem solving and locus of control will all be unique in each individual. The individuals' personal goals, past experience and training will inform their way of operating. Each individual will influence the DMU's decisions to a greater or lesser extent.

Each of these categories has two sub-categories of task and non-task-related variables. Task-related variables are directly related to the buying decision being undertaken; non-task variables are not directly concerned with the buying decision but nevertheless affect the decisions made (see Figure 4.19).

■ The Sheth framework

The Webster–Wind framework identifies and helps to assess key variables that influence organisation's purchasing decisions, but does not concentrate on the process to any great degree. Sheth (1973) developed a model that has some elements in common with the Webster–Wind framework but also has more of an emphasis on the psychology of the decision-making process.

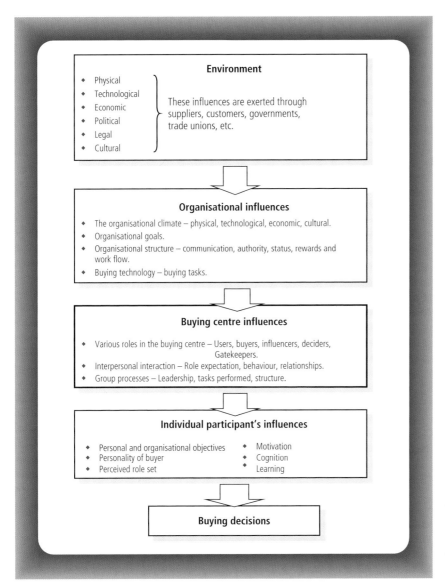

Figure 4.18
The Webster–Wind framework (*Source*: Adapted from Webster and Wind, 1972)

He identified the importance of four main factors that influence organisational buyer behaviour:

1　The expectations of the members of the DMU.
2　The factors influencing the buying process.
3　The character of the decisions-making process.
4　Situational factors.

The model is constructed so that the flow of the actual decision-making process can be illustrated (see Figure 4.20).

	Task Influences (related directly to the buying problem)	Non-task influences (extends beyond the buying problem)
Individual influences	Goal of obtaining best price	Beliefs, values and needs of the individual
Interpersonal influences	Group dynamics during meetings to agree specifications	Informal off-the-job social interactions
Organisational influences	Company policies restricting supplier choice	Criteria used for personnel evaluation
Environmental influences	Potential changes in prices	Economic and political climate in an election year

Figure 4.19
Examples of task and non-task influences on organisational buying decisions (*Source*: Adapted from Webster and Wind, 1972)

Expectations of the members of the DMU

Every individual in the DMU will have their own attitudes and particular background that shapes the way in which they judge a supplier. An engineer will use different criteria to an accountant. Individuals expectations will be determined by their educational background, their job or task orientation and their lifestyle in general.

Individuals will also be influenced by information from a range of sources. When the purchase being considered contains a high level of risk to the organisation it is likely that a rigorous process will be undertaken to identify as many sources of information as possible. This information search is likely to be undertaken by the professional buyers and can lead them to play an important gate keeping role by choosing what information is passed on to other members of the DMU.

The information provided, as with any communication, will be subject to perceptual distortion by the individuals in the DMU. Individual's expectations will also be influenced by their previous experience of the product or service.

The factors influencing the buying process

The Sheth model outlines two sets of factors that will determine the particular buying process for a specific product or service. The first set of factors relate to the product itself:

● *Perceived risk*: If the purchase is high risk then a detail search for information will take place drawing more individuals into the DMU. This could occur if the purchase was a major capital expenditure.

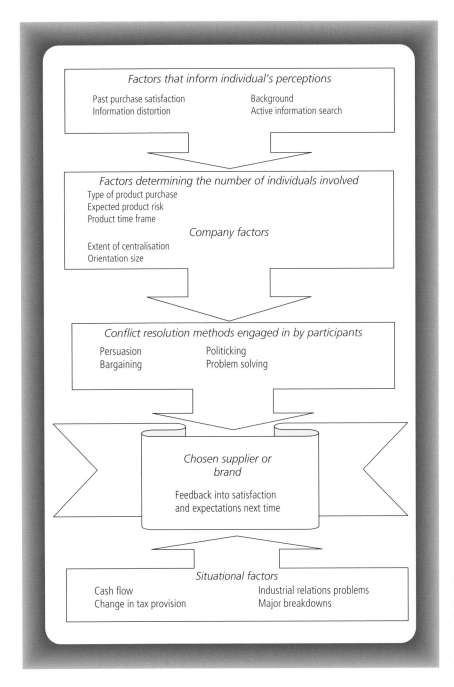

Factors that inform individual's perceptions

Past purchase satisfaction   Background
Information distortion   Active information search

Factors determining the number of individuals involved
Type of product purchase
Expected product risk
Product time frame
                    Company factors

Extent of centralisation
Orientation size

Conflict resolution methods engaged in by participants

Persuasion   Politicking
Bargaining   Problem solving

Chosen supplier or
brand

Feedback into satisfaction
and expectations next time

Situational factors
Cash flow   Industrial relations problems
Change in tax provision   Major breakdowns

Figure 4.20
A model of
organisational
buyer behaviour
(*Source*: Adapted
from Sheth, 1973)

- *Time pressure*: If a decision has to be made under time pressure a smaller number of individuals will be drawn into the DMU. The fewer people involved the quicker the decision.
- *Type of purchase*: A routine repurchase of a product is likely to be undertaken by an individual who has been delegated the responsibility.

The second set of factors that influence the buying process are related to the organisation itself:

● *The organisation's orientation*: An organisation may be engineering orientated or marketing orientated. This orientation will, to an extent, reflect the balance of power within the DMU and have an important influence on its attitude to a purchase decision. An organisation that has a dominant engineering orientation will perceive a purchase by using engineering values.

● *Size of the organisation*: A small organisation may have only one individual responsible for buying. This individual may undertake all the information searches themselves. Large organisations are likely to have more individuals involved in purchase decisions.

● *Degree of centralisation/decentralisation*: A central buying department would be common in a strongly centralised organisation. A much greater spread of individuals would be involved in a decentralised company.

● *Character of the decisions-making process*: Sheth's model identifies two types of decisions:
   1 Autonomous decisions are taken by an individual and are relatively straightforward.
   2 Joint decisions are undertaken by more than one individual. As the model has already indicated each individual has a unique set of factors influencing them and therefore some level of conflict is likely.

The manner in which these conflicts are resolved affects the final decision. The model outlines four approaches to making decisions:

1 *Problem solving*: This involves gathering information and using a systematic approach to weighing up the alternative options. A disadvantage of this approach is that it inevitably takes time.

2 *Persuasion*: Time is taken in order to get everybody to put the organisational needs and objectives above personal agendas. Again the disadvantage is this can slow the decision process down.

3 *Bargaining*: This is used in order to reach a compromise. Individuals in the buying centre trade concessions. This may result in a sub-optimal decision. Individuals may be satisfied but the decision may not be in the best interest of the organisation as a whole.

4 *Politicking*: Power and influence are used to coerce individuals into supporting majority positions within the DMU.

The model would suggest problem solving and persuasion are the most rationale approaches to decision making. Many practising managers will be well aware that the bargaining and politicking options are common practice in many organisations.

Situational factors

Finally the model highlights situational variables that are outside the control of the organisation but influence the DMU. These variables would be such things as:

● A strike at a key supplier
● A supplier is suddenly taken over by a competitor

- Financial problems
- Production breakdown
- Changes in corporate taxation

These two models illustrate the complexity of the buying process in organisations. They also give some insights into potential factors that can be used to identify organisational market segments.

◼ Approaches to organisational market segmentation

Organisational markets can be segmented according to the characteristics of the organisation, this is sometimes referred to as the macro level. Factors that would be analysed at this level would be:

- *Industry sector*: Standard industry classification codes (SIC codes) will identify an organisation's primary business activity. Different industry sectors may have unique needs from a product or service. In the computer hardware and software market, the needs of retailers, financial services companies and local government will be different.
- *Size of the organisation*: This can be judged using several variables such as the number of employees, volume of shipments and market share. This method of segmentation has to be used with caution, just because an organisation is large does not mean that it will be a large purchaser of your product. However, larger organisations will differ from smaller companies by having more formalised buying systems and increased specialisation of functions.
- *Geographic location*: Traditional industries can tend to cluster geographically, an example being the car industry in Detroit, USA. However, even emerging technologies show the tendency to locate in the same geographical area. The UK computer industry has clusters in central Scotland (Silicon glen) and along the M4 motorway in southern England. Internationally there may well be different regional variations in purchasing behaviour, for example between Western and Eastern Europe.
- *End-use application*: The way in which a product or service is used by a company has an important effect on the way the organisation views its value. A truck that is used 12 hours a day by a quarrying company may represent great value. But for a construction company who only use the same piece of equipment two hours a day it may represent a much lower value for money purchase. Establishing end-use application can help establish the perception of value that will be used in particular segments.

Organisational markets can also be segmented according to the characteristics of the DMU, this is sometimes called micro segmentation. The factors used include:

- *The structure of the DMU*: This is directly related to the models covered earlier in this chapter on organisational buyer behaviour. The type of individuals involved in the DMU of an organisation will vary, as will its size and complexity.

- *The decision-making process*: This can be short and straightforward or complex and time consuming. This will largely be dependent on the size and complexity of the DMU.
- *Structure of the buying function*: The buying function can be centralised or decentralised. Centralised buying allows an individual buyer to specialise in purchasing particular types of product categories. An individual is responsible for buying much larger volumes per purchase than under a decentralised structure. This allows them to negotiate larger discounts. In centralised structures the professional buyer has much greater influence within the DMU over technical advisors compared to buyers in decentralised systems.
- *Attitude towards innovation*: There may be specific characteristics that mark out innovative companies. Identifying companies that exhibit this profile will allow a segment to be established at which new products can be initially targeted. There are organisations that are followers and only try a product once innovators have already adopted it. Identifying these companies can also be useful to a marketer.
- *Key criteria used in reaching a decision on a purchase*: These can include product quality, price, technical support, supply continuity and reliability of prompt deliveries.
- *Personal characteristics of decision makers*: Factors such as age, educational background, attitude towards risk and style of decision making can potentially be used to segment the market (Figure 4.21).

Variables	Examples
Macro Segmentation	
• Size of organisation	Large, medium or small
• Geographic location	Local, National, European Union, Worldwide
• Industrial sector	Retail, engineering, financial services
• End market served	Defined by product or service
Micro Segmentation	
• Choice criteria	Quality, delivery, value in use, supplier reputation, price
• Structure of DMU	Complexity, hierarchical, effectiveness
• Decision-making process	Long, short, low or high conflict
• Buy class	New task, straight or modified re-buy
• Importance of purchasing	High or low importance
• Type of purchasing organisation	Matrix, centralised, decentralised
• Innovation level of organisation	Innovative, follower, laggard
• Purchasing strategy	Optimiser, satisficer
• Personal attributes	Age, educational background, risk taker/adverse, confidence level

Figure 4.21
Organisational macro and micro segmentation

A more systematic method to organisational market segmentation has been developed called the nested approach. This method moves through layers of segmentation variables starting with the demographics of the organisation (the macro level) down through increasingly more sophisticated levels reaching the complex areas of situational factors and personal characteristics. This approach effectively establishes a hierarchical structure in which to undertake the segmentation process (see Figure 4.22).

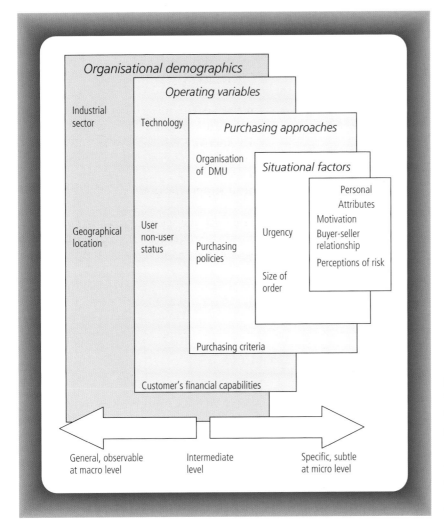

Figure 4.22
The major factors for segmenting organisational markets (a nested approach) (*Source*: Adapted from Bonoma and Shapiro, 1983)

There is a balance to be struck with this approach between the macro level which is generally inadequate when used in isolation, and the micro level which may be too time consuming and expensive to establish and operate in markets with limited potential.

■ Summary

This chapter has illustrated how an in-depth knowledge of both consumer and organisational buyer behaviour is needed to successfully identify useful segmentation criteria. This led to an exploration of a wide range of criteria that can be used to segment both consumer and organisational markets. This is the first step in the critical strategic process of establishing market segments that are available for a company to serve. Companies have to evaluate the potential of these segments and to make choices about which groups to serve (targeting) and on what competitive basis (positioning). The next steps to successful segmentation will be explored in detail in Chapter 9, Targeting and positioning and brand strategy.

■ References

Bonoma, T. V., Major sales: who really does the buying?, *Harvard Business Review*, **60**, May–June, 1982, 111–119.

Bonoma, T. V. and Shapiro, B. P., *Segmenting the Industrial Market*, Lexington Books, D.C. Heath and Company, Lexington, MA, 1983.

CACI Limited (Data source BMRB and OPCS/GRO(s)). © Crown Copyright (2004) All rights reserved. ACORN is a registered trademark of CACI limited.

De Mooij, M. K. and Keegan, W., *Advertising Worldwide: Concepts, Theories and Practice of International, Multinational and Global Advertising*, Prentice Hall, Hemel Hempstead, 1991.

Doyle, P., *Marketing Management and Strategy*, Prentice Hall, Hemel Hempstead, 1994.

Ensor, J. and Laing, S., *Cadbury's Project Gift*, European Case Clearing House, Cranfield, 1993.

Family Policy Studies Centre Report cited in Rice, C., *Consumer Behaviour*, Butterworth Heinemann, Oxford, 1993.

Lawson, R. W., The family life cycle: a demographic analysis, *Journal of Marketing Management*, **4**(1), 1988.

Maslow, A. H., *Motivation and Personality*, 2nd edn, Harper & Row Inc, New York, 1970.

Miaoulis, G. and Kalfus, D., 10 MBA benefit segments, *Marketing News*, 5 August, 1983.

Morris, M. H., *Industrial and Organizational Marketing*, Merrill Publishing Company, Columbus, OH, 1988.

Murphy, P. E. and Staples W., A modernised family life cycle, *Journal of Consumer research*, June, 1979.

Plummer, J. T., The concept and application of life style segmentation, *Journal of Marketing*, **38**, January, 1974.

Rose, D. and O'Reilly, K. (eds), *Constructing Classes: Towards a New Social Classification for the UK*, ESRC/ONS, 1999.

Sheth, J. N., A model of industrial buyer behaviour, *Journal of Marketing*, **37**(4), 1973, 50–56.

Steers, R. M., Porter, L. W. and Bigley, G. A., *Motivation and Leadership at Work*, McGraw Hill, New York, 1996.

Tinson, J., *Customer Service Interface: Implications for Maternity Service Provision*, Conference Paper, Academy of Marketing, Sheffield, 1998.

Vandermerwe, S. and L'Huillier, M., Euro-consumers in 1992, *Business Horizons*, January–February, 1989, 34–40.

Webster, F. E. and Wind, Y., A general model of organizational buying behaviour, *Journal of Marketing*, **36**, April, 1972, 12–17. Copyright American Marketing Association.

■ Further reading

Hooley, H. J., Saunders, J. A. and Piercy, N. R., *Marketing Strategy and Competitive Positioning*, 2nd edn, Chapters 9 and 10, Prentice Hall, Hemel Hempstead, 1998.

McDonald, M., *Marketing Plans. How to Prepare Them: How to Use Them*, 4th edn, Chapter 4, Butterworth-Heinemann, Oxford, 1999.

Rice, C., *Consumer Behaviour: Behavioural Aspects of Marketing*, Butterworth-Heinemann, Oxford, 1993.

CHAPTER 5

Internal analysis

The internal analysis of an organisation's resources is the final stage of the auditing process. It creates the information and analysis necessary for an organisation to identify the key assets and competencies upon which a strategic position can be built. The chapter explores the nature of organisational assets, competencies and capabilities. The auditing process used to identify these assets and competencies include the elements of an innovation audit. The use of various auditing tools to facilitate this process, in particular the portfolio models and the SWOT analysis, are also covered.

■ Introduction

So far in Part 1 the external environment, the market and the customer have been analysed. However before an organisation can begin to review its strategic options it has to evaluate the enterprise's relative ability to compete and satisfy customer needs in attractive market areas. The organisation's current and potential capabilities have to be identified and this can be achieved by evaluating the assets and competencies that make up the company's resources. Once this has been undertaken an organisation can begin to develop a competitive position that matches organisational capabilities to the needs of consumers in market sectors identified as attractive (see Figure 5.1). This approach builds on two sources of literature, a resource-based view of the firm and market orientation. A resource-based view of the firm emphases the need for an organisation to exploit its distinctive capabilities whereas market orientation emphasises the need to be responsive to market needs.

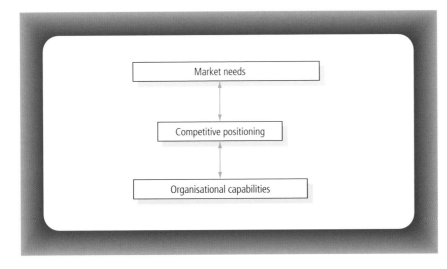

Figure 5.1
Matching organisational capabilities to market needs through competitive positioning

This chapter will explore aspects of an organisation's capabilities, before illustrating the component parts of an audit and the tools available to facilitate the audit process.

■ Organisational capabilities

In this chapter resources are defined as all the assets and competencies to which the organisation has access. Assets are given a broad definition to include both the tangible and intangible capital of the organisation. Competencies are the skills that are contained within the organisation. The application of these skills to effectively deploy the available assets, delivers the organisation's strategic capabilities in the market. Corporate capabilities are therefore defined as the combination of assets and competencies that denote the organisation's competitive capacity.

Establishing an organisation's current and potential capabilities is therefore reliant upon an evaluation of two aspects of its resources: assets and competencies.

■ Organisational assets

Organisational assets are the accumulated capital, both financial and non-financial, that a company has at its disposal. These assets are both tangible and intangible (Hooley et al., 1998) and include:

● *Financial assets*: such as working capital, or access/availability of investment finance, and credit worthiness.
● *Physical assets*: ownership or control of facilities and property. In the retail sector ownership of an outlet in a prime location could be a significant asset.
● *Operational assets*: production plant, machinery and process technologies.
● *People assets*: the quantity of human resources available to the organisation and the quality of this resource in terms of their background and abilities.
● *Legally enforceable assets*: ownership of copyrights and patents, franchise and licensing agreements.
● *Systems*: management information systems and databases and the general infrastructure for supporting decision-making activities.
● *Marketing assets*: of particular concern in the development of marketing strategy are of course marketing assets. These marketing assets fall into four main categories:
  1 *Customer-based assets*
  These are assets that the customer perceives as being important such as:
  ○ *Image and reputation*: These relate to the company and the recognition of its corporate identity.

○ *Brand franchises*: These are important because of the time and investment required in building them. Once established effective brands have high levels of customer loyalty, create competitive positions that are defendable and obtain higher margins because customers feel a higher price is merited by the added value that the brand provides them. Weak brands of course show the opposite characteristics.

○ *Market leadership*: A strong brand may not be the market leader but a brand leader enjoys distinct advantages such as excellent market coverage, widespread distribution and beneficial shelf positions in retail outlets.

○ *Country of origin*: Consumers associate particular attributes to different countries, these then become associated with an organisation or a brand that derives from that particular state. So, for instance Germany is associated with efficiency and quality. Products like Mercedes and BMW benefit from this perception of their country of origin and it reinforces their quality positioning in the market.

○ *Unique products and services*: These are key assets. Their distinctiveness in the market can be built on a number of attributes such as price, quality, design or level of innovation.

2 *Distribution-based assets*

Distributing a product or service successfully into the market is a critical marketing activity. Therefore a number of potential assets lie in this area such as:

○ *The size and quality of the distribution network*: The size of the distribution network should be seen in terms, not only of geographic spread but the intensity of that coverage on the ground. An organisation may only distribute over a specific geographic region of a national market, but have built up a strong presence in that area and be locally dominant. Quality should be seen in terms of fitness for purpose. There is a range of factors that could be used to judge quality such as ability to guarantee supply, lead times or ability to react quickly.

○ *Level of control over distribution channels*: An organisation that can exert control over the main channels of distribution in a market is at a huge advantage, making control a key marketing asset. For example, Irn-Bru is the market leader in the soft drinks market in Scotland. However Coca-Cola successfully stopped Irn-Bru being distributed through McDonald's fast food restaurants in favour of Coca-Cola. Coke were able to apply control over that channel of distribution due to their global relationship with McDonald's.

3 *Internally based assets*

There are a number of internal organisational assets that lie outside the marketing function but can be deployed to give advantages to marketing activities. It is important to identify the underlying asset rather than just the activity. It is the asset that has the potential to be deployed in new ways to create additional advantages. There is a range of organisational assets that may give advantages to marketing activities:

- ○ *Cost structure*: The organisation may be able to achieve lower costs than competitors through, higher capacity utilisation, better economies of scale or by applying newer or more innovatory technology. This could allow marketing to set lower prices for their products and services than the competition. The asset is the manufacturing cost base; this can be deployed to give advantage to the marketing activity of pricing.
- ○ *Information systems*: These can be applied to marketing research activities to collect and analyse customer, competitor and market information. These systems could also be used to create customer databases that are a marketing asset that can be exploited.

There are also some organisational competencies that lie outside the marketing function that can be used to create advantages in marketing activities such as:

- – *Innovatory culture*: The ability to be able to create and maintain a culture for innovation is an important competence. This competence facilitates activities such as new product development, customer service through empowering front-line staff to develop creative solutions to customers' problems and advertising through a willingness to adopt creative ideas.
- – *Production skills*: These may allow an organisation's production to have more flexibility, higher quality or shorter lead times, all of which can be used to advantage by the marketing function.

4 *Alliance-based assets*

There are a number of areas where the asset is linked to a formal, or informal, external relationship. These agreements with third parties can allow an organisation to gain:

- ○ *Access to markets*: through local distributors that the organisation could not cover with its existing resource base.
- ○ *Management expertise*: from outside agencies not available within the company.
- ○ *Access to technological developments or processes*: through licensing or joint ventures.
- ○ *Exclusive agreements*: with third parties, such as Coca-Cola and McDonald's already mentioned above, that effectively exclude competitors.

■ Organisational competencies

These are the abilities and skills available to the company to marshal the effective exploitation of the company's assets. The combination of assets and these skills, allow an organisation to undertake specific activities. Activities such as producing innovative products are a capability that arises out of the underlying assets and competencies of the organisation. These competencies can lie at the three decision-making tiers; strategic, functional and operational, and at three levels in the organisation's structure; corporate, team and individual level (Hooley et al., 1998):

- *Strategic competencies*: These relates to the management skills, the drive and the strategic direction of the organisation. Skills should be assessed in a range of areas. Ability to: create strategic vision, communicate, motivate, implement strategy, assess changing circumstances, learn and innovate.
- *Functional competencies*: These refer to the skills available to the organisation to manage its activities in the various functional areas such as finance, operations and marketing. The marketing function should be assessed on its skills such as handling customer relationships, channel management, product management, product innovation and new product development.
- *Operational competencies*: These skills are necessary to run the day-to-day operations across the functional areas of the organisation. As an example in the marketing function these would include skills of co-ordinating and implementing: sales force activities, promotional campaigns, public relations activities, special offers and discounts, updating product packaging and labelling. Where these activities are sub-contracted to third parties such as public relations agencies, the skills that need to be assessed are the abilities of co-ordinating and controlling these external relationships.
- *Individual competencies*: These are the abilities and skills that lie with individuals in the organisation. These competencies are based not on individual's skills in isolation, but on whether individuals have the required skills to execute the tasks they face in their area of responsibility, whether at strategic, functional or operational level.
- *Team competencies*: It is necessary for individuals in organisations to work together in teams. These may be teams formed on a formal or informal basis. Despite the specific skill base of the individuals' involved, a group also requires the skills necessary to work together as a team. A key element of successful project management relies on these team competencies.
- *Corporate-level competencies*: There are the skills, that apply to the organisation in its entirety, to execute tasks at strategic, functional and operational level. This could relate to the ability to foster innovation throughout the organisation or the ability to exploit and continually update the organisational knowledge base, by effective communication of critical learning throughout the business.

Once the assets and competencies of an organisation have been identified there are likely to be some assets that are more important than others. The relationship between these assets and competencies can be mapped to uncover the key relationships (see Figure 5.2).

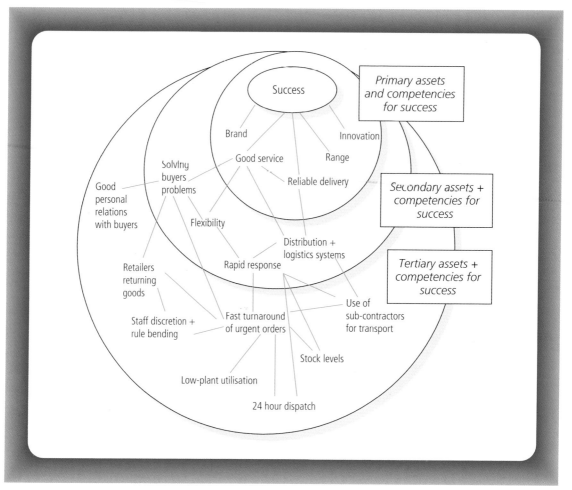

Figure 5.2
Hierarchy of assets and competencies for a consumer goods company supplying major retail outlets (*Source*: Adapted from Johnson and Scholes, 1999)

■ Initial corporate wide internal audit

As has already been stated some assets and competencies that can be deployed to create advantage in marketing activities are found in the other functional areas, besides marketing. Any audit will therefore need to carry out a thorough analysis of company's resources to establish assets and competencies, that either currently or potentially could assist the marketing function, and support strategic marketing developments. Hooley et al. (1998) suggest that these wider non-marketing assets and competencies will fall into five categories; financial resources, managerial skills, technical resources, organisation and information systems. Once this overview has taken place the specific marketing activities of the organisation should be evaluated. This can be undertaken by an internal marketing audit.

■ The internal marketing audit

The internal marketing audit is specifically aimed at reviewing the marketing activities of the enterprise and is split into five distinct areas (Kotler et al., 1996):

1 *Marketing strategy audit*: This analysis examines the organisation's current corporate and marketing objectives to establish if they are relevant and explicit. The current strategy is evaluated in terms of its fit with the set objectives. This element of the audit also highlights whether adequate resources have been allocated for the successful implementation of the strategy.
2 *Marketing structures audit*: This examines the structure of the marketing function and its relationship with other areas of the business. In particular the profile that the marketing function has, within the business, is reviewed. For instance, is the head of marketing a member of the board of directors? This is an indicator of how influential marketing considerations are in strategic decisions. Communication both within the marketing function, and between marketing and other functions, should also be analysed to see how effective the function is at co-ordinating its activities. The internal structure should be examined to establish whether marketing activities are carried out efficiently.
3 *Marketing systems audit*: This part of the audit inspects the planning systems, control measures and new product development processes in the organisation, as well as examining the information systems that support these activities.
4 *Productivity audit*: This element of the audit examines the organisation's activities using financial criteria such as profitability and cost effectiveness applied to assess the relative productivity of products, market sectors, distribution channels and geographic markets.
5 *Marketing functions audit*: This element of the audit looks in detail at all aspects of the marketing mix: the products and services the organisation produces, pricing policy, distribution arrangements, the organisation of the sales team, advertising policy, public relations and other promotion activities.

One other area that should be examined is the organisation's innovation activities. These abilities may have been identified at the initial stage in the audit when wider organisational resources were reviewed. However this area is of increasing importance to organisations and deserves further attention.

■ The innovation audit

This part of the auditing process reviews how effectively the organisation is able to deliver the level of innovation necessary to create new products, new services and new ways of undertaking activities. Success in these activities is likely to depend on the company successfully harnessing the latent creativity in individuals at all levels in the organisation. The innovation audit examines whether the necessary assets and competencies are present and examines four key areas:

1 The current organisational climate with regard to innovation.
2 Hard measures of the organisation's current performance in innovation.
3 The organisation's policies and practices that are currently used to support innovation.
4 The balance of the cognitive styles of the senior management team.

The organisational climate

There are two components to the audit of the organisation's climate: an attitude survey, and the technique of metaphorical description.

● *An attitude survey of key areas of the organisational climate that affect creativity*
  The aim of this component of the audit is to discover the current feelings of staff about the organisational climate. There are eight influential factors that are crucial in supporting innovation and four areas that act as constraints (Burnside, 1990). Support for creativity and innovation includes:
  1 *Teamwork*: The level of commitment to the current work, the level of trust between team members and the willingness to help each other.
  2 *Resources*: The amount of access to appropriate resources in terms of facilities, staff, finance and information.
  3 *Challenge*: The challenge involved in the work undertaken in terms of its importance and the very nature of the task. Is it intriguing in itself?
  4 *Freedom*: The amount of control individuals have over their work and ideas. How much freedom are they allowed to decide how a project or task will be undertaken?
  5 *Supervisor*: Managerial support in terms of clear goals, good communication and building moral.
  6 *Creativity infrastructure*: Level of senior management support and encouragement of creativity and the structures necessary for developing creative ideas.
  7 *Recognition*: The level of recognition and the type of rewards given for innovative ideas.
  8 *Unity and co-operation*: Factors such as a collaborative and co-operative atmosphere and the amount of shared vision in the organisation.

Factors that act as constraints on innovation in an organisation includes:

- *Insufficient time*: There is a lack of time in which to consider alternative approaches to undertake work.
- *Status quo*: A traditional approach, an unwillingness of managers and other staff to change the current way of doing things.
- *Political problems*: Battles over areas of responsibility and lack of co-operation between different areas of the organisation.
- *Evaluation pressure*: The evaluation or feedback systems are perceived to be inappropriate. The environment is focused on criticism and external evaluation.

Two other areas should be included in the audit of the staff's perceptions on organisational climate:

1 *Creativity*: How creative is the organisation perceived to be overall?
2 *Productivity*: How productive is the organisation perceived to be?

- *Metaphors*
  This audit is about innovation and it should therefore use proven creativity tools as part of the process. The second part of the evaluation of the organisational climate uses the technique of metaphorical description (Morgan, 1993).

  The power of the metaphor approach is that it can overcome the limitations of literal language and describe far more complex relationships and connections.

  Individuals are asked to describe their organisation in terms of a metaphor. For example: 'This organisation is like a well-oiled machine, it runs well and does not make too much noise' or 'This organisation is like a 'supertanker' it takes a long time to change direction'. These metaphors can then be analysed. They are likely to be either positive or negative observations based around seven organisational practices:

1 Managerial skills
2 Organisational structure
3 Operations
4 Organisational life cycle
5 Strategic orientation
6 People orientation
7 Power orientation

This method allows a more rounded perspective of the organisational climate to emerge.

Hard measures

There is a range of hard measures that can be reviewed to establish the current organisational performance in the areas of creativity and innovation:

- Rate of new product development in last 3 years. Davidson (1997) suggests that both total innovation development and percentage success rate are analysed (see Figure 5.3).

Innovation criteria	3 years ago	This year
Number of significant innovations in past 5 years	11	6
Number successful	4	4
Success rate (%)	36	66
Total sales in product/services launched in past 5 years (%)	16	28
Incremental sales (%)	11	14
Average annual sales per new product/service (£m)	6	12.5
Incremental payback per new product/service (years)	3	4

Figure 5.3
Product and service innovation performance measures (*Source*: Adapted from Davidson, 1997)

These product and service innovation performance measures show the following:

○ New product and service developments are lower in the last 5 years, but the rate of successful market launches has risen from 36 per cent of developments to 66 per cent.
○ Sales per new development have risen from £6 to £12.5 million.
○ Although 28 per cent of sales, in the last 12 months, are from products launched in the last 5 years (up from 16 per cent 3 years ago) only 14 per cent of these sales are new (incremental) sales. The remaining 14 per cent are sales that have cannibalised current products. This is an indication of poor planning.
○ The payback period for new developments is also lengthening.

One action the organisation could take is to have more effective segmentation and targeting processes, so that new product sales are developmental rather than cannibalising existing sales. This type of analysis allows an organisation to explore its current performance using hard output measures.

● Customer satisfaction ratings. This should be reviewed not just in terms of the actual core product but across all areas of customer service.
● Staff turnover.
● An innovation/value portfolio analysis (see Figure 5.4) should be undertaken on the organisation's strategic business units or products to establish whether they are:
  ○ *Settlers*: Businesses or products that offer the normal (me-too) market value.
  ○ *Migrators*: Businesses or products that offer value improvements over competitors.
  ○ *Pioneers*: Businesses or products that represent value innovations such as the Dyson vacuum cleaner or the Sony Walkman.

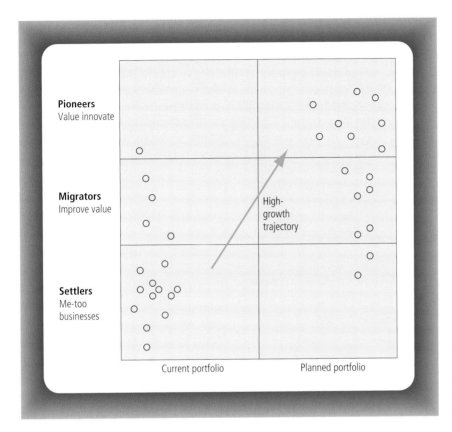

Figure 5.4
The innovation/
value matrix
(*Source*: Kim and
Mauborgne, 1998)

Research undertaken on a hundred new business launches (Kim and Mauborgne, 1998) discovered that 86 per cent of them were standard market value (me-too) launches, or only offered incremental improvements. These businesses only generated 62 per cent of launch revenues and 39 per cent of profits. The remaining 14 per cent of launches were businesses that created markets or recreated markets that were already in existence. These 'pioneering' businesses although only 14 per cent of the sample generated 38 per cent of revenues and a massive 61 per cent of profits. The clear implication of this study is that organisations that are driven by future profitability need to have a spread of business across the portfolio. Companies that find the majority of their businesses or products are in the settler area are paying insufficient attention to the innovation process.

The organisation's policies and practices that are currently used to support innovation

This consists of identifying current policies that may be in place to support innovation. It would also review whether any structures or procedures have already been developed to try and facilitate creativity and innovation.

The balance of the cognitive styles of the senior management team

The final part of the innovation audit is to evaluate the cognitive preference and behaviours of the management team. Although individuals have the capacity to make use of all their cognitive functions, one area tends to dominate. The four cognitive preferences are shown in Figure 5.5.

It is important to have a mix of cognitive styles in the senior management team that will influence the business's orientation towards creativity and innovation. Researchers have hypothesised the likely influence of a range of senior management team's potential cognitive profiles as illustrated in Figure 5.6.

The whole issue of the nature of groups and the need for balanced teams is considered further in Chapter 6.

Cognitive preference	Concerned with...	Handles these with...	Tends to be...
Intuition	Possibilities, patterns + ideas	Metaphors and symbols	Ingenious and integrative
Feeling	People and values	Force of personality	Enthusiastic and insightful
Thinking	Cause and effect things	Regulations and language	Reliable and orderly
Sensation	Activities, events	Spontaneity and action	Adaptable and practical

Figure 5.5
Cognitive styles
(*Source*: Adapted from Hurst et al., 1989)

Cognitive composition	Time orientation	Strategy orientation
Mainly intuitives with some feelers	Future	Prospecting
Mainly thinkers with some sensors	Near-term future and past	Analytical
Mainly sensors	Current	Reflective
Mostly feelers with some intuitives	Past	Preserving
Mix of intuitives, feelers, thinkers and sensors	Future through to the past	Renewing

Figure 5.6
The senior
management's
cognitive
composition and its
likely relationship to
business strategy
(*Source*: Adapted
from Hurst et al.,
1989)

■ Auditing tools

There is a range of tools that can be applied during the auditing process that are capable of providing useful insights into the companies situation.

● *Value chain*
The value chain is an obvious analytical tool to use in the internal audit. This tool specifically looks at the primary and support activities of an organisation and therefore directly relates to identifying organisational capabilities. A full explanation of this tool is undertaken in Chapter 8.

● *Portfolio analysis*
There are a number of portfolio models that are used to identify the current position of business units or products. This position will be the result of the organisation's current resources and can be seen as a symptom of the competencies and assets of the organisation. They reflect the organisation's current performance and identify strengths on which the marketing strategy can be built, or weaknesses that the strategy is required to overcome.

● *The Boston Consultancy Group (BCG) growth share matrix*
This is one of the most well known portfolio models. The growth share matrix is concerned about the generation and use of cash within a business and can be used to analyse either SBU's or products. The two axes on the model represent relative market share and market growth (see Figure 5.7). Relative market share is seen as a predictor of the product's

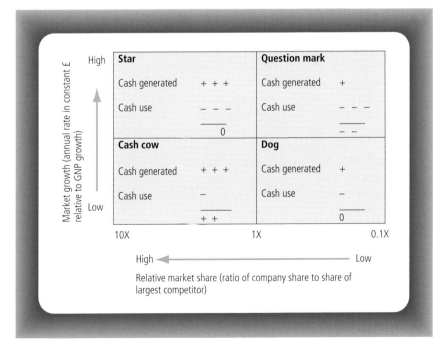

Figure 5.7
The BCG's growth share matrix

capacity to generate cash. The proposition being, that products with a dominant position in the market will achieve high sales, but will need relatively less investment as they are already an established brand and should have lower costs through economies of scale advantages. Market growth on the other hand is seen is a predictor of the product's need for cash. Products in high growth sectors require investment to keep up with the increased demand.

The model uses market share relative to competitors as an indication of the products relative strength in the market. To do this the axis uses a log scale. At the mid-point of the axis, represented by 1.0 (or 1X) on the scale, the products market share is equal to its largest competitor's market share. At the extreme left-hand side of the axis, represented by 10.0 (or 10X) a product has 10 times the market share of the largest competitor. At the other extreme of 0.1, on the axis, the product would only have a tenth or 10 per cent of the largest competitor's market share.

Products or SBU's are represented on the model by circles and fall into one of the four cells into which the matrix is divided. The area of the circle represents the products sales relative to the sales of the organisation's other products. The four cells in the matrix represent:

○ *Cash cows*: These products have high profitability and require low investment, due to market leadership in a low growth market. These products are generating high levels of cash. These products should be defended to maintain sales and market share. Surplus cash should be channelled into Stars and Question marks in order to create the Cash cows of the future. Current Cash cows will inevitably overtime loose their position as their market changes.
○ *Stars*: These are market leaders and so are generating high levels of cash, but are in areas of rapid growth which require equally high levels of cash (investment) to keep up with the growth in sales. Cash generated by the Cash cows should be channelled to support these products.
○ *Question marks*: These are also sometimes referred to as Problem Children or Wildcats. Question marks are not market leaders and will have relatively high costs at the same time these products require large amounts of cash as they are in high growth areas. An organisation has to judge whether to use cash generated by the Cash cow to try and develop this product into a Star by gaining market share in a high growth market or to invest in other areas of the business.
○ *Dogs*: These are products with low levels of market share in low growth markets. Products that are in a secondary position to the market leader may still be able to produce cash (Cash dogs). For others the organisation's decision is likely to be a choice between moving the product into a defendable niche, harvesting it for cash in the short term or divestment.

The overall aim of an organisation should be to maintain a balanced portfolio. This means investments should flow from Cash cows into Stars and Question marks in an effort to make products move round the matrix from Question marks into Stars and from Stars into Cash cows. This movement of cash and products round the matrix thus ensures the future cash flows of the business.

There have been a number of revisions and adaptations to this basic model in order to accommodate different factors. Figure 5.8 highlights the fact that products in the research and development stage also need investment which cash generation provides, an issue the standard BCG overlooks. Figure 5.9 applies the basic portfolio analysis technique but in the context of the public sector. On one axis of this matrix is the organisation's ability to effectively deliver a service within the constraints of current resources, on the other is the level of the political requirement to offer the service. This allows a key consideration of the public sector bodies, the need to provide services to satisfy political objectives, to be accommodated within a portfolio analysis approach.

The BCG is criticised for having a number of limitations amongst them are:

○ Market growth is seen as an inadequate measure of a market or of an industry's overall attractiveness. This measure does not consider such issues as barriers to entry, strength of buyers or suppliers or investment levels.
○ Market share is an inadequate measure of a products' relative ability to generate cash. Other factors such as product positioning, brand image and access to distribution channels may allow an organisation to gain higher margin and strong cash flows as a result.

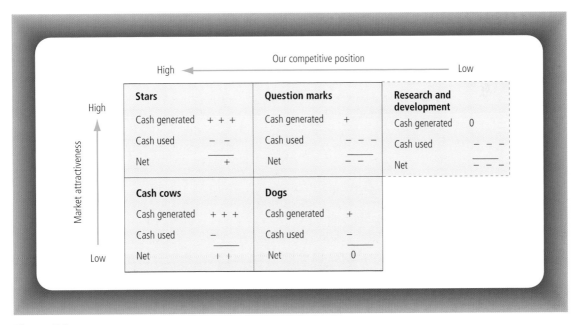

Figure 5.8
Matrix to accommodate research and development (*Source*: McDonald, 1985)

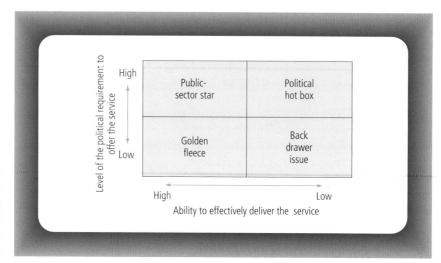

Figure 5.9
Public sector
portfolio matrix
(*Source*: Adapted
from Montanari and
Bracker, 1986)

○ The focus on market share and growth ignores fundamental issues
such as developing sustainable competitive advantage.
○ Not all products face the same life cycle. Therefore for some stars
facing a short life cycle it may be better for the organisation to harvest
them, rather than committing further investment.
○ Cashflow is only one factor on which to base investment decisions.
There are others to consider, such as return on investment, market size
and competitors.

There are a number of models that use a range of weighted criteria in
place of relative market share and growth in order to overcome some of
the limitations of the growth share matrix.

● *The General Electric multifactor portfolio matrix*
This model has two axes; market attractiveness on one axis and competitive strength on the other. Industry/market attractiveness is
assessed on a range of weighted criteria including:

○ Market size
○ Market growth rate
○ Strength of competition
○ Profit potential
○ Social, political and legal factors

Competitive strength is also assessed on a range of weighted criteria such as:

○ Market share
○ Potential to develop differential advantage
○ Opportunities to develop cost advantages
○ Channel relationships
○ Brand image and reputation

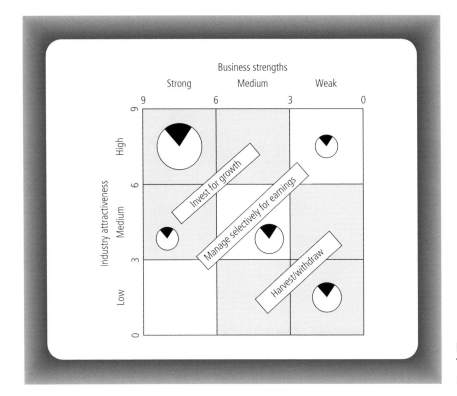

Figure 5.10
The General Electric multifactor matrix

On the basis of these criteria and on an agreed weighting scheme, a SBU or product is then positioned on the matrix, which is divided into nine separate cells, three on each axis (see Figure 5.10). The SBU or product is represented on the matrix by a circle. The circle's area represents the sales volume of the business/product as a percentage of the overall business. On occasion the circle represents the size of the market and a slice of the circle is shaded to represent the business's share of that market.

● *The Shell directional policy matrix*
  Takes a similar approach to the general electric multifactor matrix (see Figure 5.11). In both models the cells contain policy recommendations for businesses/products that fall within their boundaries. For instance for products that fall in the cell that represents high-industry attractiveness and strong-business strength, on the General Electric multifactor model, the policy recommendation is to invest for growth.
  In both these models the number of factors considered as important on both axis, and their relative weighting, are based on managers' subjective judgements. This is a major criticism of these more sophisticated portfolio models. However, this ability to use judgement, based on their knowledge of their markets and industry, does allow managers to adapt the model to an organisation's specific situation. The models are also criticised as being more difficult for managers to use and more time consuming than the BCG matrix.

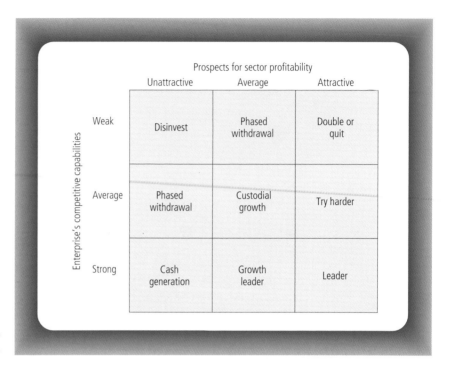

Figure 5.11
The Shell directional
policy matrix (DPM)
(*Source*: Shell, 1975)

There are also wider criticisms of portfolio models in general:

○ They are based on an analysis of current areas of business and are therefore an inappropriate tool to employ in tackling the issue of new business development.
○ They placed too much emphasis on growth, either through entering high growth markets, or through gaining high market share. Whereas there are virtues to entering stable markets that have lower growth rates.
○ These models can require information that can be difficult to obtain and are complex and time consuming to successfully execute.

In response to these criticisms, it should be pointed out that much of the information required for portfolio analysis, organisations should be collecting anyway to support strategic decisions.

The reality is also that all models have weaknesses; their very role is to try and simplify relationships to foster understanding. Managers should be using a range of portfolio models along with other analytical tools in order to establish a rounded and comprehensive view of their organisation's performance.

● *SWOT analysis*

The SWOT (strengths, weaknesses, opportunities and threats) analysis is another tool that is commonly used during the auditing process. The SWOT draws together the key strengths, weaknesses, opportunities and threats from the audit. This tool should be used to distil the critical factors that have been identified during the auditing process. It is a summary of the audit not a replacement. The strengths and weakness of the organisation have to be judged in relation to the opportunities and threats identified in the external environment. The list should therefore be limited rather than extensive. The aim of the SWOT is to highlight the critical issues in order to focus attention on them during the strategy development.

■ Summary

The internal analysis aims to identify the organisation's key resources which are its assets and competencies. Out of these arise organisational capabilities. There are a number of tools to help with this process. The aim at this stage is to identify these assets and competencies. Their current usage will already have been identified; the next stage is to decide how they may be potentially applied. This requires managers to develop a view of future changes in the environment that these assets and competencies can effectively address. The next stage before developing a marketing strategy is to generate a view of the future.

■ References

Burnside, R., Improving corporate climates for creativity, in West, M. A. and Farr J. L. (eds), *Innovation and Creativity at Work*, Wiley, New York, 1990.

Davidson, M., *Even More Offensive Marketing*, Chapter 2, Penguin, London, 1997.

Hooley, G. H., Saunders, J. A. and Piercy, N. F., *Marketing Strategy and Competitive Positioning*, 2nd edn, Prentice Hall, New Jersey, 1998.

Hurst, D. K., Rush, J. C., White, R. E., Top management teams and organisational renewal, *Strategic Management Journal*, **10**, 1989, 87–105.

Johnson, G. and Scholes, K., *Exploring Corporate Strategy*, 5th edn, Prentice Hall, London, 1999.

Kim, C. W. and Mauborgne, R., Pioneers strike it rich, *Financial Times*, 11 August, 1998.

Kotler, K., Armstrong, G., Saunders, J. and Wong, V., *Principles of Marketing: the European Edition*, Prentice Hall, New Jersey, 1996.

McDonald, M., Seminar Notes, Cranfield MBA Programme, 1985.

Montanari, J. R. and Bracker, J. S., The strategic management process at the public planning unit level, *Strategic Management Journal*, **7**(3), 1986, 251–265.

Morgan, G., *Imaginization, the Art of Creative Management*, Sage, Newbury Park, CA, 1993.

Shell Chemical Company, *The Directional Policy matrix: a New Aid to Corporate Planning*, Shell, London, 1975.

■ Further reading

Davidson, M., *Even More Offensive Marketing*, Chapter 2, Penguin, London, 1997.

McDonald, M., *Marketing Plans. How to Prepare Them, How to Use Them*, 4th edn, Chapter 5, Butterworth-Heinemann, Oxford, 1999.

Wilson, R. M. S. and Gilligan, C., *Strategic Marketing Management, Planning, Implementation and Control*, 2nd edn, Chapter 9, Butterworth-Heinemann, Oxford, 1997.

CHAPTER 6

Developing a future orientation

So far in Part 1 the strategic analysis has focused on establishing the current situation. Any strategy has to address the future, and therefore developing a perspective on possible development is necessary. This chapter explores a range of forecasting techniques, trend extrapolation, modelling, intuitive forecasting, consensus forecasting and scenario planning. Information requirements and the make up of teams undertaking forecasting are also covered.

■ Introduction

In Part 1 of this text we have been analysing the situation that any organisation currently faces and identifying current issues that may have an impact on the company's operations. However in order to make plans that are of a long-term nature an organisation has to develop a view of the future in which it will have to compete. One of the major mistakes that an organisation can make is to base decisions on the logic that explained yesterday's market. To quote L. P. Hartley (1953) 'The past is a foreign country: they do things differently there'. The future is not a replication of the past and an organisation cannot develop strategy based on a historical perspective. Over a 5-year period there can be dramatic shifts in a whole range of areas that can have a major impact on an organisation for example: aspects of consumer behaviour, distribution channel arrangements or advances in technology. An organisation that has anticipated these changes can take advantage of any opportunities they offer and establish a far stronger competitive position as a result. It is important that organisations are creative in the manner in which they address these changes. Yesterday's view of what worked is unlikely to be appropriate in the changed environment of the future. Drucker (1980) states 'The greatest danger in times of turbulence is not the turbulence: it is to act with yesterday's logic'. The first step an organisation has to take is to form a view as to what may occur in the future, the second step is to address the issues that arise creatively.

The role of forecasting is therefore crucial to developing strategy. New product development depends on forecasts of technological developments. Selecting target markets is reliant upon forecasts of their attractiveness on a range of factors. Plans have to be developed to address the future not to suit the past. How then can organisations form this view of the future?

■ Forecasting

Forecasting the future is a different activity from market research. Market research can identify the current activities and perceptions of consumers.

At an operational level relevant marketing information is likely to be readily available to support the activities that have to be undertaken. At the marketing management level marketing information will not be so easily available which is relevant to the supported activities. At a strategic level marketing information to support decisions is likely to be largely unavailable and the reliability of that information questionable (see Figure 6.1). On what basis can a manager judge the quality of marketing information relating to the future? To give an example market research could be undertaken to establish consumers' current perceptions of the future. However consumers' views of the future are based on what they currently know and they may not be in a position to take an informed view. Indeed there is no reason to believe that the view of the average customer is relevant. Is this view any more realistic than the view of a single expert in the area?

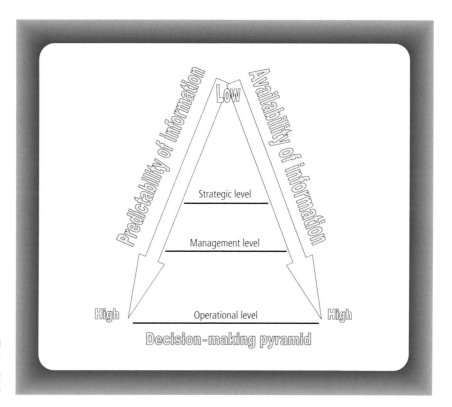

Figure 6.1
Decision-making pyramid (*Source*: Adapted from Piercy, 1997)

More and more marketing information can be produced but at a strategic level this is unlikely to be reliable.

There is no useful benefit in acquiring more and more marketing information in order to support strategic decisions. It is typical that only 1–10 per cent of a companies resources and effort in gathering marketing information is useful in supporting the strategic decision making process which is likely to generates 90–99 per cent of the value in an organisation.

(Diffenbach, 1983)

What is critical is for managers to form a fully developed understanding of the market they are in and to establish the strategic issues that could have an impact on the business in the longer term. This will allow them to establish the key areas where changes in the environment could affect critical factors such as the industry's structure, market demand or competitive reactions. Effectively this entails establishing the key questions that need to be answered in order to form a view of the future. These questions are unlikely to be important in terms of the day-to-day operation of the business but will be crucial to its long-term direction. Forecasting can be an effective way of identifying these strategic questions.

There are various forecasting techniques that can be used by an organisation (see Figure 6.2). A simple method is trend extrapolation.

Technique	Percentage of companies reporting use of techniques
Expert opinion	86
Trend extrapolation	83
Alternate scenarios	68
Single scenarios	55
Simulation models	55
Brainstorming	45
Causal models	32
Delphi projections	29

Figure 6.2 Forecasting techniques used by large industrial organisations (*Source*: Adapted from Diffenbach, 1983)

■ Trend extrapolation

This technique purely takes a historical trend overtime and extrapolates where the trend line will be if extended into the future. The general assumption is that whatever happened in the past will continue in the future. In some areas this may be an entirely suitable way to establish what the situation will be in the future. For instance demographic trends are slow moving and therefore more predictable. However trend lines can mislead planners if they fail to understand the underlying nature of a market. Car ownership in the UK has been on an upward growth curve for years. The assumption is that this will continue causing escalating problems in terms of congestion and pollution. However it is unlikely these growth estimates will be fulfilled precisely because roads will become more overcrowded and less easy to use. Consumers will switch to other forms of transport. Even where trends can provide reasonable forecasts it is usually in areas that are not of major strategic importance. Issues that have a major impact on the organisation's strategy are likely to occur where a development in the future causes the trend line to change. Identifying these discontinuities is a critical activity, which this simple technique ignores.

■ Modelling

Modelling techniques have a generally more sophisticated approach to forecasting than trend extrapolation. This technique tries to identify the key variables in a situation and to model how they interact with each other. In this way the key inputs to a particular market can be modelled. Once the model is created variables such as quantity of supply or consumers' level of disposable income can be altered to see what effect this has on the market as a whole. These variables tend to be those that can be easily quantified. The problem with this approach, when applying it to futures forecasting, is that what appear to be key variables in the current market may not be the key variables in the market of the future. The relationship between these variables may also change in the future.

To enable managers to form a more challenging view of the future other techniques have to be used that foster a more creative approach.

■ Intuitive forecasting

There can be some merit in an individual forecast or 'Genius' forecast. If an individual is an expert in a specialist area they are able to form a comprehensive overview of their area of activity. This can allow them to see potential patterns or relationships emerging that very few other individuals or groups have the perspective to contemplate.

In the 1930s military planners believed that any future war in Europe would be a repeat of the type of war fought between 1914 and 1918, with armies facing each other over fortified defences. One individual wrote a book called 'The army of the future' in France in the early 1930s forecasting that any future war would be dominated by highly mobile tanks supported by aircraft. The British and French high commands rejected this forecast. The Americans believed they understood how a mobile war should be fought due to their experiences in the 'non-mechanised' American Civil War and rejected the book's view of the future. Adolph Hitler read this book and as we now know realised the strength of the ideas it contained. The book was written by a certain Charles de Gaulle then a little known French army officer. This is a dramatic illustration of the power of an individual genius forecasting the future.

However the dangers of individual forecasts are obvious. An individual forecast is a personal judgement and is open to idiosyncratic interpretations of an individual's observations.

In reality though many company's forecasts are reliant on an individual. This may be the owner of a small company or the marketing manager in a larger organisation. Organisations also use forecasts published by an individual expert as the basis of their planning. The techniques we are going to discuss try to address the weaknesses of this individual approach. However it needs to be stressed that while there are obvious problems with relying on a single individual it has to be borne in mind that futures forecasting is largely more of an art than a science.

■ Consensus forecasting

To overcome the limitations of individual forecasting the obvious step is to involve a group of individuals in the forecast. These individuals will develop a forecast by reaching some sort of consensus. There are different methods available to reaching this consensus, a straightforward Jury system or the Delphi technique.

Jury forecasting

According to Dalrymple (1989) and Mentzer and Cox (1984) a jury of executive opinion is one of the most popular forms of forecasting used by organisations. Effectively a group of company executives (or it could be a panel of experts external to the company) are brought together to discuss their respective views of events that may occur in the future. A group forecast emerges that is the consensus view of the group. Any forecast will depend on the quality of the individuals within the group. There are several problems with a jury method. Decisions about the composition of the jury will have a major impact on the judgements the group will derive. The consensus reached by a jury, as it attempts to reach an accommodation all members can live with, may diminish the input of the more talented forecasters. An even greater threat is that persuasive individuals, or those with greater status, rather than those with the most knowledge dominate the group. The greater the cohesiveness of the group the more likely it is that they will be unwilling to listen to a dissenting individual within the group. This tendency is called 'groupthink' and can have major implications for management groups in general and jury forecasting in particular. Groupthink tends to occur with group of individuals that know each other well, enjoy being together and belonging to the same 'ingroup' (Janis, 1972; Janis and Mann, 1982). These ingroups are widespread in organisations.

Four key factors affect the way ingroups work and the level of groupthink that develops:

1 *High cohesiveness*: Ingroups display the tendency to have a high degree of cohesiveness among their members. There is a great feeling of harmony among members of the group and a mutual self-support of fellow members. This result in members of the group increasingly conforming and complying to group norms. Members are less willing to show dissent during group meetings as a result.

2 *Strong leadership*: Strong group leaders carry enormous influence within the group and this can lead to increased pressure for a unanimous group position to be taken in order to show solidarity with the leader.

3 *Lack of objective search and evaluation*: Groups develop their own way of reaching decisions; this tends to be informal because of the level of trust between members. The result is that alternative courses of action are not explored. When alternative actions *are* identified they are only considered at a superficial level.

4 *Insulation of the group*: As the group bonds increase members tend to have fewer interactions with members outside the group. Alternative viewpoints therefore are not heard on a regular basis. When they are heard they are largely rejected because the individual proposing them is not a member of the group and therefore not a reliable source.

Groupthink causes six different types of problem for jury forecasting:

1 *Illusions of invulnerability*: Because the responsibility for a decision is shared in a group, individuals do not feel the same level of responsibility for the outcome. Groups therefore are more willing than an individual to take decisions that carry a higher level of risk. This is exacerbated by the fact that the individual group members have confidence in the combined wisdom of the group and feel the group's deliberations will have identified all the potential dangers. The reality is that ingroups tend to be over optimistic and ignore warning signs taking more risky decisions as a result. Research also shows that groups tend to become more extreme, whatever they are like, so for example conservative groups become more conservative.

2 *Collective rationalisation*: Ingroups tend to develop a collective rationale to discredit any evidence that may act as a warning or a threat. Elaborate reasons are developed to explain why events did not happen as predicted. The group will find a rationale that will allow it to defend itself from criticism especially from outside individuals or groups. The overall effect is to reassure the group that its decisions are legitimate.

3 *Belief in the inherent morality of the group*: All members of the group are presumed to have a set of high moral and ethical standards. Group decisions as a result are seen as unquestionably morally right. Ingroups therefore fail to pay rigorous attention to the moral consequences of their decision making.

4 *Pressure on dissenters*: Both direct and indirect pressure to conform is applied to members of the group. A member who shows signs of dissent may be excluded from an exclusive inner circle unless they return to the conformist view. Ultimately they may be ejected from the group altogether if their dissent continues.

5 *The illusion of unanimity*: Individuals who may hold opposing opinions to other members of the group on an issue tend to practice self-censorship. They will give voice to mildly opposing views or keep quiet altogether as a way of avoiding the hostile reaction of the rest of the group. Group members may stay quiet merely because they believe that no one else shares their views which further reinforce self-censorship.

6 *Self-appointed mind guards*: Members of the group take on the role of guarding against incoming information that may threaten the group's position. Thus information is effectively filtered to stop any opposing evidence from being considered during group discussions. The absence of any contradictory evidence reinforces the unanimity of view amongst group members.

Janis regarded decisions such as the Bay of Pigs invasion, escalation of the Vietnam War and the lack of preparation for an air attack on Pearl Harbour as illustrations of the effect of group think. A more contemporary example would be the disaster of the Challenger space shuttle. There are obvious commercial examples as well including perhaps the Sinclair C5.

Ingroups cause obvious problems for organisations as they curtail critical evaluation, limit the serious reflection of alternative courses of action and foster acquiescent behaviour in individuals. However they are virtually impossible to eradicate. Ingroups exist precisely because they offer security to individuals and a sense of belonging. There are ways to minimise groupthink behaviour during forecasting and planning activities. The aim of these curtailing actions is to enforce a critical evaluation decision-making process without destroying the group. Fostering a critical evaluation can be facilitated by instituting several procedural measures (Makridakis and Wheelwright, 1989):

- A member of the group can be assigned the role of the 'Devils advocate' when specific decision-making activities are taking place. The individual undertaking this role will obviously be rotated.
- The group leader is not allowed, at least at the early stages of the discussion, to advocate a particular point of view. They have to take an impartial role and allow the group to develop its own opinions.
- The group can invite outside independent individuals to attend group discussions when critical decisions are being made. Their role could be precisely to raise alternatives or to provide alternative evidence not considered by the group.

Given that group forecasting is prevalent in organisations it is crucial that companies recognise the dangers of groupthink in their forecasting and planning activities.

Delphi forecasts

One technique that has been developed to overcome the problem with group forecasts is the Delphi forecast. A Delphi forecast purposely keeps the panel of experts involved physically apart. In many studies they will remain unknown to each other. Communication is undertaken by letter or e-mail directly to each individual from the Delphi study co-ordinator. This approach is taken in order to remove the social pressures and other undesirable aspects of group interaction. If a study examining what technological breakthroughs are desirable and achievable in the next 20 years was commissioned the following procedures would be executed. Once a panel of experts has been formed by the co-ordinator the Delphi study will have at least four phases:

Phase 1

A letter is sent to each of the experts asking them to state the scientific breakthrough and technological developments that they feel are firstly beneficial and secondly could be attainable in the next 25 years. Each expert will send his or her independent judgement back to the co-ordinator. From these lists the co-ordinator will create a comprehensive list or choose those items of particular concern to the organisation undertaking the study.

Phase 2

In Phase 2 each expert is sent the list and asked to judge for each item the probability of when each potential development will take place. The timescale would normally be broken down into 5-year bands.

Therefore one expert may reply to a question as follows:

Year	By 2005	2006–2010	2011–2015	2016–2020	2021–2025	Never
Probability	0.0	0.15	0.25	0.35	0.25	0.00

A second expert's judgement however may be different:

Year	By 2005	2006–2010	2011–2015	2016–2020	2021–2025	Never
Probability	0.5	0.10	0.15	0.25	0.45	0.00

The co-ordinator will then collate all the replies and draw up charts displaying the distribution of experts' responses for each potential development.

Phase 3

The co-ordinator will then write to each panel member enclosing the charts that have been developed as a result of Phase 2. These results will however be broken down into two areas. One set of results will have a very small spread of responses and therefore a near consensus. The other set will have a wide spread of responses and therefore be clearly non-consensus items. On each question the expert can see how far they are away from the average. They are then asked to reassess their responses. Experts that are at an extreme position from the mean can be asked to give a rationale for their prediction if they continue to maintain their position.

Phase 4

This is a repeat of Phase 3 except the experts will now consider revised charts that have been developed as a result of the reconsideration that individuals have undertaken in the previous round. Panel members can adjust their judgements in the light of the previous round in particular they may change their view once they have seen the reasoning given by the experts who took an extreme position.

Delphi forecasts aim to arrive at a consensus position and can go beyond a fourth phase in order to arrive at this position. Once a consensus has been achieved an organisation can then begin to weigh up the impact the forecasted events will have on their operations.

There are several problems with this forecasting technique:

- The process consumes a lot of time, as there can be considerable delays waiting to receive a full set of replies every round.
- The time delays cause organisational problems as panel members begin to drop out or become less motivated.
- A major problem is that Delphi forecasts appear to be heavily influenced by the ideas in fashion at the time of the survey.
- The other significant shortcoming with the technique is that experts on these studies have invariably been over optimistic on the timescales involved in developments coming to fruition.
- There are also issues about the membership of the panel in the first place. How decisions on the panel, and who involved in making those deliberations, can be subject to all the problems outlined in the jury method discussed earlier.

The advantages of the Delphi method should not be dismissed, however the technique does attempt to remove some of the problems related to group decisions making. The Delphi method also is a move away from striving to form a single view of the future. Although the aim is to narrow down the responses to as much of a consensus as possible this may not be achieved. When the process does not reach a clear consensus it can still be useful as it has identified the spread of opinion among experts in the field. A planning team therefore can consider a series of potential outcomes.

■ Scenario planning

This idea of identifying a diverse range of potential futures lies at the heart of the scenario planning process. Scenarios are normally developed by a whole management group, although they can be undertaken by a cross section of people from across an organisation. They may also include specially invited outside guests who may be able to offer an alternative perspective. It is important that all members of the group are familiar with the environmental analysis that has already taken place. There are several techniques available to develop scenarios some much more sophisticated and thorough than others. Here we are only going to explore the development of simple scenarios. There are four key stages in the development of simple scenarios:

1 *Identify the critical variables*: The first step is to use a brainstorming session to establish the factors that will drive changes in the future

Illustrative Example 6.1

The Copenhagen Institute for Futures Studies

The Copenhagen Institute for Futures Studies (CIFS) is an academic group specialising in futures forecasting. The institute's view is that society in future will be driven by creativity and innovation. This will lead to the phenomena of the 'Creative Man' (CIFS, 2004) born out of a number of trends. At a social level CIFS has identified a growth in peoples' individual need for greater personnel growth while developments at a technological level permit greater individual self-expression in the production of products and services. In Europe and other developed economies the growth of automation in manufacturing is also leading to a shift in the balance of employment to the service sector where these new technologies allow higher levels of self-expression.

CIFS believes this shift to a creative and innovative society will lead to profound changes in consumption patterns. In a society where having a high level of income is more common and brands are everywhere it will become difficult to demonstrate one's social standing simply through the exhibition of high-priced status brands. In future individuals will wish to demonstrate their status through building on the wealth they exhibit by also having a creative part in the design of the products and services they display. This ability to co-design products is a service that companies are already beginning to offer. For example, in Poland consumers can buy a designer white sofa that comes with an embroidery set. This allows the customer to add their own embroidery to the sofa making their own customised version of the product. CIFS believe this development will accelerate and move, at a fundamental level, the centre of power away from companies and towards consumers. Market segments will become highly fragmented making current market communication strategies obsolete. At the same time organisations will need to have a much deeper level of engagement with individual customers. These developments will have a major impact on the culture of companies and the nature of their value chains.

environment. Longer-term time horizons should be used so that participants' do not simply extrapolate from present trends. The focus is on the external environment not the organisation and its current relationships. Once these drivers for change have been identified they should be evaluated on the basis of their importance to the organisation and the level of certainty associated with the manner in which that driver of change will actually develop (see Figure 6.3).

2   *Develop possible strings of events*: The key drivers of change will be ones that are identified as being important but not predictable in which way they will develop. There will be more than one view or interpretation on which way these drivers will manifest themselves in the future. These will form the building blocks for the scenarios. The important drivers that are certain to develop may also appear in the scenario but these will appear in every scenario on the same timescale. The next

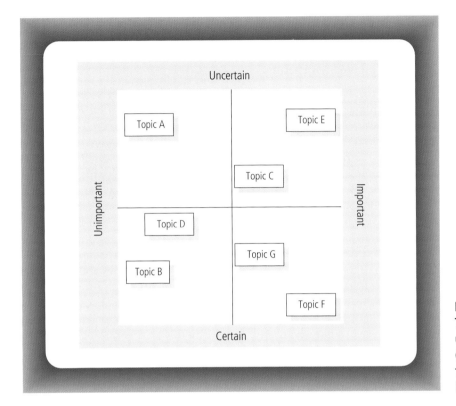

Figure 6.3
The importance/
uncertainty matrix
(*Source*: Adapted
from Van Der
Heijden, 1997)

step is to again have a brainstorming session that puts these drivers into alternative sequences of events overtime. One way of operating is to write each driver of change on a separate note of paper. These can then be moved to change their position as each alternative scenario is developed. The whole aim is to build scenarios that start from the situation today and develop into a future position that was not pre-planned, by the planning group, at the beginning of the scenarios development.

3   *Refine the scenarios*: Once a whole range of scenarios have been developed using the same key drivers for change they will need to be evaluated. Scenarios have to be challenging and have an internal consistency. A scenario would not for example be internally consistent if it had the UK government cutting interest rates dramatically below the rate of other European countries, while at the same time the Pound (Sterling) was dramatically strengthening against the Euro. Scenarios also should be credible and recognisable. Once the weakest scenarios have been discarded it is important to test the remainder for their robustness. One useful approach is to test the scenario from the perspective of organisations or individuals that are actors in the story line. Do their actions appear to be compatible with the logic of that actor's position?

4 *Identify the issues arising*: The robust scenarios that have survived the evaluation process should then be reviewed to see whether any critical event or outcomes have been identified that would have a major impact on the organisation.

There is no reason to assign a probability of the likelihood of a scenario actually happening. If the reasoning behind a scenario is sound then it is a potential future that could happen and management needs to be aware of the impact that future could have on their organisation. The technique was used to great affect by Shell in the early 1980s. Shell developed a range of scenarios aimed at developing a view of economic development and the demand for oil that would accompany them covering the 1980–1985 timescale. One scenario created a surprise result that demand for oil would fall as consumers began to implement conservation measures to lower energy use as a result of the second oil shock (OPEC's second oil price increase). The general consensus in the oil industry was that demand would be sustained at normal levels. At the time there were worries about the outbreak of the Iran–Iraq war, customer orders were strong and therefore the general feeling in the industry was towards expansion. Oil companies in 1980–1981 competed heavily to win supply contracts and increase drilling activity massively. However, early in 1981 there were the first signs that the scenario of less demand for oil was beginning to develop in the real economy. Further scenario work leads them to refine this scenario to include more detail.

With the benefit of hindsight in 1980–1981 oil companies clearly overestimated future demand. The scenario technique allowed Shell to see this early and to have prepared appropriate plans if this scenario actually started to develop. In 1981 Shell reduced oil stocks much earlier and at a greater level than the industry as a whole. This had the added benefit of allowing them to sell before prices decreased (Wack, 1985).

The scenario technique is obviously open to similar group dynamic problems as the jury method. They may also be open to the problem of currently fashionable ideas being given too high a profile. There are however clear benefits to the scenario planning process:

● It is a useful technique to help managers understand the critical issues that lie at the heart of the future of the organisation. It can help create a framework within which to understand events as they evolve.
● Prepares managers for the possibility that there may be discontinuities in the external environment.
● Critically, it helps to place fundamental strategic issues on the management agenda.

The key dimension of scenario writing is not so much forecasting the future but helping managers to understand the factors that could have a major impact on their business. Graham Galer of Shell states 'Accuracy has to be judged, I think, in terms of whether the scenarios got the right things on the management agenda' (Galer, 1998).

Illustrative Example 6.2

New Solutions

New Solutions is one of a number of consultancy practices that employ scenario planning as a method of creating perspectives on the future consumer environment. In one exercise the consultancy explored the emerging pattern of consumer behaviour using a model with two key dimensions. On one axis was a range with 'work dominated life' and 'a balanced life' at either extreme, and on the other axis was a range from 'acceptance of risk' to 'aversion to risk' at either extreme. Four scenarios were thus developed using these consumer characteristics, as shown in Figure 6.4.

Scenario title: The Kaleidoscope

In this scenario consumers are more self-assured and are happy to experiment and lead non-conformist lifestyles. Success is a matter of achieving a balance in the activities of one's life. In this environment a diverse range of highly differentiated brands emerges to satisfy the wide spectrum of disparate consumers.

Scenario title: The Fast Show

In this scenario consumers attempt to squeeze as much into life as possible. They are extremely committed to both work and play. In order to achieve this full lifestyle they need domestic services such as those offered by nannies and cleaners. The scenario envisages the Victorian world re-emerging with a rich middle and upper class dominating society supported by a domestic service class ('below stairs').

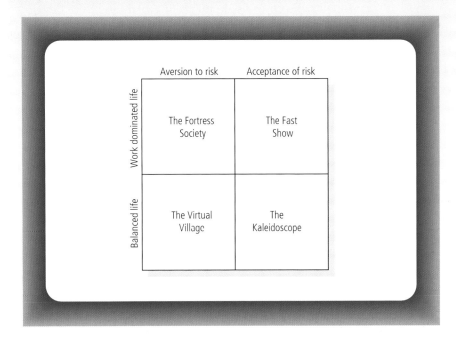

Figure 6.4
New Solution's
four scenarios
(Continued)

Illustrative Example 6.2 (Continued)

Scenario title: The Fortress Society
This is a society marked out by anxiety. Individuals with employment find work is an unrelenting treadmill. Those without employment are marginalized and have no relevant role in society. The price of a brand becomes the major factor in consumer choice as lifestyle brands become the domain of a shrinking social elite.

Scenario title: The Virtual Village
Here personal identification is tied to a sense of community. Consumers work only in order to live rather than work for its own sake. Virtual as well as real markets are vehicles in which to trade skills. Successful brands in this environment have to earn the trust of stakeholders by portraying a commitment to community values.

   This is one example of scenario planning allowing organizations to explore visions of the possible consumer environments that might emerge in the future.

■ Market sensing

There is some overlap between the aims and operation of scenario planning and market sensing as an approach. With market sensing the emphasis is on the need for managers to understand the market (Piercy, 1997). The role of individuals who co-ordinate marketing planning is to develop a process whereby managers can gain a more in-depth understanding of the fundamental dynamic forces in their industry.

   The emphasis with market sensing is similar to scenario planning and is to establish the impact on the organisation of critical events that may take place in the environment and decide upon the probability of that event occurring.

   Whichever approach is taken to developing a view of the future one key feature is that the critical strategic questions facing the organisation have to be identified.

■ Strategic questions

There have been a range of studies by psychologists that show that in judgmental situations predictive ability does not improve as the amount of information increases (Alpert and Raiffa, 1982). The main effect of additional information is to lead to an overconfidence in the judgements made. In fact the studies show that the optimal amount of information reaches a plateau reasonably early in the process (Makridakis and Wheelwright, 1989). Once past this point additional information only increases the confidence of those involved in the judgement but does nothing further to enhance the quality of the forecast. Thus increasing amounts of marketing research beyond the threshold is wasting the resources of an organisation.

Forecasting activities help to identify the key factors underpinning an organisation's position in the market, the follow up is to monitor and evaluated developments in those areas on an ongoing bases. This allows an organisation to focus the marketing research requirements and planning efforts into the critical areas for strategic development (see Figure 6.5). Where an event has a high impact on the organisation and the probability of it happening in the near future is high and then the company needs to undertake more in-depth analysis and develop a strategy that addresses the impact of the development. Where the impact of an event is high but the probability of it happening is low, or the event is only likely to happen far into the future, then the organisation should monitor and analyse data and begin developing contingency plans. Events that only have a low impact will be given a much-reduced emphasis in terms of monitoring and analysis undertaken by the company.

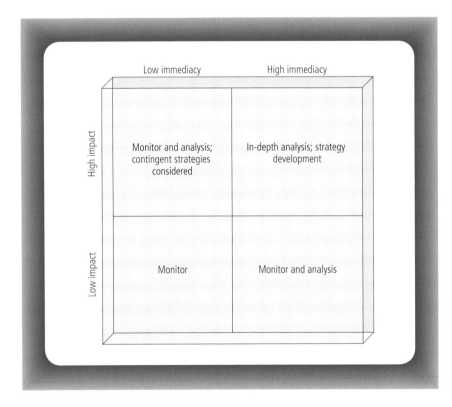

Figure 6.5
Categories of responses to strategic events forecasted in the external environment (*Source*: Adapted from Aaker, 1995)

■ People involved

The mix of people involved in the forecasting process will have an impact on the effectiveness of the exercise. Part of the essence of the environmental analysis and futures forecasting is to build an understanding across the organisation of the issues that it faces. Therefore this has to be a team activity that is widely spread. There are a number of issues that have to be considered when creating this team:

- *Ownership*: The managers who will be responsible for creating and delivering the strategy that flows from any analysis have to be involved in the process. If they are involved in developing the forecasts there is a higher likelihood that they will take ownership of resolving the issues the process raises.
- *Subordinates inputs*: A study by Aguilar (1967) illustrated that 23 per cent of information about the external environment came from subordinate executives. Alternatively only 9 per cent came from superiors and meetings. The clear implication is that lower status executives have to be involved in the process. Some forecasters also believe it is easier for younger people to envision the future because they have been brought up and socialised in the latest social technical and political environment. Older individuals have come to the current situation holding values and beliefs developed when a different environment existed. Therefore an individual brought up with e-mail and CD ROM technology may have a clearer perception of the technologies potential than an individual whose formative education was based on paper-based information sources. These individuals again are likely to come from more junior executive positions in an organisation. Although there should not be too much emphasis placed on this issue having a group of individuals of mixed experience could help to provide a more rounded perspective.
- *Challengers*: Creating a team that all have the same values and attitudes to the company is likely to develop a view of the future that does not challenge the status quo. Individuals who do not conform to the company stereotype are more likely to challenge and test the conventional attitudes and beliefs that predominate (see Figure 6.6). Mavericks and rebels are the type of non-conformists that will challenge conventional wisdom, these are of course the very individuals that ingroups tend to exclude.
- *Cross-functional teams*: Any team is obviously stronger if it is made up of individuals from across the company's operations. Not only does each individual bring an in-depth knowledge of their particular area of expertise but also helps to build support for marketing plans within other functional areas.
- *Outsiders*: As has already been mentioned under scenario planning there can be advantages in including outside experts in any team. This can be widened to include representatives of both customers and suppliers.

Obviously there are likely to be weaknesses with any group that is formed. It is unlikely that all the above factors can be covered in any particular team. However consideration of the above issues should be undertaken by anyone who is responsible for co-ordinating forecasting activity.

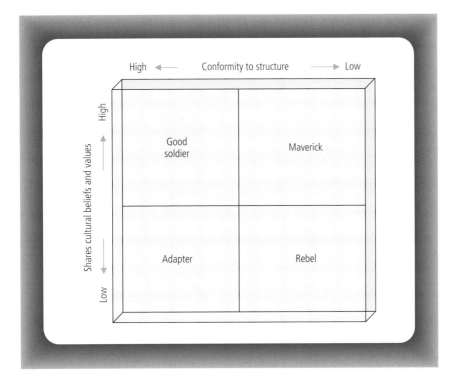

High ←——— Conformity to structure ———→ Low

| | Good soldier | Maverick |
| | Adapter | Rebel |

Shares cultural beliefs and values — High / Low

Figure 6.6
Individual's fit in corporate culture (*Source*: Adapted from Sathe, 1988)

■ Summary

Developing a view of the future is a clear step in the development of strategy. Without it we are merely planning for the past. There is a range of forecasting techniques available to planners. Scenario planning is a useful way of identifying the important issues facing by a company. It can also help mangers achieve a greater understanding of how the market they operate within actually works. This ties in well with the idea of market sensing. The crucial step is then to motivate managers to develop creative approaches to deal with future issues the organisation may face. Formulating elegant strategies to address the future, that this part of the strategic analysis has identified, is the next significant step in the planning process.

■ References

Aaker, D., *Strategic Market Management*, 4th edn, Wiley, Brisbane, 1995.

Aguilar, F. J., *Scanning the Business Environment*, Macmillan, New York, 1967.

Alpert, M. and Raiffa, H., A Progress report on the training of probability assessors, in Kahneman, D., Slovic, P. and Tversky, A. (eds), *Judgement under Uncertainty: Heuristic and Biases*, Cambridge University Press, New York, 1982.

Dalrymple, D. J., Sales forecasting practices from a United States survey, *International Journal of Forecasting*, **3**, 1989, 379–392.

Diffenbach, J., Corporate environmental analysis in large US corporations, *Long Range Planning*, **16**(3), 1983, 111.

Drucker, P., *Managing in Turbulent Societies*, Heinemann, London, 1980.

Galer, G., Shell Group Planning, in Mercer, D. (ed.), *Marketing Strategy: The Challenge of the External Environment*, Sage, London, 1998.

Hartley, L. P., *The Go-Between*, Hamish Hamilton, London, 1953.

Janis, I. L., *Victims of Group Think*, Houghton Mifflin, Boston, 1972.

Janis, I. L. and Mann, I., *Decision Making: A psychological Analysis of Conflict, Choice and Commitment*, 2nd edn, Free Press, New York, 1982.

Makridakis, S. and Wheelwright, S. C., *Forecasting Methods for Management*, 5th edn, Wiley, New York, 1989.

Mentzer, J. T. and Cox, J. E., Familiarity application and performance of sales forecasting techniques, *Journal of Forecasting*, **3**, 1984, 27–36.

Piercy, N., *Market-Led Strategic Change*, 2nd edn, Butterworth-Heinemann, Oxford, 1997.

Sathe, V., *Culture and Related Corporate Realities*, Irwin, Homewood, IL, 1988.

The Copenhagen Institute for Future Studies (CIFS), *Creative Man*, Gyldendal, Denmark, 2004.

Van Der Heijden, K., *The Art of Strategic Conversation*, Wiley, New York, 1997.

Wack, P., Scenarios: shooting the rapids, *Harvard Business Review*, November/ December, 1985, 139–150.

■ Further reading

Mercer, D., *Marketing Strategy: The Challenge of the External Environment*, Chapters 2, 5–8, Open University/Sage, London, 1998.

Piercy, N., *Market-Led Strategic Change*, 2nd edn, Chapter 10, Butterworth-Heinemann, Oxford, 1997.

PART 2

Formulation of Strategy

- Strategic intent
- Strategy formulation
- Targeting, positioning and brand strategy
- Product development and innovation
- Alliances and relationships

Part 1 examined the elements that make up a strategic analysis. This analysis is the foundation upon which strategic decisions are constructed. Part 2 explores the process involved in formulating strategy.

Chapter 7 examines the strategic intent of an organisation. The influences on an organisation's mission and the creation of a mission statement are explored. The development of specific goals and objectives are then discussed.

Strategy is formulated to achieve the mission and objectives of an organisation. Chapter 8 explores the process of strategy formulation: competitor advantage, industry position and product/market strategies. A number of strategic models are also covered.

Chapter 9 explores the issues concerned with developing a specific competitive position, through targeting, positioning and branding strategy.

Chapter 10 examines the crucial areas of product development and innovation. Specifically product development strategy and the new product development process is discussed. The chapter then examines management methods that can facilitate innovation in an organisation.

Chapter 11 considers the increasing importance of alliances and joint ventures. Relationship marketing is also examined.

Chapter 12 examines the strategic marketing plan, and focuses on corporate and marketing planning. The analytical, behavioural and organizational aspects of planning which help to overcome the barriers to success are also discussed.

CHAPTER 7

Strategic intent

An organisation has to have key objectives that define the aims that any strategy attempts to fulfil, this is the realm of strategic intent. This chapter explores the issues surrounding an organisation's mission, goals and objectives. The hierarchy of objectives in an organisation is discussed, as is the use of the balanced scorecard approach.

■ Introduction

Before an organisation starts to make judgements about how it is going to compete, fundamental decisions about the organisation's overall method of operation and the areas it wishes to serve have to be articulated. A conscious statement of the primary direction and purpose of the organisation has to be the key foundation upon which objectives and strategy are based. This rationale behind the company's existence usually comes in the form of a mission statement and is meant to act as a guiding light to all personnel within the organisation.

■ Mission

The mission of the organisation is the unique purpose that distinguishes it from other companies and defines the boundaries of its operations. The mission statement is a proclamation of the organisation's primary objective that encapsulates its core values. The organisation's aims and aspirations are the result of a series of influences (see Figure 7.1).

There are four major sources of influence acting upon the core meaning behind an organisation's existence. Johnson and Scholes (1999) refer to these as:

1 *Corporate governance*: To whom should the organisation be accountable and within what regulatory framework should executive decisions be overseen and reviewed? With any organisation these issues which relate to accountability, will have an influence on the overall direction of the institution. Some groups that the organisation is meant to serve, such as small shareholders, can be very removed from the managers actually running the company. Thus the regulatory framework acts to constrain management freedom and protect the rights of stakeholders.
2 *Stakeholders*: Stakeholders in an organisation include such groups as customers, suppliers, shareholders, employees, financiers and the wider social community. In reality even operating within the corporate governance framework, organisations may be inclined to further the

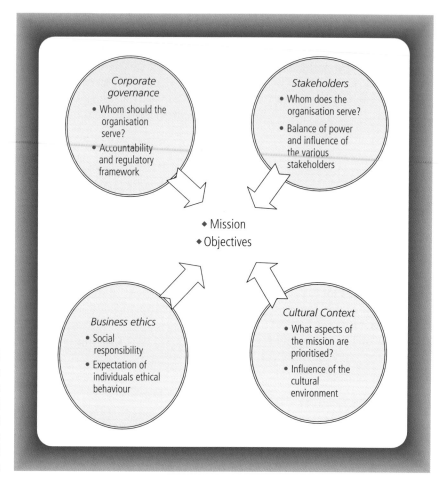

Figure 7.1
Influences on an organisation's mission and objectives (*Source*: Adapted from Johnson and Scholes, 1999)

interests of particular stakeholder groups according to the power and influence the groups actually wield.

3   *Business ethics*: An ethical dimension also affects the mission and object-ives that an organisation should fulfil. This mainly relates to the corpo-ration's social responsibility to stakeholder groups, in particular those whose power and influence is marginal, such as a local community. Although expectations of an individual's ethical behaviour has a sig-nificant influence, this ethical domain is subject to cultural attitudes and beliefs.

4   *Cultural context*: The aspects of mission that are prioritised will reflect the cultural environment that surrounds the corporation. This influ-ence will occur at several levels: at a broad level wider national cul-tures will be influential, individuals in functional areas will be influenced by the culture of their professional reference groups, there will also be internal sub-cultures operating at divisional or functional level within the company.

A mission statement then is subject to these influences and needs to address their interests in a manner that allows it to satisfy their diverse demands. In essence the mission statement ought to characterise the organisation's principles and priorities and define the broad product, market and technologies that are core to the business. Missions can be framed with a very narrow view of the business or be given a much broader frame of reference.

- *Narrow focus*: Some organisations choose to frame a mission statement with a very narrow focus. An example is Newport News Shipbuilding. The advantage is that it gives a very clear description the organisation's primary business. However creating a narrow focus may set unnecessary constraints on the company's activities in terms of the markets served, the product/service offered or the technology employed.

Newport News Shipbuilding
Mission statement – unchanged since the company was founded in 1886

We shall build good ships here – at a profit if we can – at a loss if we must – but always good ships.

Source: Cosco, 1995.

The Scottish Power Mission statement

To be recognised as a highly rated utility-based company trading in electricity other utility and related markets providing excellent quality and service to customers and above average total returns to investors.

- *Broad focus*: The use of a broad mission statement is fairly common and generally refers to all the various stakeholders in the business: shareholders, customers and employees as well as the area of business to be served. Scottish Power's mission statement has this broader focus, although it has a reasonably defined business scope. One noticeable stakeholder group not referred to in this mission statement is, surprisingly, the employees. In general, broad mission statements can address the problem of giving too narrow a focus on the business's area of operation, but can fall into the trap of failing to clearly define the market and product areas that are core to its operation. Richer Sounds is a company that retails hi-fi equipment, however its mission statement makes no reference to the product or market areas it is concerned with as a business. It does however engender a clear vision on the way that business should be undertaken.

Mission statement of Richer Sounds
The Richer Way

In our business, our aim is to give customers friendly, efficient service and value for money second to none. We believe that by giving excellent customer service we will earn their loyalty and word of mouth recommendation to others. This is the only way to ensure our future success and so, looking after the customer must be an absolute priority at all times, and we really do expect our colleagues to give above average service.

We also believe that work should be fun. We believe that if people enjoy what they do, they will do a better job. We also believe at all times in aiming to be the best. This means that we expect and demand superior performance from our people with both quality of service, attention to detail in the presentation of our stores and in everything we do. We believe that if customer service is the top goal, this will create loyalty, and long term revenue and profitability will naturally follow.

Source: Drummond and Ensor, 1991.

Successful mission statements have to demonstrate the following characteristics:

- *Credibility*: The mission statement has to set realistic ambitions for the organisation. In particular they have to be believable in the eyes of stakeholders', in particular the employees.
- *Uniqueness*: The mission has to relate to the particular organisation. It should not be a statement that could be generically applied to a range of other organisations. The mission has to relate to the company and its stakeholders in a unique fashion.
- *Specific capabilities*: The mission should also embrace the core capabilities of the organisation and emphasise their core role in the future of the organisation.
- *Aspirational*: The mission needs to motivate individuals by giving them a statement that has significance to the work they undertake. A vision that is meaningful in terms of more than just making profits. It should engender a vision to which individuals feel they wish to contribute.

A mission statement should also define the boundaries of the business's ambitions. What is the territory that the business wishes to operate within? This is commonly referred to as the scope of the business or the competitive domain. There are several dimensions that have to be considered when defining the organisation's scope:

- *Product Scope*: This is defined in terms of the goods and services the enterprise supplies to customers. A critical aspect of defining product scope is deciding how to categorise the organisation's products. Some products may fit into a collective category easily; some more important products may be better served listed separately. The product could be defined in terms of its technology.

- *Market Scope*: Market scope can be difficult to define but it is an important exercise. Market scope should depict the consumers and customers who utilise the company's products. There are a number of criteria that are helpful in defining market scope such as:
  - Type of industry sector targeted
  - Channels of distribution
  - Demographics
  - Salient features of the consumer
- *Geographical Scope*: This should be defined at an appropriate level of aggregation. This may be defined in strictly local terms, for a small business, through to national and international regions for large organisations

Definitions of the scope of the business based on markets are likely to be safer than a product definition. Particular products and technologies ultimately become obsolete but the consumer's need for those products or technologies used to address may endure. There is a danger of marketing myopia developing (Levitt, 1960) if a business's competitive domain is defined solely according to a product type rather than a market need. Pharmaceutical companies are beginning to re-define their competitive domain in terms of the customer benefits of 'good health' rather than purely product terms of 'drugs' (Green, 1995). SmithKline Beecham now sees the scope of its business covering four key areas of the health care market: prevention, diagnosis, treatment and cure, rather than just research and development of drugs. Products and services that address these primary market needs may change but the underlying market areas are likely to remain.

Stakeholders also have to be considered when developing a mission statement. Stakeholders are individuals or groups who rely on an organisation to achieve some of their own personal objectives, at the same time the organisation is reliant on these individuals (Johnson and Scholes, 1999). There are a number of different stakeholders that companies try to address and accommodate in a mission statement:

- *Internal*: These are the people most directly involved with the organisation, therefore the values and attitudes of these groups are a key influence on the aims and objectives of the organisation. Internal stakeholders include owners or shareholders, managers, employees and unions.
- *External*: These groups do not have the same close relationship with the organisation as internal stakeholders do, never the less they can be a major source of influence over the direction of an enterprise. External stakeholders can be split into two groups primary and secondary external stakeholders:
  1 *Primary external stakeholders*: These are external groups that have a direct relationship with the organisation. They include crucial groups such as customers, suppliers, financiers and competitors.
  2 *Secondary external stakeholder*: These have a less direct relationship with the company and includes groups such as government agencies

(local, national or international), political pressure groups, the financial community at large and society in general. These groups can exercise influence over the organisation through such things as legislation and ethical campaigning.

Criticisms of mission statements are that many are too bland and ill defined and therefore fail to give clarity to the business's endeavours. This could well be the result of the development of a statement that attempts to satisfy the interests of all stakeholders in the business. There are also some who feel mission statements are too brief to clearly depict the organisation's strategic intent.

■ Statement of strategic intent

Some writers see strategic intent, or the corporate vision, as a concept separate from the mission. They would argue that a mission statement merely states what the organisation is currently doing and that a statement of intent, or a vision statement, is also needed. A statement of strategic intent describes what the organisation aspires to become. However many companies strive to achieve both objectives within the single mechanism of the mission statement.

■ Nature of support for the mission statement

Mission statements can be put to use in different ways depending on which stakeholders have the dominant influence and what the nature of their support for the vision is. The dominant stakeholder will either be internal or external to the organisation. Stakeholders' attitudes can be split into passionate campaigners for the mission and those who will afford more equivocal support (see Figure 7.2).

- *Faint support*: A mission statement is likely to be paid lip service where strategic decision making is dominated by internal managers that view other stakeholders and corporate governance in general merely as constraints. In these circumstances a mission statement has little influence on the strategic developments of the organisation.
- *Passionate support*: Where the strategic process is dominated by internal managers who have a close identification with the values and philosophy of the organisation, the mission statement will be central to their actions. These managers will use the mission statement as a vehicle to drive the corporate aims and aspirations through the organisation.
- *Dissipated mission*: If strategic decisions are the territory of external stakeholders, whose overriding concerns are to do with corporate

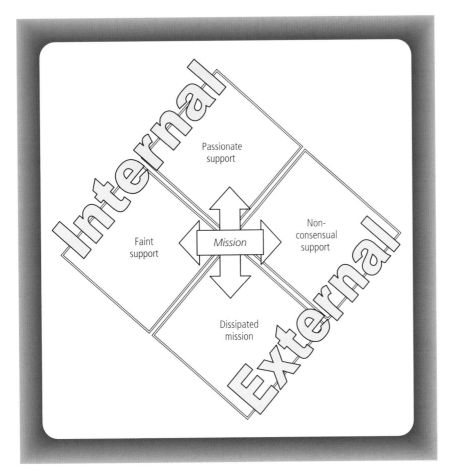

Figure 7.2
Level of adoption of
a mission statement
(*Source*: Adapted
from Johnson and
Scholes, 1999)

governance then regulation and process will dominate the enterprise. The mission will become lost in the day-to-day routines of compliance to the regulations. Bureaucracies are classic examples of this type of organisation, where the original mission of the organisation is lost in the day-to-day paperwork and strict regulations that have to be adhered to at all times.

• *Non-consensual mission*: The opposite of the previous situation is where external stakeholders, that hold passionate ideological views, dominate the strategic process. When this occurs it can become difficult to develop a mission statement that is acceptable to the different stakeholder groups alternatively the mission becomes a highly political one. One example is of state-owned industries that needed to shed production capacity and jobs in order to become competitive. These industries suffered because stakeholder groups, such as governments, could not support the organisation's strategic decisions because of their own political/ideological position. European governments and unions currently feel unable to support the closure of car plants even though there is clear overcapacity and therefore lack of profitability in the industry.

In summary the mission statement, or mission and statement of strategic intent, operate as a guiding light that acts as a reference point when making strategic decisions in general and when forming objectives in particular.

■ Goals and objectives

The mission statement acts as a guide and leads to the development of a hierarchy of objectives. Objectives are the specific intended outcomes of strategy. There are differing views on the definition of goals and object-ives. Some writers see goals as being less specific than objectives. Strategic goals are general aspirations that the organisation needs to achieve but are difficult to measure or put within a specific time scale. Objectives there-fore are more specific than goals and state what is to be achieved; they are given a quantifiable measure and a specific time scale. These objectives are seen as needing to be:

- *Specific*: Objectives that are specific should be set so that there is clarity throughout the organisation as to what is to be achieved.
- *Measurable*: Objectives that are stated clearly, with tangible targets, what is to be achieved. Objectives can then be measured overtime.
- *Aspirational*: Objectives that are set at a level that provides a high-enough challenge to motivate individuals although not so high that it demoralises them. Different groups or functions will have various per-ceptions of the level of challenge set by the objectives. One way to address this problem is to set distinct objectives for each specific group.
- *Realistic*: Objectives that are achievable based on a thorough strategic analysis. Companies can fall into the trap of developing objectives that reflect an unrealistic, but desired for, position that does not reflect the current reality of their situation.
- *Time scaled*: A time scale should be put on the achievement of an object-ive. This again allows the organisation to measure their performance against a set deadline.

These quantifiable objectives are normally referred to by their acronym SMART. Examples of SMART objectives are 3 M's financial objectives.

Minnesota Mining and Manufacturing's Financial objectives

- To achieve 10 per cent annual growth in earnings per share.
- To achieve 20–25 per cent return on equity.
- To achieve 27 per cent return on capital employed.

Source: Wheelen and Hunger, 1998.

Other writers however argue that both quantifiable and non-quantifiable objectives can be set. They would argue that some important objectives such as technology leadership might be impossible to quantify (Johnson and Scholes, 1999). Obviously with specific objectives it is easier for an organisation to gauge whether those objectives have been achieved. However a less specific objective, such as technology leadership, can still be assessed by comparing the organisation with the performance of competitors'.

There are dangers though if all objectives are couched in such qualitative terms in that it becomes difficult to know whether they have been achieved or not.

Whichever perspective is taken on this matter successful objectives also need to demonstrate the following characteristics:

- *Acceptability*: Internal managers are more likely to wholeheartedly support objectives that are in line with their own inclinations. As with the mission statement some of the organisations long-term objectives are drawn up to be acceptable to groups external to the organisation.
- *Flexibility*: Objectives have to be flexible enough to be adaptable when discontinuities in the external environment occur (see Chapter 6). Here again is the issue of a trade-off between flexible and SMART objectives.
- *Comprehensibility*: Managers and staff at all levels have to understand what is to be achieved and know the main criteria by which their performance will be judged.

Peter Drucker (1954) suggests that there are a number of key areas within which organisations should develop objectives:

- *Market standing*: This relates to the organisation's success in the market. Objectives can be a statement of the total sales or the market share the organisation seeks.
- *Innovation*: Targets can be set for innovation in: product and service development, cost reduction, financing, operational performance, human resources and management information.
- *Productivity*: Objectives can be set for of the productive use of resources. A common approach is to state the number of items produced or the number of services performed per unit of input. Sometimes productivity can be stated in terms of decreasing inputs whilst retaining the same outputs. For example an objective could be to decrease overtime while at the same time maintaining production levels.
- *Physical and financial resources*: An organisation can state objectives about the acquisition and use of resources.
- *Profitability*: A range of targets can be established for financial returns including earnings per share or return on equity.
- *Manager performance and development*: Objectives can be framed to set performance criteria for managers.
- *Employee performance and attitude*: Specific performance criteria can be set against which actual achievements can be measured. Objectives relating to aspects of employee relations are seen as beneficial in gaining employee's loyalty.

- *Public responsibility*: Objectives can be set for an organisation's wider social responsibilities, in particular an effort could be made to be seen as responsible corporate citizens. They may establish objectives for contributions to charities, community action, urban renewal or other forms of public and political activity.

There are dangers for organisations that see objectives in one of these areas as overriding. Komatsu concentrated so much on competitive positioning objectives that its main concern became its position relative to its main competitor, Caterpillar. As a result Komatsu ignored emerging areas where there were opportunities for growth. This began to lead to a decline in the organisation's profitability until corrective action was taken (Pearce and Robinson, 1997).

■ Hierarchy of objectives

Objectives are not only developed across a range of key areas they also exist at a number of levels within an organisation. Objectives cascade down through an organisational structure effectively forming a hierarchy. The fictitious Edinburgh Hotel is given as a useful example to illustrate this hierarchy of objectives (see Figure 7.3).

	Objectives	Strategy
Corporate (over 3 years)	• Increase gross operating profit by 30 per cent	• By becoming market leading luxury hotel in Edinburgh with 25 per cent share
Marketing (over 3 years)	• Achieve 25 per cent share of Edinburgh luxury hotel market	• By providing best facilities for key market segments • By providing best standards of service • Promote it
Marketing mix (1–3 years) Product	 • Provide best facilities for key market segments	 • Build more informal restaurant • Refurbish hotel to higher standard • Add fitness club • Improve bus facilities
Service	• Provide best service standards	• Retrain staff, etc.
Promotion	• Create awareness of improved facilities, service, etc.	• Promote new restaurant • 'Relaunch' hotel

Figure 7.3
The Edinburgh Hotel's hierarchy of objectives (*Source*: Adapted from Revuelta, 1996)

Edinburgh Hotel's objectives include:

- *Corporate objectives*: Objectives at a corporate level relate to the organisation's overall direction in terms of its general attitude towards growth. At this higher level, managers of the Edinburgh hotel are likely to be concerned with long-term profitability. (*Note*: In a not-for-profit organisation the key objectives are more likely to relate to the efficient use of resources rather than profitability.) In this case the hotel management wishes to increase operating profit by 30 per cent over 3 years. The method proposed to achieve this objective is by growing market share to 25 per cent of the Edinburgh market. At this corporate level expanding market share becomes a strategy for achieving the organisation's principal objective.
- *Functional objectives*: At a functional level expanding market share becomes an objective. Each functional area: finance, human resources, operations and marketing will develop a strategy to support this objective. In terms of the marketing function it is concerned about which products/services should be sold into which markets. At a fundamental level marketing strategy is about products and markets. In this example the strategy at the marketing function's level is to provide the best facilities in Edinburgh for key market segments, provide the best standards of service and ensure they are adequately promoted.
- *Operational objectives*: At this level the functional level marketing strategy becomes the objective. Strategies have to be developed for each element of the marketing mix to support these operational objectives.

This hierarchy ensures that at each level the objectives that are developed are consistent with the objectives that lie at the level above them. However there has to be strong co-ordination between functional areas otherwise conflicting actions may be taken as each functional area conducts independent actions in order to fulfil their objectives. The key corporate objective could be to increase profitability by 10 per cent over the next 3 years. If independent actions are taken, marketing could develop strategies to increase sales in order to meet this objective. At the same time production could be operating at optimum capacity any increase in throughput would increase its costs. Without co-ordination and communication functional areas can effectively be working against each other.

In many situations there will be more than three levels to this hierarchy increasing the complexity of the situation even more:

- *Strategic Business Unit (SBU) Objectives*: In an organisation with a divisional structure this hierarchy will have an additional level of the business (or S.B.U. level) objectives that will be derived from the corporate level objectives and strategy and then feed into the functional level objectives.

■ Long-term versus short-term goals

There is some tension between long-term and short-term objectives. Long-term objectives are an integral part of the planning horizons of up to

5 years ahead. Shorter-term objectives for 12 months are more likely to drive the activities at the operational level. However short-term objectives have to fall within the overall direction of the longer-term objectives. Budgets and targets generally are based on these short-term objectives and are essential for management control. But unless they are developed within a long-term framework they are not strategic in nature.

According to Aaker (1995) short-term financial measures such as sales, return on investment and market share are the dominant objectives in businesses. Even where other objectives exist they are eclipsed by these quantitative ones. This often leads to a bias in strategic choice towards squeezing a business and starving it of investing in order to improve the short-term financial performance. One way to avoid this bias is to use the balanced scorecard approach – this would also have helped Komatsu to avoid their concentration on one key objective.

■ The balanced scorecard

Objective setting is not an isolated process. As has already been discussed there is a need for managers to know the key criteria by which their performance against objectives will be measured. There is a clear link between setting objectives and the setting of performance measures. The balanced scorecard (Kaplan and Norton, 1992, 1993) is an approach that more clearly links these two activities. Kaplan and Norton suggest that a balanced set of objectives should be created and at the same time a coherent set of performance measures should be developed alongside them.

At the core of the balanced scorecard approach is the belief that managers have to be able to look at a business from four key perspectives:

1 *Customer perspective*: How customers see a business is critical, but financial measures alone do not provide this view. Customers are generally concerned with, quality, performance, service and time. For each of these categories the organisation should develop objectives and performance measures. Obviously how these categories are defined has to be from the customer's perspective. This will allow the organisation to track how customers view the business overtime.
2 *Internal perspective*: Managers have to identify the critical internal processes that will allow them to satisfy customer needs. Identifying the processes that are important to customer satisfaction allows managers to identify the functions and competencies in which they need to excel.
3 *Innovation and learning perspective*: An organisation's ability to create value is inextricably linked to its capacity to continually improve through innovation and learning.
4 *Financial perspective*: This allows the organisation to see how the business looks from the shareholders point of view. This financial performance measures the success, not only of an organisation's strategy, but also of its implementation.

The balanced scorecard widens the view managers have of the business rather than concentrating purely on financial criteria. For each of these perspectives the organisation has to create distinct objectives and at the same time develop the accompanying performance measures. This process also forces managers to understand many complex relationships and to surmount some of the traditional functional barriers that hamper strategic development (see Figure 7.4).

	Strategic objectives	Strategic measures
Financial	F.1 Return on capital F.2 Cash flow F.3 Profitability F.4 Profitability growth F.5 Reliability of performance	→ ROCE → Cash flow → Net margin → Volume growth rate versus industry → Profit forecast reliability → Sales backlog
Customer	C.1 Value for money C.2 Competitive price C.3 Customer satisfaction	→ Customer ranking survey → Pricing index → Customer satisfaction index → Mystery shopping rating

Internal	I.1 Marketing
	  • Product and service development
	  • Shape customer requirement
	I.2 Manufacturing
	  • Lower manufacturing cost
	  • Improve project management
	I.2 Logistics
	  • Reduce delivery costs
	  • Inventory management
	I.4 Quality
		→ Pioneer percentage of product portfolio
		→ Hours with customer on new work
		
		→ Total expenses per unit versus competition
		→ Safety incident index
		
		→ Delivered cost per unit
		→ Inventory level compared to plan and output rate
		→ Rework

Innovation and Learning	I.L.1 Innovate products and services I.L.2 Time to market I.L.3 Empowered workforce I.L.4 Access to strategic information I.L.5 Continuous improvement	→ Percentage revenue from pioneer products → Cycle time versus industry norm → Staff attitude survey → Strategic information availability → Number of employee suggestions

Figure 7.4
The balanced scorecard (*Source*: Adapted from Kaplan and Norton, 1992, 1993)

The balanced scorecard approach also addresses one other potential problem that of ensuring consistency between objectives. This can be difficult in practice because objectives are formed in a range of areas, at different levels and on different time scales (effectively objectives are formed both horizontally and vertically through the organisation).

■ Gap analysis

The process of strategic analysis explored in Part 1 of this text effectively establishes the current situation that the company finds itself in and allows forecasts to be made of how the company will perform in the future. The objectives that are set by the organisation allow it to project what the company's actual performance will need to be to achieve those objectives. It is at this point that the organisation can calculate the gap between these two positions. This is commonly referred to as the gap analysis (see Figure 7.5).

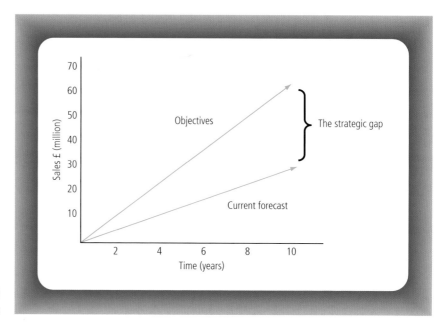

Figure 7.5
The gap analysis

   The gap between these two positions represents the divide that the marketing strategy has to address. The rest of Part 2 of this book addresses how an organisation can develop strategy to allow it to meet its objectives by crossing this gap.

■ Summary

This chapter has explored the issues surrounding corporate mission, in particular influences acting upon the development of an organisation's mission statement. The nature of strategic objectives was discussed, as well as the hierarchy of objectives and strategies. The possible tensions between functional objectives and strategies were highlighted. Strategies are developed to achieve the mission and objectives of the organisation.

The next step in the process is for the organisation to formulate strategies to ensure that the organisation can cross the gap between its current position and the fulfilment of its primary objectives.

■ References

Aaker, D. A., *Strategic Market Management*, 4th edn, Wiley, New York, 1995.

Cosco, J., Down to the sea in ships, *Journal of Business Strategy*, November/December, 1995, 48.

Drucker, P., *The Practice of Management*, Harper & Row, New York, 1954, pp. 65–83.

Drummond, G. and Ensor, J., *Teaching note for the Richer Sounds case study*, European Case Clearing House, 1991.

Green, D., Healthcare vies with research, *Financial Times*, 25 April, 1995, p. 34.

Johnson, G. and Scholes, K., *Exploring Corporate Strategy*, 5th edn, Prentice Hall, London, 1999.

Kaplan, R. S. and Norton, D. P., The balance scorecard: measure that drive performance, *Harvard Business Review*, **70**(1), 1992, 71–79.

Kaplan, R. S. and Norton, D. P., Putting the balanced scorecard to work, *Harvard Business Review*, **71**(5), 1993, 134–147.

Levitt, T., Marketing myopia, *Harvard Business Review*, July/August, 1960, 45–56.

Pearce, J. A. and Robinson, R. B., *Strategic Management*, 6th edn, Irwin, Homewood, IL, 1997.

Revuelta, J., Seminar, Napier Business School, Edinburgh, 1996.

Wheelen, T. L. and Hunger, J., *Strategic Management and Business Policy*, 6th edn, Addison Wesley, New York, 1998, p. 11.

■ Further reading

Johnson, G. and Scholes, K., *Exploring Corporate Strategy*, 5th edn, Chapter 5, Prentice Hall, London, 1999.

McDonald, M., *Marketing Plans; How to Prepare them; How to Use Them*, 4th edn, Chapter 6, Butterworth-Heinemann, Oxford, 1999.

CHAPTER 8

Strategy formulation

Marketing strategy aims to generate sustainable competitive advantage. The process is influenced by industry position, experience curves, value effects and other factors, such as product life cycle (PLC). In any given market place, businesses must adopt defensive and attacking strategies. Such actions aim to maintaining and/or increasing market share. Organisations need to ensure their strategic position is relevant to current/future market conditions.

■ Strategy formulation – an overview

Chapter 6 outlined the basic principles of setting objectives. It is important to recognise that alternative methods of achieving objectives exist. The ability to identify and evaluate these alternatives forms the essence of strategy development. The goal is to obtain sustainable competitive advantage within predetermined markets. Figure 8.1 summarises the process.

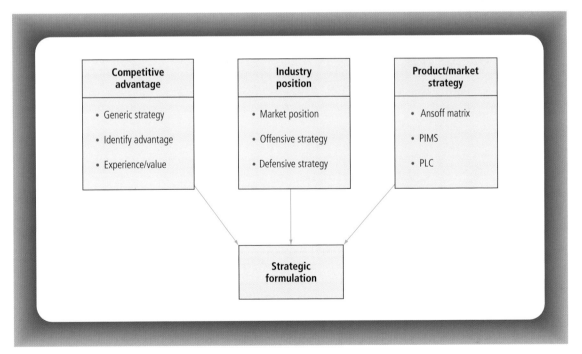

Figure 8.1
The formulation of strategy

■ Competitive advantage

The notions of competitive advantage and marketing strategy are intrinsically linked. Competitive advantage is the process of identifying a fundamental and sustainable basis from which to compete. Ultimately, marketing strategy aims to deliver this advantage in the market place.

Porter (1980) identifies three *generic strategies* – fundamental sources of competitive advantage. These are: cost leadership, differentiation and focus. Arguably, these provide a basis for all strategic activity and underpin the large number of marketing strategies available to the organisation. Additionally, management needs to define the competitive scope of the business – targeting a broad or narrow range of industries/customers (see Figure 8.2). Essentially either operating industry wide or targeting specific market segments. Each generic strategy is examined in turn.

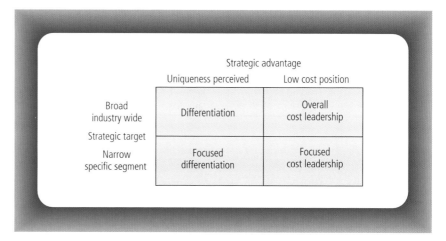

Figure 8.2
Competitive advantage (*Source*: Adapted from Porter, 1980)

Cost leadership

One potential source of competitive advantage is to seek an overall cost leadership position with an industry, or industry sector. Here the focus of strategic activity is to maintain a low cost structure. The desired structure is achievable through the aggressive pursuit of policies such as controlling overhead cost, economies of scale, cost minimisation in areas such as marketing and R&D, global sourcing of materials and experience effects. Additionally, the application of new technology to traditional activities offers significant opportunity for cost reduction.

Difficulties can exist in maintaining cost leadership. Success can attract larger, better resourced competitors. If market share falls, economies of scale become harder to achieve and fixed costs, such as overheads, are difficult to adjust in the short-to-medium term. Additionally, cost leaderships and high volume strategy are likely to involve high initial investment costs and are often associated with 'commodity' type products where price discounting and price wars are common.

Remember, low cost does not need to equate automatically to low price. Products provided at average, or above average, industry price (while maintaining cost leadership) can generate higher than average margins.

The basic drivers of cost leadership include:

- *Economy-of-scale*: This is perhaps the single biggest influence on unit cost. Correctly managed, volume can drive efficiency and enhances purchasing leverage. Additionally given large-scale operations, learning and experience effects (see later) can be a source of cost reduction.
- *Linkages and relationships*: Being able to link activities together and form relationships can generate cost savings. For example, a 'Just-in-Time' manufacturing system could reduce stockholding costs and enhance quality. Forging relationships with external organisations is also vital. If industry partners were to share development and distribution costs, or activities were 'outsourced' to specialist operators, a substantial reduction in overheads is possible.
- *Infrastructure*: Factors such as location, availability of skills and governmental support greatly affect the firms cost base. Given the development of information technology and the global economy, it is possible to have a worldwide infrastructure and selectively place activities in low cost areas.

Differentiation

Here the product offered is distinct and differentiated from the competition. The source of differentiation must be on a basis of value to the customer. The product offering should be perceived as unique and ideally offer the opportunity to command a price premium. Will customers pay more for factors such as design, quality, branding and service levels?

The skills' base is somewhat different from a cost leadership strategy and will focus on creating reasons for purchase, innovation and flexibility. Remember, often it is the perception of performance as opposed to actual performance that generates differentiation.

There are several 'downsides' to this type of strategy. Firstly, it can be costly with associated costs outweighing the benefits. Secondly, innovation and other initiatives can be duplicated by competitors. Thirdly, customer needs change with time and the basis of differentiation can become less important as customers focus on other attributes. For example, in the car market, safety may now be seen as more important than fuel economy.

Common sources of differentiation include:

- *Product performance*: Does product performance enhance its value to the customer? Factors such as quality, durability and capability all offer potential points of differentiation. Performance is evaluated relative to competitor's products and gives customers a reason to prefer one product over another.

● *Product perception*: Often the perception of a product is more important than actual performance. Hopefully, the product has an enduring emotional appeal generating brand loyalty (see Chapter 8). This is commonly achieved through marketing communications (advertising, branding, endorsement, etc.) and direct experience of customer groups.
● *Product augmentation*: We can differentiate by augmenting the product in a way that adds value. For example, high levels of service, after sales support, affordable finance and competitive pricing all serve to enhance the basic product offering. It is common for distributors, such as retailers, to provide the added-value augmentation. Product augmentation is dealt with in Chapter 9.

Focus

The organisation concentrates on a narrower range of business activities. The aim is to specialise in specific market segment and derive detailed customer knowledge. This focus, or niche, strategy can also generate the benefits of cost leadership or differentiation within a defined market segment (see Figure 8.2). For example, it may be possible to obtain cost leadership within a chosen segment or that segment may regard your product offering as differentiated.

Success within a specialist niche can attract competitors – perhaps much better resourced. Additionally, the narrow business base means more susceptibility to downturns in demand from key customer groups.

A focus strategy is based on factors such as:

● *Geographic area*: Using geographic segmentation allows a product to be tailored to local needs. The local association may offer the potential to differentiate the offering (e.g. Champagne comes from a specific French region) and protect the market from larger predators. Another rationale for such segmentation is to serve markets too small or isolated to be viable on a large scale (e.g. rural communities).
● *End-user focus*: It is possible to focus on a specific type of user as opposed to the entire market. Specialisation offers the opportunity to get 'close' to customers and have a better understanding of their needs (e.g. specialist hi-fi manufacturer). Additionally, within a narrow segment, the focused organisation may be able to offer the choice, service and economy-of-scale not available to more broadly based competitors. This strategy often works by selecting specific points on the price/quality spectrum within a given market (e.g. discount food retailer).
● *Product/product line specialist*: The organisation focuses on a single product type or product line. Value is derived from the specialisation in terms of skills, volume and range (e.g. industrial power supplies).

Consistency and the alternative view

The 'Porter' (1980) view of generic strategy supports the need for consistency of approach. The organisation needs to adopt a definite generic strategy. Attempting to mix the above strategies, within a defined market place, may result in failing to achieve the potential benefits and result in the organisation being stuck in the 'middle-of-the-road' – either low cost, differentiated or focused (Figure 8.3).

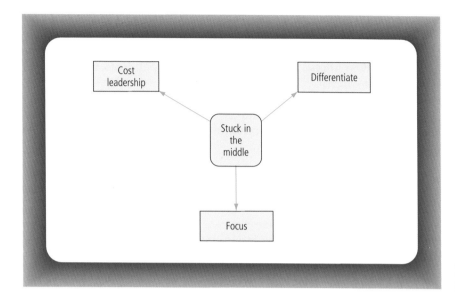

Figure 8.3
Inconsistent strategy

Illustrative Example 8.1

SimplyOrg@nic Food Company Ltd: A niche 'e-tailer'

The food retailing business is highly competitive, with large supermarket chains (e.g. Tesco) dominating the market place. However, potential exists for specialist retailers. The SimplyOrg@nic Food Company stocks a range of over 1500 organic products. These include fruit and vegetables, meat, fish, wine and beer, groceries, dairy and infant products. Telephone and Internet home shopping allows easy ordering, with products delivered to UK customers before noon, on a day of their choice. The company has recently expanded its organic range to cover non-food products – gifts, fabrics and home care items.

While the large supermarket chains offer a range of organic goods, they operate on broad retail bases as opposed to SimplyOrg@nic's specific focus. As a home shopping 'e-tailer' – a dot.com company selling to the general public – focusing on organic goods, the potential exists to create and sustain competitive advantage.

Porter's concept of competitive advantage advocates pursuing one generic strategy and thus avoiding a low profit 'stuck-in-the-middle' position. Alternative views exist. The adoption of common production, quality, marketing and management philosophies by industry competitors may mean that effective differentiation or absolute cost leadership is rarely achieved. Additionally, what managers aren't concerned with controlling costs? Therefore differentiation strategies need a cost focus. It is also possible to follow *'hybrid strategies'* aiming to offer added value and lower cost. Indeed it has been pointed out that the two strategies (cost leadership and differentiation) are not mutually exclusive. For instance, total-quality-management programmes have resulted in superior quality and cost reductions.

The reality of modern business is that many successful organisations are 'stuck-in-the-middle' within their competitive environments. This is not to decry the importance of establishing competitive advantage and consistency of approach. It merely serves to illustrate the competitive nature of modern business and the importance of uncovering and optimising all available sources of competitive advantage. It is a question of how best to add value within the context of the strategic business environment.

■ Identifying sources of competitive advantage

Having an understanding of generic strategy; it is possible to consider how such general strategy can be translated into specific competitive advantage. A prerequisite to competitive advantage is sustainability. The organisation must be able to sustain its competitive advantage over the long term. In order to be sustainable the competitive advantage must be:

● *Relevant*: It must be appropriate to current and future market needs. Additionally, it must be relevant to the organisation – achievable within the available resource base.
● *Defensible*: There must be barriers to replication, otherwise success will simply be duplicated by competitors. Such barriers tend to be: (i) Asset based – tangible factors controlled by the organisation such as: location, plant and machinery, brands and finance. (ii) Skills based – the skills and resources required to make optimum use of the assets. Examples include: quality management, brand development, product design and IT skills.

Clearly competitive advantage must be appropriate to the strategic nature of the industry. An interesting template that evaluates the strategic competitive environment has been developed by the Boston Consultancy Group (3). This matrix identifies four types of industry (see Figure 8.4). The industries are classified in terms of: (i) size of competitive advantage and (ii) number of possible ways to achieve advantage.

● *Stalemate industries*: Here the potential for competitive advantage is limited. Advantages are small and only a few approaches exist to achieving these advantages. Technological advances are commonly adopted by all industry 'players' and we see rapid convergence in product design/performance. Such industries tend to be mature, highly competitive and often akin to commodity type products where price is the key buying criteria (e.g. manufacturing desktop computers).
● *Volume industries*: Here few but high significant advantages exist. These industries are often capital intensive and are dominated by a few large players who achieve economies of scale (e.g. volume car manufacture).

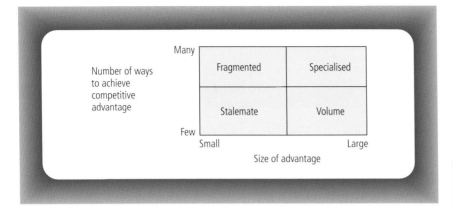

Figure 8.4
BCG strategic advantage matrix

- *Fragmented*: The market's needs are less well defined and numerous ways exist to gain advantage. The industry is often well suited to niche player and profitability may not be linked directly to size. Commonly, organisations grow by offering a range of niche products to different segments – a multi-segmentation strategy (e.g. computer software).
- *Specialised*: The potential advantage of differentiation is considerable and numerous ways exist to achieve this advantage. Profitability and size are not automatically related. Such industries include those developing customised solution to specific problems (e.g. management consultancy) and firms involved in the development/application of innovative technology (e.g. biomedical engineering).

Understanding generic strategies and the application of competitive advantage to the business environment is fundamental to success. Davidson (1997) offers an alternative view and states that competitive advantage is achieved: '*… whenever you do something better than competitors. If that something is important to consumers, or if a number of small advantages can be combined, you have an **exploitable** competitive advantage.*' Instinctively, this view appeals to the industry practitioner. The most potent sources of competitive advantage can be summarised as:

Source of competitive advantage[1]	Examples
1 Actual product performance	Robust, economic, easy to use
2 Perception of product	Brand image, product positioning
3 Low cost operations	Location, buying power
4 Legal advantage	Patents, contracts and copyright
5 Alliances and relationships	Networking, procurement
6 Superior skills	Database management, design skills
7 Flexibility	Developing customised solutions
8 Attitude	Aggressive selling, tough negotiation

[1] Adapted from Davidson (1997).

Such advantages are underpinned by the previously summarised generic sources of competitive advantage (Porter) and Figure 8.5 illustrates this concept.

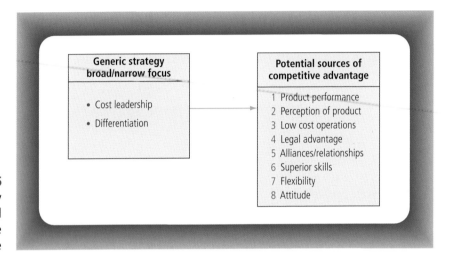

Figure 8.5
Generic strategy
and potential
competitive
advantage

■ Experience and value effects

Perhaps it is to state the obvious to say experience and ability to create value are closely linked and a major factor in successful marketing strategy. In considering these factors, two useful models are presented below.

The experience curve denotes a pattern of decreasing cost as a result of cumulative experience of carrying out an activity or function. Essentially, it shows how learning effects (repetition and accumulated knowledge) can be combined with volume effects (economy-of-scale) to derive optimal benefits (Figure 8.6). With experience, the organisation should produce better and lower cost products. The main influence of experience effects has been to promote a high volume/low cost philosophy aiming at a reduction in unit cost. However, in today's competitive business world, organisations can't simply rely on a 'big is beautiful' strategy based on economy-of-scale and market share. It is important to recognise the importance of learning effects on factors such as product quality and service levels. Such factors hold the key to future success and greatly influence the ability to 'add value' to product offerings.

Eventually, cost and learning effect will display diminishing returns and an optimum level is reached. However, the process never stops. The advent of new technologies may mark a shift in experience and offer new challenges. For example, the large monolithic market leader could be in danger as newer, more forward thinking competitors readily embrace new technology and the subsequent benefits it brings to today's business environment.

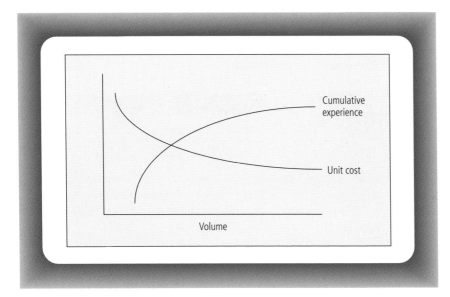

Figure 8.6
Experience curve

The concept of a *value chain*, developed by Porter (1980), categorises the organisation as a series of processes generating value for customers and other stakeholders. By examining each value creating activity, it is possible to identify sources of potential cost leadership and differentiation.

The value chain (Figure 8.7) splits activities into: (i) *primary activities*: inbound logistics, operations, outward logistics, marketing/sales and service and (ii) *secondary activities*: infrastructure, human resource management,

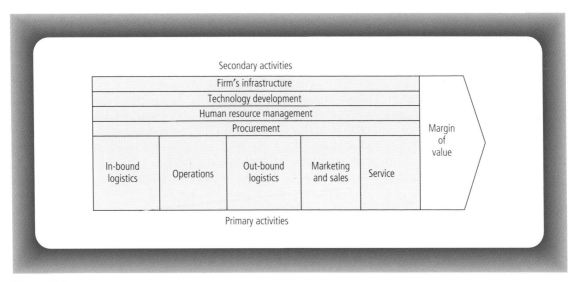

Figure 8.7
The value chain (*Source*: Porter, 1985)

technology development and procurement. These secondary activities take place in order to support the primary activities. For example, the firm's infrastructure (e.g. management, finance and buildings) serves to support the five primary functions.

Illustrative Example 8.2

Citigroup Acquires Egg

Citigroup has agreed to buy EGG, the online banking group owned by Prudential. EGG is a purely Internet-based provider of a range of financial services including: credit cards, loans, mortgages and savings accounts to approximately 3 million customers. The company has strong brand recognition and a reputation for innovation.

The combined grouping will quadruple Citigroup's UK customer base and establish a broad-based financial services provider.

George Awad, CEO, Citigroup Global Consumer Group, Europe, Middle East and Africa, said: 'We like Egg's brand; we like Egg's platform; we like Egg's customer engagement model; and we like Egg's customer set. This is a terrific acquisition for Citigroup because it provides us meaningful scale in consumer financial services in the UK, a key strategic market, and enables us to enhance the value proposition for customers. We will deliver growth by combining Egg's leading edge online products and distribution with Citigroup's global banking expertise and scale. We look forward to working with the team at Egg.'

Source: www.citigroup.com/citigroup/press, January 29 2007, Accessed 31/1/07.

While each activity generates 'value', the linkages between the activities are critical. Consider the interface between in-bound logistics and operations. A just-in-time logistics system, supported by computerised stock ordering (technology development – secondary activity) could reduce stock costs and enhance the quality of products manufactured in the operations phase of the chain. Thus enhancing the overall value generated by the process. The value generated is shown as the 'margin of value' in Figure 8.7.

The value chain provides an additional framework to analyse competitive advantage. It helps identify the key skills, processes and linkages required to generate success. Additionally, the concept can link organisations together. A series of value chains can be analysed as one overall process. For example, the value chains of a component manufacturer and equipment manufacturer could be merged into one system, with common support activities. This could have the effect of reducing overall costs and improving co-ordination between the companies.

■ Industry position

Clearly, strategy formulation must consider the position held within a given industry and the organisations resource base relative to competitors.

Successful strategy amounts to implementing plans that meet customer need while effectively dealing with rival competitors. This section examines strategies relative to the competition.

Competitive marketing strategy draws heavily on military strategy. Indeed, many strategic principles can be traced to the analogy of the market place as a battlefield with competitors as enemy forces. It could be argued that Sun Tsu[2] – 'The Art of War', provides as much of an insight into the principles of modern day strategic marketing as it does to military campaigns.

Market position

The position of the organisation (or product) within a given market will clearly influence the strategic options available. For example, when comparing the market leader with a smaller 'niche' competitor, it is likely that marked differences exist in: aims, capabilities and resources. When considering a market, competitors break down into four general categories: market leaders, market challengers, market followers and market nichers. Each will be examined in turn.

Market leaders

A market leader is dominant within the given industry or segment. This dominance is normally due to market share. However, some organisations may achieve 'leadership' through innovation or technical expertise. Additionally, the organisation may only be a leader in a given segment (e.g. geographic area). Be careful how the term 'market' is defined when talking about market leaders.

The market leader will be a constant target for aggressive competitors and must remain vigilant and proactive. Common strategies include:

- *Expanding the market*: If the total market expands, the leader tends to gain the largest share of this expansion. This can be achieved by finding new users or new uses for the products and by encouraging more use by existing customers.
- *Offensive strategy*: By aggressively pursuing market share, the fight is taken to the competitors.
- *Defensive strategy*: Equally, it is important to protect your existing customer base and ensure that market share is retained.

Offensive and defensive strategies are applicable to all industry 'players' not just market leaders. These strategies are more fully discussed in section Offensive and defensive strategies.

Market challengers

Market challengers will seek confrontation and aggressively pursue market share. Often, such organisations are large and well resourced. They are

---

[2] Sun Tsu – 'The Art of War' – A classic work defining ancient military tactics and philosophy.

seeking market leadership and present a long term sustained challenge to the current leader.

Strategies available to challengers include:

- *Selective targeting*: The challenger can target specific competitors. It may attack smaller (perhaps regional) competitors or firms that are equivalent in size and resources. Basically, the challenger is looking to attack weaker competitors – those failing to satisfy the customer in some way, or those underfinanced or resourced. By picking-off weaker competitors, challengers enhance their market position.
- *Attack the leader*: The challenger can directly challenge the dominant player. This is often a long-term war of attrition and it is unlikely that market leadership will change overnight. Commonly, direct attacks sustained over time erode market share gradually.

Market follower

Being in second, third or even further down the rankings within an industry may still be an attractive position. Market followers tend to 'shadow' the market leader as opposed to challenge them, unless there is a high degree of certainty that a challenge will be successful – they follow the leader. In simple terms, followers duplicate (to greater or lesser degree) the actions and product offerings of the bigger industry players and avoid 'rocking the boat'.

Typical strategies are:

- *Duplication*: The product offering is duplicated in every possible way, even down to the packaging and promotion. Such strategies are potentially open to legal challenge in the areas of patents and copyright.
- *Adaptation*: Here we adapt the basic product offering. If we can improve on the concept, then potential exists to differentiate ourselves. For example, we may sell the same/similar products but have a reputation for higher levels of customer service.

Market niche

Niche players focus on specific market segments. They are more specialised in nature and seek to gain competitive advantage by adding value in some way appropriate to specific target groups.

Focus strategies, adopted by niche players were outlined in section Focus and commonly involve: geographic, end-user or product line specialisation.

Offensive and defensive strategies

Two fundamentals exist in the battle for market share – the ability to gain market share and being able to retain existing market share. To achieve these objectives, organisations need offensive (attacking) and defensive strategies.

Kotler et al. (1998) identify a number of attacking and defensive strategies. Such strategies are used in combination by organisations in order to successfully compete in the modern business world.

Offensive strategies, designed primarily to gain market share are shown in Figure 8.8. Each is summarised in turn.

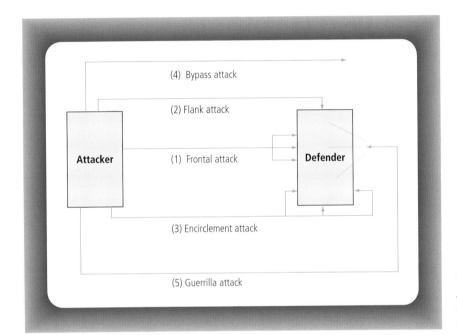

Figure 8.8
Attacking strategies
(*Source*: Kotler
et al., 1999)

1 *Frontal attack*: This is an all-out attack on a competitor. Generally, such an attack requires a sustained effort. Attackers must be certain they, have the resources to endure a long hard struggle and survive potentially heavy initial losses. They are likely to face a well-established competitor with broadly the same product offering. Therefore, the attacker needs a clearly defined advantage. For example, the attacker may have a cost advantage or its brands may be perceived more positively.

2 *Flank attack*: To draw on the analogy of the battlefield, where the flanks were always the weakest point of any army. Equally, this can be the case in the business world and 'flanking' is achieved by attacking selective market segments where the competitor is relatively weak. By concentrating resources on narrow areas it is possible to achieve superiority. The key to success is to identify worthwhile, underserved segments. For example, a computer manufacturer may feel a rival only offers a limited, and somewhat dated, range of lap-top computers. This could be a weak 'flank' vulnerable to attack.

3 *Encirclement attack*: Here we aim to offer a range of products that effectively encircle the competitor. Each of these products will tend to stress a different attribute and leave the competitor's product facing a series of more focused rivals. For example, in marketing soap powder, the market leader could be encircled by three rival products each stressing a different attribute: cleaning power, low cost and environmentally friendly. The combined effect of the three rivals is to undermine the positioning of the market leader.

One obvious danger of this strategy is that it leads to a proliferation of products. These may compete with each other and are likely to drive up cost.

4 *Bypass attack*: Perhaps more a policy of avoidance as opposed to attack. The attacker moves into areas where competitors are not active. This may involve targeting geographic areas, applying new technologies or developing new distribution systems. For example, a tour operator could bypass existing retail distribution outlets and sell direct to the public through mail-order.
5 *Guerrilla attack*: Tactical (short term) marketing initiatives are used to gradually weaken the opposition. Sudden price cuts, burst of promotional activity or other such tactics are used to create product awareness and slowly erode market share. Such attacks may be a precursor to a longer, more sustained attack. Additionally, guerrilla attacks are not restricted to marketing – legal action such as law suits can be used to harass and restrict competitors. The key to success is the unpredictability of such attacks and their ability to destroy morale and deplete resources, such as management time or finance.

It is true to say that for every offensive move a defensive counter exists. Indeed, the 'backbone' of any marketing strategy must be to maintain market share. Regardless of market position, firms must continually defend their current business against competitors. A strong defence should deter, as well as repel, rivals and allow the organisation to build on its strengths. Common defensive strategies are summarised by Kotler (1999) in Figure 8.9.

1 *Position defence*
   A position defence aims to strengthen the current position and shut out the competition. The aim is to use the distinct competencies and assets of the organisation to build an unassailable position in the market place. If the defending firms can offer a differentiated, value-added product to customers its market position will be maintain, if not enhanced. Defending a market position is often dependent on brand management, service levels and distribution.
2 *Flank defence*
   Not only do organisations need to protect their main areas of operation, but they must also protect any weak spots (flanks). Firstly, managers

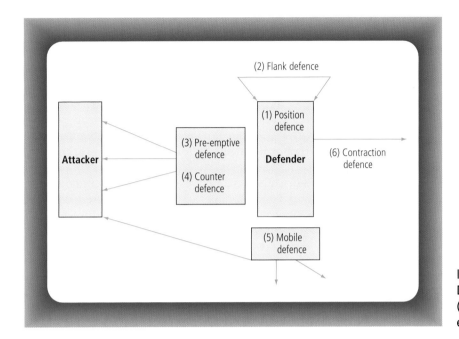

Figure 8.9
Defensive strategies
(*Source*: Kotler
et al., 1999)

Illustrative Example 8.3

Chelsea versus Manchester United, the global game

Chelsea FC have recently launched a Mandarin language version of the football club's website, Working in partnership with Sina, China's largest Internet portal provider, the club aims to access a market in excess of 100 million. Sina will convert Chelsea's Internet content into Mandarin and will examine football from a local viewpoint. Given the growth potential of the Chinese market, it is not surprising to find other 'giants' of European football – Manchester United, Real Madrid, etc. – actively targeting the South East Asian market. Chelsea view the web development, coupled with support for football at a local level, as a key element in gaining market share. The strategy differs from Manchester United, who have endeavoured to open themed outlets.

Chelsea team manager, Jose Mourinho, welcomed Chinese fans to the new website in the following statement:

> 'Hello to all our fans in China. I know that you pay close attention to our performances and today on behalf of everyone at Chelsea I want to thank you for your support, we do appreciate it very much. The new Chinese Chelsea official website will build a bridge between us.'
>
> (www.chelsea.fc.com, Accessed 30/01/07)

must identify weak areas and the potential impact of an 'attack' on the core business. Secondly, they need to be sure that the flank defence is sustainable. For example, a food retailer may see its flank as frozen products. Here it competes with specialist frozen food retailers. The flank could be protected by maintaining several 'loss leader' (sold at below cost) products.

3 *Pre-emptive defence*

This involves striking at potential competitors before they attack you. The aim is to pre-empt their actions and reduce the potential competitive threat. This may involve using, or threatening to use, the attacking strategies (e.g. guerrilla attack) shown in Figure 8.8. Large, powerful 'players' deter competitors by routinely threatening, but seldom actioning, price cuts or increased promotional expenditure. They warn others to back-off.

4 *Counter defence*

When attacked, most organisations will respond with a counter attack. The counter attack may be immediate or a more considered response might be made once the situation has settled down. By nature, counter defences are reactive, and if the position defence is strong enough no additional counter may be necessary. For example, a strong well-established brand loyalty may see off a price cutting competitor.

5 *Mobile defence*

A mobile defence involves a flexible and adaptive response, allowing the defender to switch into new areas of interest as threats or opportunities materialise. It is achieved by broadening current markets or by diversifying into unrelated activities. To illustrate, an insurance company may broaden the range of financial services offered to customers or diversify into areas such as estate agency and property management. The key is to build a strategic presence in a range of lucrative areas/segments.

6 *Contraction defence*

It may prove impossible to defend all operational activities. Therefore, a selective strategic withdrawal could be the best option. By sacrificing some activities, resources are freed to defend core activities. For example, consider a computer company. It could withdraw from the high volume/low margin personal computer market and focus on more profitable areas, such as maintenance and software development.

■ Product and market strategies

Product/market strategies are detailed in nature. They address the specific market impact of a product or product line. This section examines three concepts useful in formulating such strategies: the product/market matrix, PIMS analysis and the PLC.

Product/market matrix

Ansoff (1975) developed a policy/market matrix (or 'Ansoff' matrix) which provides a useful linkage between products and markets. The matrix (Figure 8.10) considers four combinations of product and market. Each combination suggests a growth strategy.

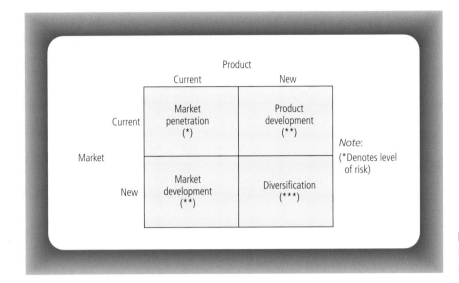

Figure 8.10
Product/market
matrix

The organisation's potential is determined by the combination of current and new products within current and new markets. Additionally, the element of risk must be considered. As organisations move away from existing markets and products the potential risk factors increase.

- *Market penetration*: The aim is to increase sales of existing products in current markets. An aggressive marketing drive, through factors such as competitive pricing, sales promotion or advertising can expand the share of an existing market. Dealing with familiar customers and products is low risk and provides a starting point to planned growth. However, the potential for market penetration is often limited and strategic plans may require additional options to be pursued.
- *Market development*: Referring to Figure 8.10, market development aims to find new markets for existing products. This could involve new geographic market (e.g. exporting), adding distribution channels or finding new market segments. For example, a manufacturer of sports clothing may try to position its products as fashion items and target a different set of retailers.
- *Product development*: Organisations must update their product portfolio to remain competitive. Ideally, a balanced product portfolio should exist, with established products generating funds for product development.
- *Diversification*: This involves moving beyond existing areas of operation and actively seeking involvement in unfamiliar activities. Diversification can be related – having linkages to existing activities, or unrelated – venturing into totally new activities. While unrelated diversification may spread risk, it can be difficult to achieve.

The product/market matrix can be expanded to consider the degree to which new activities are related or unrelated (Figure 8.11) to the core business. As previously stated, it is more difficult to achieve success in unrelated activities. Hence, unrelated diversification of product and/or markets is often tackled through joint ventures, mergers and acquisitions (see Chapter 10).

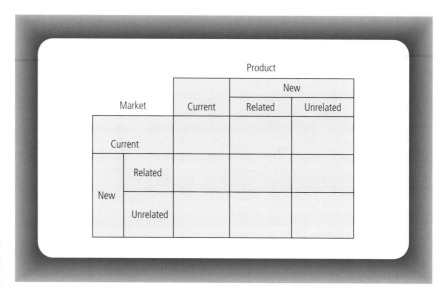

Figure 8.11
Expanded
product/market
matrix

Illustrative Example 8.4

Tesco takes on Microsoft

Not content with taking on global retailers such as Wal-mart, Tesco now has Microsoft in its sights, with the launch of a range of own-brand software. Tesco is offering own-label software for less than £20. The range includes a word processing, spreadsheet and database package designed to rival Microsoft Office, plus security and photo-editing software. Packages are compatible with Word, Excel, etc. files and have similar interfaces. The product is available in selected stores or over the Internet.

PIMS analysis

Many influential marketing studies have examined the link between profit and marketing strategy. These PIMS (profit impact of market strategy) studies aimed to identify the key drivers of profitability and have recognised the importance of market share as such a driver. Generally speaking, profits will increase inline with relative market share. This relationship (Figure 8.12) has influenced marketing thinking, promoting actions aimed at increasing market share as a route to profitability.

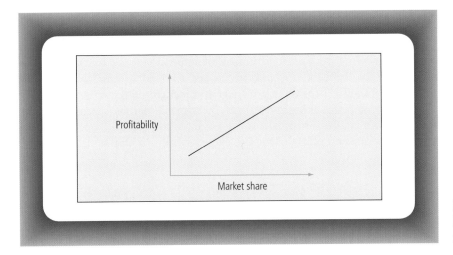

Figure 8.12
Profit related to
market share

While such a relationship is often true, it is not universal, and some industries display a 'V-shaped' relationship. Here, profitability can initially fall until a critical mass, in terms of market share, is reached. The effect of the 'V-curve' is polarisation – industries with small niche players and large dominant companies. Medium-sized firms see profits fall until critical mass is reached. This makes it very difficult for small/medium companies to grow. Figure 8.13 shows the relationship.

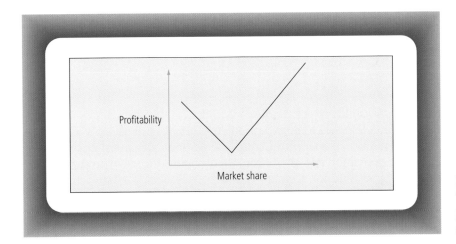

Figure 8.13
'V-shaped'
profit/market share
relationship

Clearly, the marketing strategist must consider the nature of these relationships and not blindly pursue market share. It should be possible to determine the optimal market share/profitability position.

The PLC

The PLC has been described as the most quoted but least understood concept in marketing. Any strategy considering products and markets will be influenced by the PLC. Organisations are advised to ensure they fully understand the PLC for their products and industry segments.

The basic concept (Figure 8.14) can be summarised as – products pass through four stages: introduction, growth, maturity and decline. Sales will vary with each phase of the life cycle.

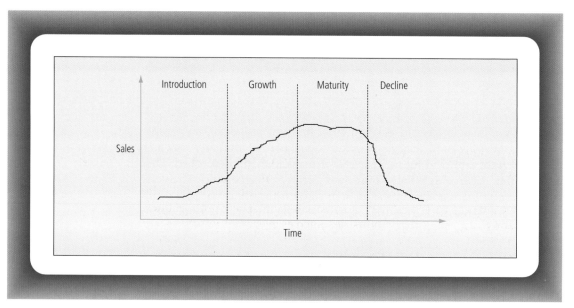

Figure 8.14
Product life cycle

Introduction

It takes time for sales to grow and the introductory phase sees awareness and distribution of the product increasing. Some organisations will specialise in innovation and aim to consistently introduce new products to the market place. Common strategies include: (i) *Skimming*, where a high price level is initially set, in order to capitalise on the products introduction and optimise financial benefit in the short term or (ii) *Penetration*, with pricing being used to encourage use and build market share over time.

Growth

This phase sees a rapid increase in sales. Additionally, competition begins to increase and it is likely that prices will be static, or fall, in real terms. The growth stage sees the product being offered to more market segments, increasing distribution and the development of product variations.

Maturity

Here product sales peak and settle at a stable level. This is normally the longest phase of the PLC, with organisations experiencing some reduction in profit level. This is due to the intense competition common in mature markets. As no natural growth exists, market share is keenly contested and marketing expenditure is increased. Marketers may try to expand their potential customer base by encouraging more use or finding new market segments.

Decline

The decline stage can be gradual or rapid. It is possible to turn-around declining products and move them back into the mature phase of the cycle. The alternative is replacement. A residual demand will exist, with current users needing parts, services and on-going support. Often the decline phase offers a choice, re-investing (turn-around/replace) or a 'harvesting' strategy that involves maximising financial returns from the product and limiting expenditure.

To fully utilise the PLC, managers need a detailed understanding of concept and the following points merit consideration.

- *Industry and product line*: The PLC concept can also apply to overall industry sales. Clearly, the PLC for individual product lines needs to be considered in relation to this. For example, if industry is entering the decline phase of its PLC, it may be unwise to launch new product lines. Currently, high-technology industries, such as telecommunications, are in the growth phase. However, individual products lines have very short PLC's as they are rapidly replaced by more advanced technology. Make sure you understand where the industry is in terms of overall PLC and how your portfolio of products fits into this overall pattern.
- *Shape of the PLC*: While the PLC normally conforms to the classic 'S-shape' curve (see Figure 8.14), it is not always the case. PLCs can take different forms. They can display: (i) cyclical/seasonal trends, (ii) constant demand, where a steady level of sales is reached or (iii) rapid growth and fall, common to fashion or fad products (see Figure 8.15).

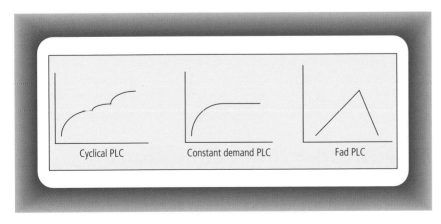

Figure 8.15
Variation in PLC shape

- *Volatility*: Any sales person will tell you that sales levels will fluctuate over time. The reality of the PLC is that sales will vary and the smooth graph shown in most text books will in fact display considerable volatility. This makes predicting your exact position in the life cycle difficult. Does a fall in sales mean we have reached the point of decline or is it a temporary blip? Only time will tell. Examine Figure 8.14 and you will see the variation in the curve.
- *Duration of stages*: Some would argue that the length of each PLC phase is closely related to marketing decisions and not simply a natural cycle. Effective marketing should be able to extend and sustain the growth or maturity of a product offering. Equally, ineffective marketing would hasten its decline.

■ Strategic wear-out

The adage – *'nothing lasts for ever'* – is certainly true of marketing strategy. Care must be taken to avoid strategic wear-out. This occurs when the organisation no longer meets customer needs and the pursued strategy is surpassed by competitors. Davidson (1997) summarises the causes of strategic wear-out (see Table 8.1).

Table 8.1 Reasons for strategic wear-out
1 Changes in customer requirements
2 Changes in distribution systems
3 Innovation by competitors
4 Poor control of company costs
5 Lack of consistent investment
6 Ill-advised changes in successful strategy
Source: Davidson (1997)

Future business requires active steps to ensure that your strategy does not 'wear-out' and the role strategy formulation is to develop/maintain a marketing orientation. This is based on the premise of defining customer need and prospering through customer satisfaction and loyalty. Sound general and financial management should underpin this orientation and the entire corporate focus should relate to key asset of any business – customers.

■ Difficult market conditions

Marketing strategy is often linked to a premise of favourable market conditions. For example, strategies tend to work well when we are experiencing incremental growth – the market demand grows annually. However, many industries (arguably the majority of industries) are now experiencing static or declining demand. Such markets are hostile in nature and feature factors such as: volatility, over capacity, price discounting, reduced profit margins and 'downsizing'.

Given these conditions Aaker (1995) advocates a number of strategic options for declining and/or hostile markets these include:

- *Generate growth*: Can we revitalise the industry by finding growth? This could be possible through: (i) encouraging existing users to increase usage, (ii) developing new markets for our products and (iii) finding new applications for existing products or technologies/skills. The 'Ansoff' matrix (see Figure 8.10) provides a useful analytical framework for this purpose.

Illustrative Example 8.5

Kronenberg 1664: The premium lager marketing decline

The UK drinks market contains many segments. Currently, the premium lager market displays many characteristics associated with difficult market conditions. Sales are generally falling as consumers move to other drinks. Additionally the market is dominated by well-resourced providers willing to fight for market share.

France's favourite beer – Kronenberg 1664, was first introduced into the UK in the 1950s. The premium lager segment of the drinks market has proved challenging in recent years, with Kronenberg coming second to market leader 'Stella Artois'. Stella has cultivated an image of quality through a carefully orchestrated 'reassuringly expensive' brand position established over many years. Kronenberg has launched a number of brand variations (see below) including a white beer, 'Kronenberg Blanc', designed to compete with the speciality beer 'Hoegaarden'. Kornenberg aims to position the brand, through an advertising strategy, as a drink to sit and saviour. TV advertising portrays the message that 1664 was a great year for beer – 'Sit, Savour, 1664'.

Premier Cru
A slow brewed beer (6 per cent ABV), which has a sophisticated taste characterised by a robust flavour and dark golden colour and provides a perfect accompaniment to food.

Blanc
White beers use wheat in the brewing process. This can give the beer a cloudy appearance. It is pale in colour and 5 per cent ABV.

(ABV denotes strength of the product)

Note, a 'problem-based learning' version of this case is available to Tutors through the companion website.

- *Survival*: Organisation can survive by effectively managing cost and clearly signalling their commitment to the industry and its customers. Clearly, there is a need to manage cost structures, with experience effects and economy-of-scale becoming vital. Organisation may rationalise their product portfolios and focus on larger more profitable customers. Conversely, perhaps correctly, organisations may actually expand their product range, aiming to cover the maximum number of customers by offering a wide range of price points. We may witness takeovers, mergers and acquisitions as organisations aim to reduce cost and generate economies of scale. A portfolio approach can be taken, with 'cash cows' supporting operations/products with are currently struggling but are deemed to have long-term potential. A useful strategic option is to reduce industry exit barriers by selectively buying-out elements of competitor's current business. For example, we could take over their commitment to supplying spare parts and maintain existing products. This 'shake-out' inevitable leaves the industry with fewer but larger competitors.

● *Exit strategy*: If business conditions are particularly unfavourable, prudence may dictate that we withdraw from the industry. Such action will involve overcoming exit barriers such as the costs associated with downsizing (e.g. redundancy, legal costs of breaking contracts, etc.) and handling commitments to existing customers. Exit strategy can be rapid – withdrawing immediately – or a slow phased withdraw with activities being gradually run-down. Remember exiting a market may have repercussions for other actives and products, as it affects 'goodwill' and customer confidence.

■ Summary

Strategy formulation offers alternative methods of achieving objectives. The process has three components: (i) competitive advantage, (ii) industry position and (iii) product/market strategies. The importance of having constant and sustainable strategies cannot be underestimated.

Three generic (fundamental) strategies exist – cost leadership, differentiation and a focused approach. Porter (1980) stresses the importance of adopting one generic source of competitive advantage and thus avoid the strategic equivalent of 'being stuck-in-the-middle'. These strategies can be expanded upon to generate specific sources of competitive advantage. For example, superior products, perceived advantage or scale of operation are all exploitable competitive advantages. Additionally, it is important to understand the effects of experience curve and value chains within your industry. The primary and secondary activities of a value chain, coupled with experience effects, should support the organisation's strategic thrust.

Companies need to examine their position within the market place. They can occupy the role of market leader, challenger, follower or niche player. Marketing strategy needs to be appropriate to the position occupied, relative ambition and resource base. All organisations actively pursue offensive and defensive strategies. The need exists to protect your core business and your flanks (weak areas), while taking the fight to competitors through appropriate offensive options (e.g. bypass or guerrilla attacks).

Ansoff's product/market matrix provides a useful summation of product and market strategies. Organisations can consider market penetration, market development, product development or diversification as key marketing initiatives. Much product/market strategy focuses on gaining market share. PIMS analysis has proved highly influential and has linked market share to profitability. While this relationship is often true – don't blindly chase market share as it is not universally applicable.

Additionally, an awareness of the PLC is important. The strategist needs to understand the PLC shape and how the marketing mix varies in the introduction, growth, maturity and decline phases.

Organisations need to be watchful and avoid the pitfall of strategic wear-out and strategies need to address hostile and declining markets.

■ References

Aaker, D., *Strategic Market Management*, 4th edn, Wiley, New York, 1995.

Ansoff, I., Strategies for diversification, *Harvard Business Review*, **25**(5), 1975, pp. 113–125,

Davidson, H., *Even More Offensive Marketing*, Penguin, London, 1997, p. 285.

Hooley, G., Saunders, J. and Piercy, N., *Marketing Strategy and Competitive Position*, 2nd edn, Prentice Hall, Hemel Hempstead, 1998.

Kotler, P., Armsrong, G., Saunders, J. and Wong, V., *Principles of Marketing*, 2nd edn, Prentice Hall, New Jersey, 1998.

Kotler, P., *Principles of Marketing*, 2nd European edn, Prentice Hall, 1999, p. 531.

Kotler, P., *Principles of Marketing*, 2nd European edn, Prentice Hall, 1999, p. 528.

Porter, M., *Competitive Strategy: Techniques for Analysing Industries and Competitors*, Free Press, Macmillan Publishing Co., New York, 1980, p. 39.

Porter, M., *Competitive Advantage*, The Free Press, Macmillan Publishing, 1985, p. 6.

■ Further reading

Aaker, D., *Strategic Market Management*, 4th edn, Chapter 14, Wiley, New York, 1995.

Wilson, R. and Gilligan, C., *Strategic Marketing Management*, 2nd edn, Chapters 9, 10, Butterworth-Heinnemann, Oxford, 1998.

CHAPTER 9

Targeting, positioning and brand strategy

The subject of targeting and positioning builds on the segmentation techniques that were covered in Chapter 5. This chapter now explores criteria by which the attractiveness of a market segment can be judged. The targeting process is then examined before a discussion on a range of product positioning techniques is undertaken. Central to this discussion is the issue of brand strategy.

■ Introduction

At a fundamental level, marketing strategy is about markets and products. Organisations are primarily making decisions about which markets to operate in and which products/services to offer to those markets. Once those essential decisions have been taken the company then has to decide on what basis it is going to compete in that chosen market. Segmentation is therefore at the heart of strategic marketing decision making. In essence it is a strategic rather than an operational issue and has to be treated as such.

Initially any organisation has to identify how it can, in general, gain competitive advantage. The stage that we will now explore is concerned with creating a specific competitive position. The first crucial step is to decide in which specific market segments to operate. Chapter 5 examined the criteria that can be used to identify discreet segments within a market. Once segments have been identified they then have to be evaluated in order that an organisation can decide which particular segments it should serve. Target marketing, or targeting, is the common term for this process.

Once target markets have chosen an organisation, then it has to decide how it wishes to compete. What differential advantage can it create that will allow the companies product or service to hold a distinctive place in the chosen market segment. This process is normally called positioning. Targeting and positioning are critical processes that require the attention of senior management.

■ Evaluating market segments

To effectively evaluate different market segments it is necessary to systematically review two issues: the market attractiveness of the competing segments and the organisation's comparative ability to address the needs of that segment. There are a number of criteria that can be used to judge the attractiveness of a market segment. These fall under three broad headings: market factors, the nature of competition and the wider environmental factors. At this point it is important to stress that marketers need to recognise that many of the criteria that can be used to evaluate the attractiveness of a market segment are qualitative rather than quantitative in nature. This has implications for the manner in which the process is managed. We will return to this topic later in the chapter. Firstly we need to review the criteria themselves.

Market factors

When assessing market attractiveness the particular features of a market will affect any evaluation.

- *Segment size*: A large segment will generally have greater sales potential. This in itself will make it more attractive but it may also offer the potential of gaining economies of scale because of the larger volumes involved. Large segments with their potentially larger sales can justify the higher investments that may be necessary for organisations wishing to operate within them. However large segments may not always be the most attractive. Large segments can be more competitive as their very size will attract other companies into them. Smaller organisations may not have the resources to address a large market and therefore may find smaller segments more appropriate for their attention.
- *Segment's rate of growth (measured in terms of real revenue growth after inflation)*: Segments that are growing are normally seen as being more attractive than segments where growth has peaked or even begun to decline. Segments in growth are seen as having a longer-term potential and therefore justify any investment necessary. Once again, however, these segments are likely to be more competitive as other companies also recognise their potential.
- *Segment's profitability*: What is the total profitability of the segment. If you are already operating in this segment it's not your organisation's profitability alone that should be reviewed. In order that all segments are evaluated on a consistent basis it is the profitability of all companies operating in the segment that should be calculated. This will have to be an estimate based on analysing competitors' activities.
- *Customers price sensitivity*: Segments where consumers have low price sensitivity are likely to be more attractive as higher profit margins can be gained. Consumers will be more concerned about quality and service rather than price alone. Price sensitive segments are more susceptible to price competition, which leads to lower margins.
- *Stage of industry life cycle*: Entering a segment that is in the early stages of an industries life cycle offers the advantages of potentially high growth in the future. In the early stages there are also likely to be less competitors. However, the early stages of the industry life cycle are characterised by the need for high investment in new plant, promotional activities and securing distribution channels. This occurs at a time when there may only be modest sales revenue. There will be a drain on cash into the new area of business that the company has to be able to fund. Business's that are more interested in cash generation or profits

in the short term may consider mature markets more favourable. These markets are likely to require a more modest level of investment.

● *Predictability*: The potential value of a market will be easier to predict if it is less prone to disturbance and the possibility of discontinuities. In the long term a predictable market is likely to be more viable.

● *Pattern of demand*: The attractiveness of a segment will be affected by any seasonal or other cyclical demand patterns it faces. A large percentage of sales in the gift and card market take place at Christmas in western countries. An organisation has to be able to withstand the cash flow implications of this skewed demand. The same problem occurs in other industry sectors such as travel and tourism.

● *Potential for substitution*: In any market there is the potential for new solutions to be developed that will address consumers' needs. An organisation should review markets to establish whether new innovations could be used in the segment. Where substitutions are likely an organisation may decide not to enter on the basis that it makes the segment less attractive. If, however, the organisation has the ability to deliver that innovatorary approach it may make the segment a prime target as the company has the skills to change the nature of competition to their advantage.

Nature of competition in the target market and the underlying industry structure

● *Quality of competition*: Segments that have weak competition are more attractive than segments where there are strong and aggressive competitors. It is not the number of competitors operating but the nature of their competition that is critical in judging an opportunity.

● *Potential to create a differentiation position*: A segment will be more attractive if it contains unsatisfied customer needs that allow the company to create a differentiated product or service and gain a higher margin by charging a premium price. If it is a commodity market then competition is likely to be driven by price and the segment will be less attractive.

● *Likelihood of new entrants*: Segments that currently have limited competition may appear attractive. However the potential for other companies to enter this market has to be taken into account.

● *Bargaining power of suppliers*: An organisation will be in a stronger negotiating position where there is a range of potential suppliers. If, however, supply is in the hands of a few dominant companies the balance of power in negotiations will lie with the suppliers making a segment less attractive.

● *Bargaining power of customers*: Customers may be the end customer but they can also be a customer in the channel of distribution (i.e. a major supermarket). If customers are in a strong negotiating position they will try and push suppliers' prices down reducing margins. A market segment will be less favourable when a few major customers dominate it or the channels of distribution.

- *Barriers to entry in the market segment*: There may be entry barriers to a segment that will reduce its appeal. These can be in the form of patents, new specialised plant or machinery necessary, or the need for high promotional expenditure. It may be that the overall level of investment necessary to successfully enter an area may be unrealistic for some companies. These same barriers may also put off other potential entrants. Therefore if a company calculates that it can overcome these barriers it may be able to enter a segment where there is little direct competition.
- *Barriers to exiting the market segment*: There may be barriers that make exiting a segment difficult. Expensive facilities may have to be built that can only be used in servicing a particular market segment. Therefore withdrawing from this segment would leave redundant expensive plant. Other barriers could include service agreements to provide spare parts to customers for a number of years into the future, or plant and machinery that would be expensive to decommission. Organisations would have to anticipate the potential barriers to exit when they are initially evaluating a segment's attractiveness.

Environmental factors

Social
Social changes can lead to newly emerging segments that are not currently served by any organisation. There can be a significant advantage to companies that are the first to move into these areas. Organisations also need to review the impact that any likely changes in social trends will have on a particular segment.

Political
Changes in the political environment can create new segments in a market. The deregulation of the utilities market created several new market segments that organisations could address. The political environment may also make certain segments less attractive. Segments that are located in particular geographic areas may be affected by political instability. There may also be regulatory changes that will affect a sector such as pharmaceuticals.

Economic
Economic trends may make segments more or less attractive. The growing affluence of older people in western economies is making them a much more attractive group than 20 years ago.

Technology
Technological changes have to be taken into consideration when evaluating a segment. A judgement will have to be made as to whether new entrants will be able to enter a segment competing on a different basis by using technology to create innovative ways of delivering a product or service.

Environmental

Consumers and governments concerns about environmental issues have become much more important in recent years. Therefore an evaluation of the environmental issues that may affect an organisation's ability to service a segment will have to be considered.

Companies will not be capable of supplying every attractive segment that is identified. Having analysed a segment's market attractiveness it is then necessary to compare the needs of that group of consumers with the organisation's capabilities. An organisation's strengths can be judged by analysing its assets and competencies.

■ Establishing organisational capability

Organisational capabilities will be made up of specific assets and competencies. The key areas to identify are where the organisation is superior to the competition.

In summary, assets are organisational attributes, tangible or intangible, that can be utilised to gain advantages in the market (see Figure 9.1).

Scale advantages	• Market share • Relative and absolute media weight • Leverage over suppliers	• International presence • Sales/distribution service coverage • Specialist skills due to scale
Production processes (Plant, machinery + information systems)	• Level of contemporary practice • Level of flexibility	• Economies of scale • Capacity utilisation • Unique items
Customer franchises	• Brand names • Brand franchises • Databases	• Customer relationships • Unique products/services • Patents
Working capital	• Quantity • Ready access	• Location • Access to credit
Sales/distribution service network	• Coverage • Relationships with external distributors	• Size • Quality
Relationships with other organisations	• Suppliers • Financial institutions • Joint ventures	• Joint exploitation of assets (technology or distribution)
Property	• Type • Location	• Ability to expand • Quality

Figure 9.1
Examples of assets that create a competitive advantage (*Source*: Adapted from Davidson, 1997)

Obviously assets should not be viewed in isolation, it is also important to establish any competencies that give the organisation advantages. The value chain is a useful framework to use to identify these areas of unique competence. Key competencies may lie in primary activities. These include activities such as in-bound logistics (e.g. inventory control), operations (e.g. manufacturing), out-bound logistics (e.g. global delivery), marketing (e.g. brand development) and service (e.g. installation). Other key competencies may lie in support activities such as procurement, technology development, human resource management and the organisation's infrastructure.

When trying to identify these competencies rather than using the generic value chain it may be more effective to develop a value chain that reflects the specific operations that face a particular business sector. The primary activities for an organisation offering management consultancy are outlined in Figure 9.2.

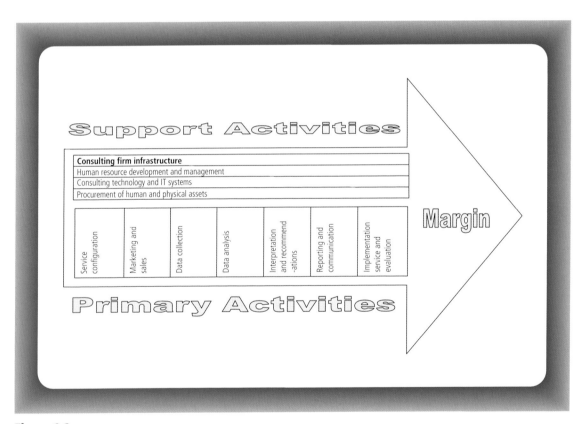

Figure 9.2
The value chain of a management consultancy practice (*Source*: Adapted from Buckley, 1993)

An organisation's key competencies once identified will normally fall into the areas of marketing, selling or operations (see Figure 9.3).

Marketing	• New product development • Business analysis • Category management • Brand extension • Brand equity measurement • Unique market research techniques • Planning skills • Database management	• Advertising development • Customer service • Marketing process • Spending efficiency • Customer relationships • Customer targeting • Testing Design
Selling	• Supply-chain management • Account management • Relationship development • Customer service • Building partnerships • Motivation and control • Planning	• New account development • Merchandising • Presentation skills • Space management • Negotiation • Pricing and promotion • Trade marketing
Operations	• Motivation and control • Process engineering • Industrial relations • Inventory control • Cost management • Productivity improvement • Planning • Health and safety • New facility development • Management training and development	• Speed of response • Flexibility • Total quality management • Purchasing • Payment systems • Capacity utilisation • Commercialisation of new products or services • Method of supplier management • Property skills • Global operation

Figure 9.3
Examples of competencies that create a competitive advantage (*Source*: Adapted from Davidson, 1997).

■ Strategic alignment of assets and competencies (targeting)

The critical stage in the segmentation process is matching the capabilities of the organisation to attractive market segment opportunities. At a largely operational level management analyse organisational assets and competencies to identify the skills and resources available to build low cost or differentiated positions. Where these assets or competencies currently, or with development could, surpass the competition, they form the basis for creating a specific competitive position in a target market. Company capability should always be judged relative to the competition.

Figure 9.4 illustrates some questions that should be asked when attempting to match assets and competencies with potential market segments (Jobber, 1995).

> **Marketing assets**
> Does the market segment allows a company to take advantage of its current marketing strengths? Successful situations are more likely to occur where a company's current brand identity, or method of distribution, is consistent with those required to enter the new target market.
>
> **Cost advantages**
> Entering a price sensitive segment would be consistent with the capabilities of an organisation that has a low cost base.
>
> **Technological strengths**
> Where the organisation has access to superior technology is its use compatible with the market segment, and will it allow the company to gain any advantage?
>
> **Managerial capabilities and commitment**
> Does the company have the technical and managerial skills necessary to successfully enter a market segment?

Figure 9.4
Examples of assets and competencies matching with potential market segments

Overall the organisation has to establish whether entering a particular segment is consistent with its long-term aims and objectives. If not then no matter how tempting entering the segment should be resisted. It will only divert company resources and management time away from the core goals of the enterprise.

Once the key areas of a company's capabilities have been identified they can be aligned with the attractive market segments already identified. An organisation should enter segments that allow it to exploit current assets and competencies, or will allow potential capabilities to develop into strengths. This is an area where adapting portfolio models, more normally used to evaluate current products or business units, can be useful. The shell directional policy matrix for instance can be adapted to analyse market segment opportunities against corporate strengths. An adapted version of this model is shown in Figure 9.5.

Weighted criteria are used as in the traditional usage of the model. In this case a selection of market attractiveness factors, from those discussed earlier, that are considered relevant in evaluating a particular sector are weighted according to their importance as judged by the organisations' management. The same exercise is then undertaken of selecting a range of assets and competencies deemed relevant to this particular sector. These are again weighted. Choosing factors in relation to the specific area being considered ensures that the model is custom made to the particular situation and organisation under review.

Every potential market segment is then evaluated on a rating scale normally of 1 to 10 (1 = poor 10 = excellent) on each of the criteria. The

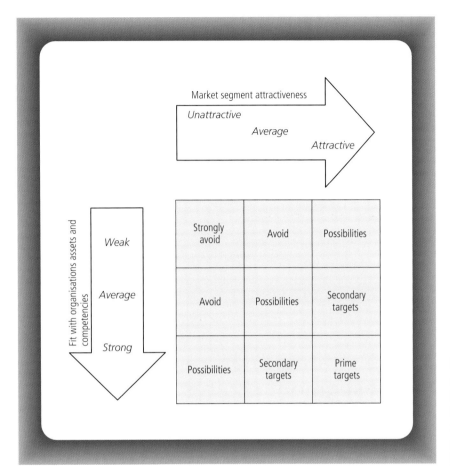

Market segment attractiveness

Unattractive

Average

Attractive

Fit with organisations assets and competencies

Weak

Average

Strong

Strongly avoid	Avoid	Possibilities
Avoid	Possibilities	Secondary targets
Possibilities	Secondary targets	Prime targets

Figure 9.5
Adapted Shell directional policy matrix applied to target market selection (*Source*: Shell, 1975)

overall position of the segment on each axis is established by multiplying the ratings by the weighting given to each factor (see Chapter 6 for full details). The result of such an exercise for an imaginary situation and organisation is shown in Figure 9.6.

The most attractive segment is B as it lies in the box that is attractive on the horizontal axis representing segment attractiveness and has a strong fit with the company's assets and competencies as represented on the vertical axis. This segment should be a priority for the company. Segment A is an attractive market but has only an average fit with the organisation's assets and competencies. This may have potential and would be a higher priority for the organisation than segment E. Segment E has medium attractiveness and medium fit with the organisations and should be selectively managed. The model suggests that targeting segments C and D is likely to be a poor investment.

This example illustrates how an adapted portfolio model can act as a screening device for identifying market segments that should be targeted.

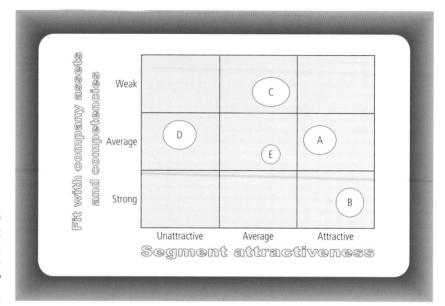

Figure 9.6
Evaluating market
segments for an
imaginary
organisation/
situation

■ The strategic nature of making target segment choices

However, as has already been stated segmentation is a strategic process where qualitative and creative judgements have to be taken. Opportunities have to be evaluated on their strategic fit. Not only do the assets and competencies of the organisation have to have synergy with a particular market segment, but wider issues have to be considered as well. Opportunities also have to be evaluated on the following somewhat subjective criteria:

● Ability to allow the creation of a sustainable market position.
● Compatibility with the corporate mission.
● Consistency with organisation's values and the culture. Segments that are a radical departure from current practice may challenge the prevailing values in the organisation and the established status quo. The new segment may challenge the current power structure within the organisation, which will create influential barriers to implementation.
● Ability to provide a focal point for action and future development in the organisation.
● Ability to facilitate an innovative approach to market entry.
● Ability of the current organisational structure to service the target market. Does this opportunity lie between two areas of responsibility in the current organisational structure. This may lead to the opportunity never being seriously addressed.
● Compatibility with current internal information flows and reporting lines. Difficulties will arise where a segment does not sit easily with

the current data collection or distribution systems. Segments in an innovative area may cause managers problems in terms of how to allocate targets and monitor progress. If this is linked to the problem already discussed under organisational structure, it may complicate issues such as areas of responsibility and reporting lines even further.

These factors of compatibility with the internal practices of an organisation are likely to prove critical to the successful implementation of a new segmentation strategy. The newly entered segment has to have clear departmental ownership. Reporting lines and information flows have to be able to monitor its progress. In short individuals within the organisation have to wholehearted embrace the development of the new segment or failure will follow no matter how attractive the segment or how well the organisations overt assets and competencies might fit.

A successful selection process will have identified a market segment or segments that are in alignment with the company's assets and competencies and is also compatible with the wider organisational issues.

■ Positioning

Having selected a target market or markets the organisation then has to decide on what basis it will compete in the chosen segment or segments. How best can it combine its assets and competencies to create a distinctive offering in the market? This has to be done in such a way that consumers can allocate a specific position to the company's product or service within the market, relative to other products. Consumers have to cope with a huge amount of product information. Customers will position a product in their mind in relation to other products on the market based on their perception of the key attributes it contains. Consumers will see the key attributes of Volvo as safety and durability. BMW's main attributes are based on performance hence the 'The Ultimate Driving Machine' advertising slogan. When consumers consider the car market, these two companies' products will be positioned relative to each other based on these perceptions. Companies can attempt to associate various qualities to their product as a way to help shape consumers perceptions of their position in the market. A brand can be positioned using a range of associations such as (Kotler et al., 1996):

Product attributes: Heinz positions it products on the attributes of no artificial colouring, flavouring or preservatives.

Product benefits: Volvo positions itself using the product benefits of safety and durability.

Usage occasions: The convenience store SPAR eight-till-late shops are positioned on the usage occasion. Customers use the shops when they need to shop out of normal hours or near to their home. Kit Kat (have a break have a Kit Kat) links the brand to tea and coffee breaks in the UK market.

Users: Ecocover cleaning products are positioned as environmentally friendly products for the green customer.

Activities: Lucozade is positioned as an isotonic drink for sporting activities.

Personality: Harley Davidson motorbikes are positioned as macho product with a free spirit.

Origin: Audi clearly illustrates it German origins in the UK market by the use of the 'Vorsprung durch technik' slogan. The hope is the product will be linked to the German reputation for quality engineering.

Competitors: Pepsi-Cola are positioned as the choice of the next generation reflecting the fact that in blind tasting tests younger people preferred Pepsi over competitors' offerings.

Product class: Kellogg's Nutrigrain bars are positioned as 'morning bars', a substitute for the traditional breakfast.

Symbol: Esso petrol has used the symbol of the tiger to position itself in the market.

These are the various ingredients that can be used by an organisation endeavouring to influence consumer's perceptions of the product offering. Companies have to decide which of these they can use and more importantly how they wish to position their product in the market vis-à-vis the competing options.

Four factors are of critical importance for successful positioning (Jobber, 1995):

1 *Credence*: The attributes used to position the product have to be perceived to be credible by the target customers. It would be very difficult for a Nuclear power generator to position itself as environmentally friendly.
2 *Competitiveness*: The product should offer the consumer benefits which competitors are not supplying. Clairol launched a new shampoo Herbal Essences in the USA in 1995 which emphased the brand's wholesome ingredients. By 1997 this was the fastest growing brand on the market and ranked number two behind Pantene.
3 *Consistency*: A consistent message over time is invaluable in helping to establish a position against all the other products and services fighting for a share of the consumers mind. An organisation that changes its positioning on a regular basis causes confusion in the consumer's mind. This will mean they have an unclear perception of exactly what are the key characteristics of the product.
4 *Clarity*: The positioning statement an organisation chooses has to create a clearly differentiated position for the product in the minds of the target market. A distinct message such as 'Bread wi' Nowt Taken Out' underlines the wholemeal old world nature of Allison's bread.

■ Perceptual mapping

Mapping consumer perceptions can allow an organisation to see where it is currently placed compared to competitor's offerings. A simple perceptual

Illustrative Example 9.1

Silverjet

In January 2007 Silverjet started operating a low cost 'full-frills' business class only airline service between London Luton airport and New York's Newark airport. The company offers return fares starting at £999 with some promotional fares as low as £799. This not only under-cuts traditional carriers' business class prices but also the prices of other business class only rivals, such as, Eos and Maxjet. Silverjet's service consists of 100 business class flat beds, personal in-flight entertainment systems, individual food service, ladies-only toilets and a quiet zone. The company provides a free passenger pick-up from London Luton Parkway station to take passengers to Silverjet's dedicated passenger terminal which operates a luggage concierge service rather than the traditional check-in operation and provides free wi-fi Internet access, plasma screen televisions, drinks and a mini Foyles library. Passengers, however, are only required to arrive at the terminal 45 minutes before the flight. The airline claims, it is the first carbon neutral airline as it charges passengers a mandatory carbon offset payment within its fares.

Silverjet believe there is a market segment that wants a business class level of service but doesn't wish to spend up to £4000 for the privilege. In March 2007 Silverjet's average load factor was 60 per cent well ahead of plan. The company now plans to buy two further aircraft and increase its operations starting with an additional daily flight from London to New York.

map is based upon two axis representing key attributes in a particular market. These attributes are identified through market research and are determined by consumer's perceptions of the important factors in a market. This could for example be price and quality, or style and performance or a range of other issues. Products/companies or more particularly brands can then be placed according to their position on these attributes (see Figure 9.7).

In the case of Figure 9.7, in the Hotel market the key attributes are deemed to be the price and the facilities. Hotel A on this map is seen as expensive but with a full range of facilities. The Hotel B is perceived to be inexpensive but with limited facilities. Both of these are reasonable consistent offerings. Hotel C, however, is seen as expensive but with intermediate level of facilities. This position does not offer any unique aspects. There may of course be more than two key attributes in a market. Figure 9.7 doesn't map out quality. Hotel C may be seen as having high service quality for instance. To gain a fuller picture obviously more than one positioning map can be developed. There are also more sophisticated three-dimensional mapping techniques available for marketers to use.

Through the use of perceptual maps marketers can establish the current situation in a particular market. There will then be a number of alternatives from which to choose.

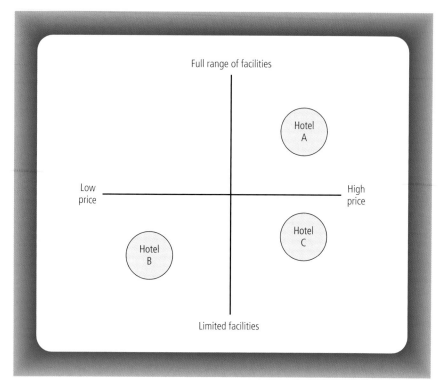

Figure 9.7
A perceptual map of
various hotels

Illustrative Example 9.2

Coca-Cola

Recent research using brands scans revealed that consumers reacted differently to the Coca-Cola brand than they did to the Pepsi-Cola brand. When the individuals participating in the experiment were shown the company logos prior to tasting the product, the Coca-Cola brand stimulated responses in the areas of the brain associated with cultural knowledge, memory and self-image. Pepsi failed to initiate these brain responses. This effect was so strong that researchers could identify what drink the individual had been shown merely by looking at the brain scan. The Director of the Brown Human Neuroimaging Laboratory at Baylor College, Houston, Texas, Dr Read Montague, is quoted as saying 'There is a huge effect of the Coke label on brain activity related to the control of actions, the dredging up of memories and self-image. There is a response in the brain which leads to a behavioural effect'. When the consumers were subjected to a blind product tasting between the two brands there was no preference for one product over the other. However when they were shown the label prior to tasting the product 75 per cent stated they preferred the taste of the Coca-Cola product. The researchers believe the label is so influential, stimulating responses in the brain the Pepsi brand failed to reach, that it actually altered the individual's perception of the taste of the product.

■ Positioning alternatives

In a seminal work Ries and Trout (1981) claim that when considering positioning there are three principal alternatives open to an organisation:

1 An organisation can build on a current position to create a distinctive perception of the brand by consumers. Avis famously uses the 'We Try Harder' slogan to make a virtue out of being number two in the market.

2 Having established the attributes that are most important to the consumer, see if there are any unoccupied positions that are desirable in consumer's minds and therefore viable opportunities. IDV Ltd used this approach when it launched Croft Original Sherry. The key product attributes in the sherry market from a consumer's perspective were the colour and the taste of the product. Consumers favoured a sweet taste; they also perceived that a light-coloured sherry was more sophisticated than the traditional, darker-coloured sherries (see Figure 9.8). There was at the time no sherry that had a light colour and a sweet taste and yet this combination was highly desirable to consumers. Croft Original entered the market with this unique positioning and now is the best selling sherry brand in the UK market.

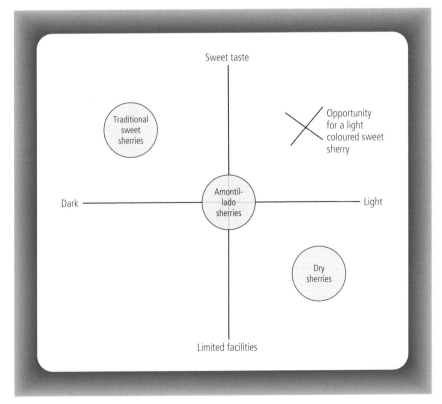

Figure 9.8
Perceptual map of the sherry market

3 Due to changes in consumer behaviour or where perhaps there has been of a failure of the original positioning a third alternative can be considered which is to reposition the brand. Campari has recently been re-launched in an effort to shake off its 1970s image as endorsed by Lorraine Chase. The new repositioning has a more macho feel, it even includes a notorious London underworld character 'Mad' Frankie Fraser in the advert. Both the soft drink Tango and the snack Pot Noodle have successfully been repositioned in recent years. However, repositioning can be difficult to achieve and there are several examples of brands that have been less successful at moving their position. Babycham, originally a product aimed specifically for the female market, abandoned the famous deer symbol and the trademark green bottle for a more masculine image in 1993. By May 1997 it revived both the bottle and the Babycham deer and went back to its original more female-orientated positioning.

There are alternative views on the correct approach to successful product/brand positioning. One view is that an organisation should identify one unique selling proposition (USP) for a product and concentrate purely on that aspect. The whole focus of this approach is to be seen as the brand leader on that key attribute. For example, Gortex fabric is seen as the leading fabric for breathable, waterproof, lightweight clothing material. The most effective USPs are based on quality, service, price, value or advanced technology (Ries and Trout, 1981).

An alternative approach to stressing a USP, based on a functional aspect of the product, is to concentrate on an emotional selling proposition (ESP). The product can be distanced from functionally similar rivals by appealing to unique emotional associations. An example of this is Alpha Romeo's positioning on the heritage and image of the traditional Italian sports car.

Both these approaches stress one key aspect of the product, however there is a view that more than one factor can be used to position a product. As has been mentioned earlier, Volvo is positioned on safety and the compatible factor of durability. Whichever approach is taken, there are a number of positioning mistakes that can be made by an organisation:

● *Underpositioning*: In this situation consumers have only a very limited perception of the brand and are unaware of any distinguishing features.
● *Overpositioning*: Consumers have a perception that the brand is only active in a very focused area, when in fact the brand covers a much broader product range.
● *Confused*: Consumers have an unclear view of how the brand relates to competitive offerings.

Positioning is concerned with establishing an organisation's product in the mind of a customer, in a position relative to other products in the market. Inevitably, therefore, making decisions about branding strategy will be a crucial aspect of this process.

Illustrative Example 9.3

Saga

Saga produces a wide range of products, including magazines, radio programmes, financial and travel services for its estimated 6.5 million customer base of over 50s. In 2005 the company was bought in a management buyout for £1.35 billion. However, the over 50s market is changing and that has implications for the Saga brand. Recent surveys have revealed that a new over 50s market is emerging, one that has been termed the 'middle youth' market. Sainsbury Bank undertook a survey of individuals in their 50s, 60s and 70s and found many had the mindset of people in their 40s. Another GreyPower survey undertaken by Millennium, an agency that specialises in the mature market, found that 75 per cent of consumers in their 50s and 60s would not consider taking a Saga holiday. In fact 40 per cent of those in their 60s, 70s and 80s thought the brand would be more suitable for people older than themselves. Saga now finds itself being challenged for the over 50s market by brands such as Secondlifestyle, which position themselves on the association of being for the active and young in customer's mind.

■ Creating brand equity

The overall aim of branding decisions is to create an identity for the product or service that is distinctive and also in line with the targeting and positioning decisions already taken. Organisations should strive to produce a brand equity that delivers value to the consumer. This will result in either the customer showing greater brand loyalty or being willing to pay a premium price for the product. Brand equity according to Aaker is 'a set of assets and liabilities linked to a brand's name and symbol that add to or subtract from the value provided by a product or service to a firm and/or that firm's customers' (Aaker, 1991).

Brands that contain high equity have strong name awareness, strong associations attached to the brand, a perception of quality and have high levels of brand loyalty (see Figure 9.9). To create a brand that exhibits these characteristics takes time and investment. For instance of the top 50 UK grocery brands, four have their origin's in the 1800s; 16 from the period 1900 to 1950; 21 between 1951 and 1975 and only 9 have been introduced to market in the years since 1975 (Hooley et al., 1998). Once established, however, a successful brand will become a valuable asset to an organisation in its own right.

■ Brand valuation

There has been a trend in recent years for companies to try and turn the general concept of brand equity into giving these organisational assets a specific financial valuation and to account for them on their company

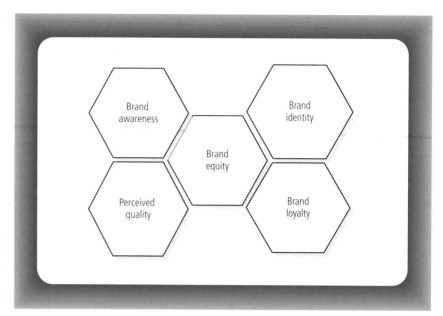

Figure 9.9
The constituents of
brand equity
(*Source*: Aaker,
1995)

balance sheets separately from goodwill. Accountants have largely been at the forefront of this approach and have developed a range of factors seen as indicators of a brand's value. All are linked to the ability of the brand to sustain higher returns than competitors. These factors include:

- *Market type*: Brands operating in high margin, high volume and stable markets will carry higher valuation than brands in less profitable or stable sectors. The confectionery or beer markets have traditionally been seen as less liable to changes in technology or fashion. Deciding on the potential of a market type, however, is full of difficulties. Even the drinks industry now shows signs of more regular changes in consumers' behaviour. It should also be borne in mind that one of the aims of developing a strong brand is to allow a company to compete on other factors than price allowing them to make strong margins even in what could be seen as commodity markets. The Andrex brand of toilet roll has consistently made strong margins in the UK market. More importantly it has gained higher margins than any of its competitors over the last 30 years from what is essentially a commodity product.
- *Market share*: Brands that are market leaders are deemed to command a premium because competitors will find it difficult to overcome consumers' tendency to buy the dominant brand. In effect holding the market leadership position is seen as a barrier to entry for other brands.
- *Global presence*: Brands that either do, or carry the potential to be, exploited internationally obviously carry more value than brands within a purely domestic market. Development in e-commerce may lower barriers to establishing a global brand name and therefore do set

a potential challenge to the high values placed on current global brands. There is also, obviously, the potential for the current global brands to end up as the dominant players in the e-commerce market thereby reinforcing their position and value.

- *Durability*: Some brands manage to maintain a contemporary appeal and retain their relevance to customers over a long period of time. These brands tend to have created strong customer loyalty and become an established player in the market. A study by Blackett found that brands such as Cadbury in the chocolate market, Gillette in razors, Kodak in film and Colgate in toothpaste, all were the brand leaders in their market areas over the period 1931–1991 (Murphy, 1991). Such long-term brand leaderships are therefore likely to generate high valuations.

- *Extendibility*: Brands that have the ability to be extended into related markets or stretched in new markets offer greater value than brands with more limited options. The Bic brand, for example, has been successfully extended from disposable pens into a number of other disposable markets such as cigarette lighters and razors. Andrex in 1987 had 39 per cent of the toilet paper market by 1994 this share had dropped to 28 per cent due to increased competition from discounters (Kapferer, 1997). However, the potential to extend the brand allowed the company to enter related markets for products as such as kitchen paper, paper tissues, etc.

- *Protection*: Brands that have some protection from coping through patents or registered trademarks or designs, potentially offer greater value. However, this protection has in reality been limited. In particular, retailers have launched own label products with similar packaging to market leading brands.

Illustrative Example 9.4

Red Bull

The energy drinks market has been a fast-growing sector over the last few years and current sales are around £775 million a year in the UK. In Western Europe Red Bull holds around two-thirds of the market. This is a market that a company can enter with relatively low levels of investment and this has resulted in a rash of brands with similar characteristics to Red Bull being launched. Some drinks have used similar names, such as, Red Rhino and Red Bat, some have used similar style packaging. In order to defend its brand Red Bull has resorted to legal action. So far it has won its case against a drink called Shark in the UK and other cases in the Netherlands and Australia. It is believed Red Bull has also settled out of court with up to 12 other drink brands in the UK. Red Bull believes unless it takes action, not only will their brand suffer a lack of differentiation in the market but also the whole category will be damaged by the resulting customer confusion.

The factors considered so far have generally been developments from an accountancy perspective. However there is a range of other significant factors marketers perceive to be crucial in terms of judging the brands potential value.

- *Superior products and services*: Brands that offer the consumer superior products and/or services than competitors create greater value. Brands that are perceived to deliver clear benefits to the consumer such as quality, style or cheapness present the company with a clear asset in the market.
- *Country of origin*: The identity of the country of origin can either attach or deduct value from a brand. Association with Scotland is seen as attaching value to fresh food products in countries such as France. Association with Britain, however, has been deemed to have a negative image by consumers in certain market sectors such as telecommunications. This resulted in organisations such as British Telecom re-branding themselves as BT as a way of distancing themselves from their country of origin and appearing more international. Conversely, in the clothing market in the USA association with Britain is seen as positive much to the benefit of brands such as Barbour (jackets, etc.) and Church's shoes.
- *Market domination*: The brand's ability to gain extensive coverage in the market, a dominant position in the distribution channels and the ability to command good shelf positions are all assets of considerable value. Most of these attributes accompany brand leadership and merely add to the potential that market position gives a brand. There is some limited evidence however that affluent customers are now moving away from the major brands as a way of standing out from the crowd. In Japan there has even been the development of a retail clothing store, Seibu, successfully selling high quality clothing that carry no branded labels.

■ Strategic brand management

Successful brand development is reliant on far more than creating a strong image through the marketing communication mix. This is the area of which the consumer will be most aware but the less visible elements are crucial ingredients in creating a strong brand (see Figure 9.10). Factors such as providing product quality, continuous product development and high levels of service are potential components of a successful brand yet are not as visible as elements of the communications mix. Significantly marketing communication skills are generally co-ordinated by agencies outside the organisation, whilst the other components of successful brand development have traditionally been reliant on the company's internal assets and competencies. However, a number of alternative approaches to the structure and ownership of crucial elements of brand development and delivery have emerged over the last 30 years. Organisations now are

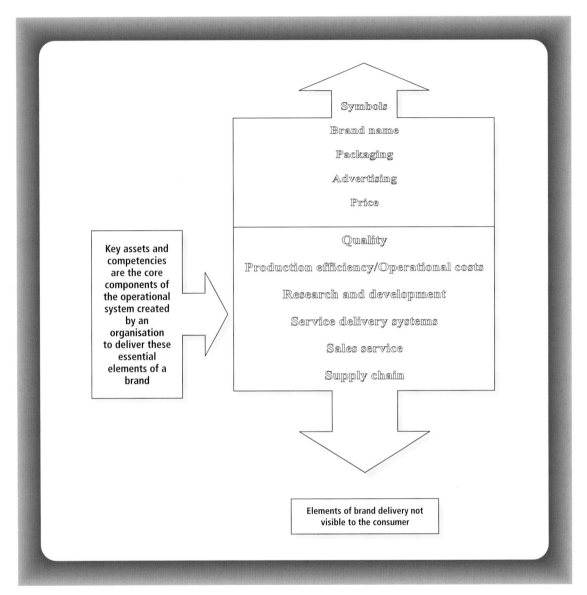

Figure 9.10
The visibility of core elements of a brand (*Source*: Adapted from Davidson, 1997)

faced with a number of decisions on the best way to gain access to the assets and competencies needed to successfully support a brand. This had led to a number of alternative ways of structuring the business functions that support successful brands. Organisations have the option of co-ordinating these activities without necessarily owning all the assets and competencies needed. The capability to support a brand can be obtained through various forms of relationships and alliances (see Figure 9.11).

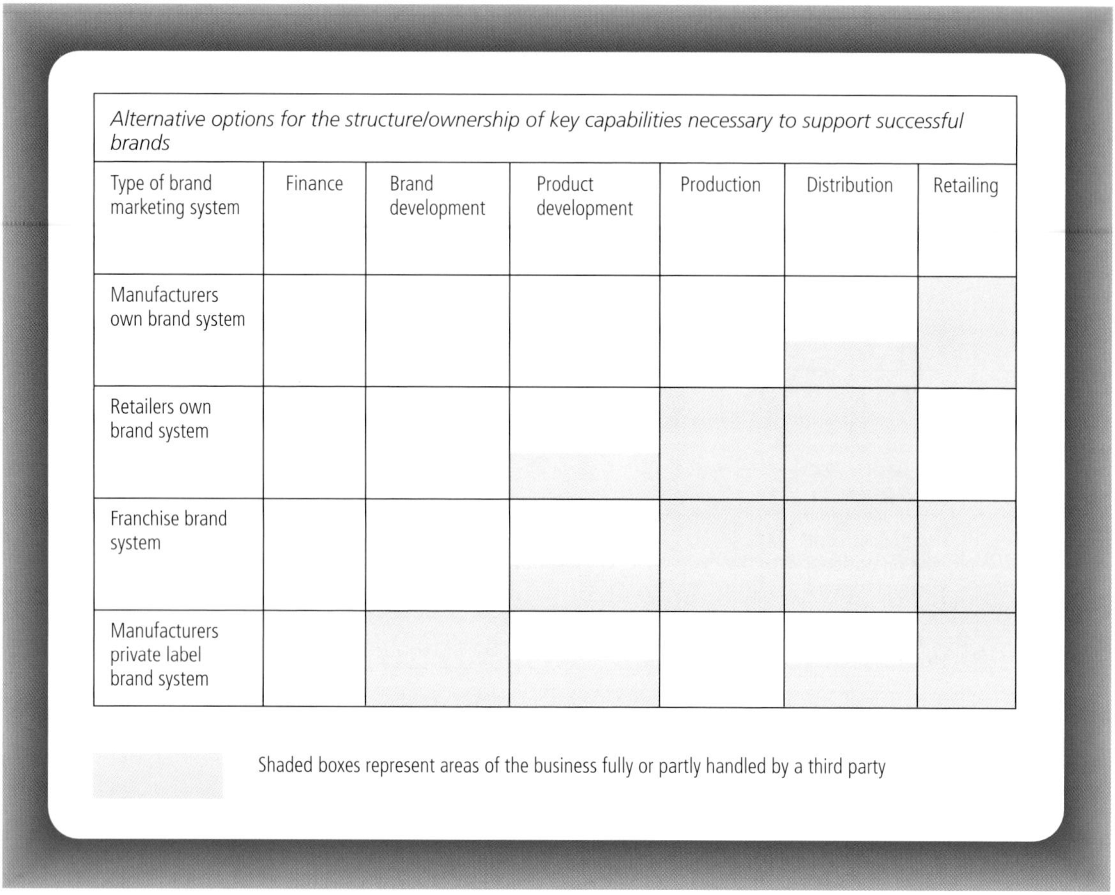

Alternative options for the structure/ownership of key capabilities necessary to support successful brands						
Type of brand marketing system	Finance	Brand development	Product development	Production	Distribution	Retailing
Manufacturers own brand system						
Retailers own brand system						
Franchise brand system						
Manufacturers private label brand system						

Shaded boxes represent areas of the business fully or partly handled by a third party

Figure 9.11
Alternative options for the structure/ownership of key capabilities necessary to support successful brands (*Source*: Adapted from Davidson, 1997)

Organisations have tended to use one of four main options in structuring their operations to gain access to the assets and competencies they require:

1 *Manufacturers brand system*: Companies such as Kellogg only produce products under their own brand name. Kellogg owns the majority of the business operations except for the retail outlets selling the product. In some areas third party distribution systems may be utilised.
2 *Retailers own brand system*: Retailers such as The Gap or Marks & Spencer only supply goods carrying their retail brand name. Manufacturers under contract to the retailer carry out production. Often distribution is contracted out. Product development is sometimes undertaken by a third party, such as a design agency, but more frequently it is a shared activity with the retailer taking an active role.

3 *Franchise brand system*: Organisations such as Benetton and Burger King are franchise operations. Benetton, it contracts out parts of its manufacturing activities. Key skills relating to core aspects of the brand's quality, such as pattern cutting and dying operations are however kept in-house. Warehousing is also kept inside the company operations and is an area were considerable investment has been made to allow fast distribution around the globe. The retail outlet are mainly franchise operations. Although these retail outlets are one of the most visible aspects of the brand this is not a core area of competence owned by the organisation. Key competencies lie in the areas of product design, brand development, management of key areas of production and distribution, supplier and retail franchise management.

4 *Manufacturers private label brand system*: Some companies concentrate on manufacturing products to be sold under a retailer's own label such as Marks & Spencer. These companies have no control over branding or the retail outlets instead they create their competitive position through highly efficient manufacturing skills, customer service and new product development abilities. There are examples of organisations, such as Weetabix, producing both their own branded products and goods for retailer's own brands.

Optimising the assets and competencies available to an organisation is obviously a crucial step in creating appropriate operational systems to support a brand.

■ Brand name strategy

The operational structure an organisation develops is not the only area of strategic decision making associated with brand management. An organisation also has to decide its policy for naming brands across all its products and services. Branding decisions for any new products can then be taken within this framework. The focal point of decisions on branding strategy is about the emphasis the organisation wishes to place on creating a distinctive offering in the market against the weight it wishes to place on the origin of the product or service (see Figure 9.12).

Between the extremes offered by these two approaches lie several options available to an organisation when considering an overall brand strategy:

● *Corporate brand*: Organisations following this approach, use one corporate name across all its products. Heinz would be a classic example of this unified approach. Individual products merely carry a descriptive name under the corporate umbrella Heinz brand, hence Heinz Baked Beans, Heinz Cream of Mushroom Soup, Heinz Tomato Ketchup. Linking the individual products together creates a strong overall image. It also gives the opportunity to create economies of scale to be developed in marketing communication and possibly distribution. The clear danger is that if there is a problem with an individual product the reputation of

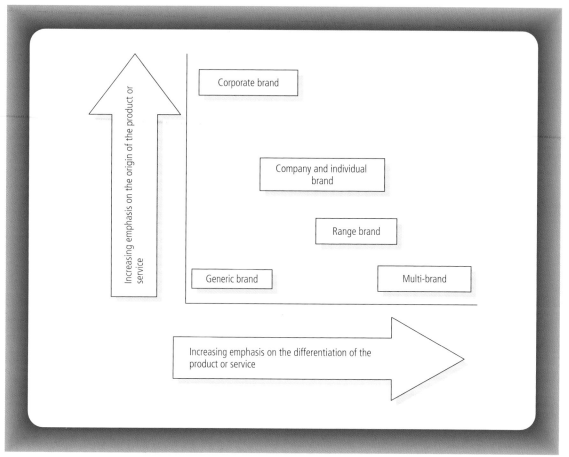

Figure 9.12
Alternative branding strategies (*Source*: Adapted from Kapferer, 1997)

all the products may suffer. Virgin has used the corporate brand name across their entire product portfolio. Their high profile problems with the Virgin rail franchise in the UK may over time have a negative impact across their other operations. The fact this does not yet appear to have happened is a testament to the strength of the core brand name.

● *Multi-brand*: Multi-branding or discreet branding is the complete opposite of the corporate branding approach. With multi-branding each product is given its own unique brand name. The aim is to build completely separate brand identities. This is appropriate, if the organisation is competing in a number of different segments and the consumers' perceptions of a product's position in one segment may adversely affect the consumers' perceptions of another product. A classic example of this approach would be Proctor & Gamble who produce a range of washing powders aimed at discreet sectors of the market such as Daz, Ariel and Bold.

- *Company and individual brand (endorsed approach)*: Traditionally Unilever practised a multi-brand approach with its washing powders but recently has been moving closer to the strategy of linking a company name to an individual brand name. Their products now have Lever Bros. as a high-profile endorsement on the individual brands such as Persil, Radion and Surf. This can be used in different ways. Endorsing a product with the corporate name gives new product credibility whilst at the same time allowing the new brand some degree of freedom. A fixed endorsed approach entails the corporate brand name being given a consistent profile against each individual product's brand name in the range. For example, all Kellogg's products give individual product brand names the prominent position on the pack, while the same secondary weighting is given to the company brand name. (*Note*: This is different to Heinz where the prominence of the corporate brand is sacrosanct.) Cadbury's take a more flexible approach to the corporate endorsement, it is more or less prominent depending on how independent they choose to make the brand.
- *Range branding*: Some organisations use different brand names for different ranges of product in effect creating a family of products. Ford has done this to an extent using Ford for its mass-market car range and Jaguar for the up-market executive car range. Volvo, another Ford acquisition, has its own distinct brand values that appeal to a particular market segment and therefore has become another brand family for the Ford group.
- *Private branding (distributors own brand)*: An organisation may decide to supply private brands in particular retail brands. In this case the private brand is owned and controlled by the distributor who will make decisions regarding the product's position in the market. The distributor is likely to use either a strategy of corporate or a company and individual brand for its products.
- *Generic branding*: This strategy involves the product having no brand name. The product's packaging merely states the contents of the package for instance flour or washing up liquid.

Each of the approaches to branding outlined above has advantages and disadvantages. These are summarised in Figure 9.13.

■ Combined brand strategies

Obviously large organisations may use a mixture of brand strategies to manage their large product portfolios. 3M employs a number of approaches to brand its broad range of products.

The 3M brand name is used as an umbrella brand on all products aimed at the professional market including camera, overhead projectors and video tapes. On Post-it notes, the individual brand name is accompanied by the 3M Company brand name. This is also true of the company's general

Branding strategy	Advantages	Disadvantages
Corporate brand	• The strength of the corporate brand is conveyed to all products • Promotional costs are spread across all products	• Any new product failure has the potential to damage to the corporate brand • The positioning of the corporate brand constrains decisions on the quality and pricing for individual products
Multi-brand	• Allows individual differentiation of brands • Allows products to be occupy different positions in the same market i.e. a premium and a discount brand from the same parent company • Current brands are insulated from any new product failures	• Each brand requires a separate promotional budget • Market sectors have to contain enough potential to support more than one brand • Highly focused brands are hard to reposition once a market enters decline
Company and individual brand	• Product can be supported by the reputation of an existing corporate brand while at the same time the individual characteristics of the specific offering can be emphasised	• A new product failure has the potential to cause some damage the company brand • The positioning of the company brand constrains decisions on quality and pricing of the individual product
Range brand	• The strength of the brand is conveyed to all the products in the range • Promotional costs are spread across all the products in the range	• Any new product failure has the potential to damage the range brand • The positioning of the brand constrains decisions on quality and pricing for individual products
Private brand	• Demands little promotional spend by producer • Producer can concentrate on gaining cost efficiency through volume production	• Marketing decisions controlled by distributors • Removes the producer from direct contact with the market
Generic brand	• Little promotional budget, reduced packaging costs	• Competition becomes based mainly on price and service levels

Figure 9.13
Advantages and disadvantages of brand strategies (*Source*: Adapted from Brown and MacDonald, 1994)

consumer products where 3M is used as an endorsing brand name in small print.

The Umbrella brand Scotch is used on most consumer products. This includes the companies video tapes aimed at the consumer market where the presence of a 3M connection is hard to identify. Initially 3M consumer scouring pads were sold under the generic product name and the

Scotch-Brite brand. In response to competitor's actions, the scouring pad product was given the specific individual brand identity of Raccoon.

There are also some variations on these major branding themes within 3M. For instance, aerosol glue aimed at the professional market is branded with a large 3M logo but also carries the Scotch brand name in smaller print.

Each of these branding decisions at 3M has been taken to make the greatest competitive impact in a particular market. 3M is not alone in having such a sophisticated brand portfolio, many large organisations have quite complex brand structures.

The approach an organisation adopts to branding is a crucial decision relating to the overall strategy of the company has decided to pursue. The branding policy should be developed in the light of:

- the nature of the product or service,
- the pattern of consumer behaviour in the specific market,
- the company's competitive position.

When companies develop new products the branding decision will invariably be taken according to the general branding strategy of the organisation. Multi-brand-orientated companies will tend to always create a new brand for the new product. For other companies the decision will depend on the nature of the target market. If it is very different from the organisations current markets they may decide to introduce a new brand. Toyota did this when they entered the up-market executive car market, introducing the Lexus brand. This is a rational approach where the target market is large enough and has the potential profitability to justify investing in creating a new brand. Companies may however choose to use a current brand name and opt for a brand extension or brand stretching policy.

■ Brand extension

There are occasions where an organisation will try to extend the use of a brand name to new products in the same broad market. Brands that carry high brand equity are candidates for brand extension as they have the ability to increase the attractiveness of the new products. PD Enterprises, a Hong Kong-based garment producer, acquired the Pretty Polly brand in the summer of 2006. Recent market research has shown that the unprompted brand awareness of the Pretty Polly brand is still very high and therefore it is likely that the new owners will be able to exploit the brands strength by adding a range of brand extensions.

■ Brand stretching

Brand stretching takes place when an organisation stretches a brand into new unrelated markets. Virgin is an obvious example of this moving from the record industry to airlines, railways, financial services and cola drinks. Marks & Spencer and Tesco have both moved from mainstream retailing into financial services. Both are examples of brand stretching. This policy is more likely to be successful where the original brand values are compatible with the aspirations of the new target group.

Over a period of time, it is likely that an organisation will be required to undertake actions to improve the performance of a brand. This can occur for a number of reasons such as the advent of new technology, changing consumer behaviour or new competition. The options open to a company in these circumstances are either to increase sales volume or to raise the brand's profitability. Brand revitalisation and Brand repositioning are two approaches that can be employed to increase the sales volume of a brand.

■ Brand revitalisation

Brand revitalisation involves gaining sales volume by expanding the market for a brand. Four significant opportunities exist that can expand a market:

1 *Enter new markets*: One approach is to expand into new geographical areas. Irn Bru the Scottish soft drinks brand has recently expanded into the Russian market as a way of increasing sales.
2 *Exploit new market segments*: Once the initial market segment has been fully exploited, a company can then expand by targeting new market segments. Johnson & Johnson's baby shampoo was stagnating until they moved the brand into a new market segment of adults who wash their hair frequently.
3 *Increase the frequency of use*: This can be achieved by actions such as:
   ● Appealing to consumers to use products on new occasions can increase a brand's sales. Kellogg have been attempting to increase sales of their Cornflakes brand by promoting the proposition that the product should be eaten as a suppertime snack as well as a breakfast cereal.
   ● Providing incentives to purchase such as frequent flyer programmes which promote the sale of airline tickets.
4 *Increase quantity used*: This can be achieved by:
   ● Increasing the size of the 'normal-sized container' such as the popcorn or soft drink containers offered in cinemas. If consumers accept this size as normal, then consumption will increase. Alternatively, undertake advertising such as Weetabix promoting larger portions as normal. In that case it suggests eating three Weetabix at a time rather than two.
   ● Removing barriers to consumption. Thus companies can offer low-calorie chocolate or soft drinks as a way of removing a major obstruction to consumer purchase.

■ Brand repositioning

Brand repositioning is undertaken in order to increase a brand's competitive position and therefore increase sales volume by seizing market share from rival products. When repositioning companies can change aspects of the product, change the brands target market or both. This gives four repositioning options (see Figure 9.14):

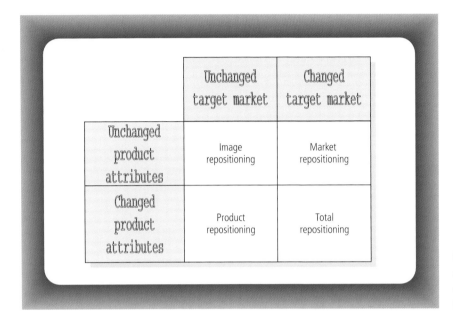

	Unchanged target market	Changed target market
Unchanged product attributes	Image repositioning	Market repositioning
Changed product attributes	Product repositioning	Total repositioning

Figure 9.14
Alternative options available for brand repositioning

1 *Image repositioning*: This takes place when both the product and the target market remain unchanged. The aim is to change the image of the product in its current target market. In the early 1990s Adidas were seen as reliable but dull. The company created an image of 'street credibility' in an attempted to reposition the brand to appeal to the consumer in the sports shoe market. Tango, the Britvic soft drink, has been transformed during the 1990s from a minor UK brand into a brand showing dynamic growth. This has been achieved by creating an anarchic image for the product through a major promotional re-launch that was aimed to appeal to consumers in the critical 16–24-year-old age group.

2 *Market repositioning*: Here the product remains unchanged but it is repositioned to appeal to a new market segments. Lucozade a brand of carbonated glucose drink was originally targeted as a product for individuals suffering from illness, particularly children. In recent years it has been repositioned as an isotonic drink at young adults undertaking sporting activities.

3 *Product repositioning*: In this situation the product is materially changed but is still aimed to appeal to the existing target market. In the early 1990s Castlemaine XXXX larger was altered with its alcohol content being increased from 3.7 per cent to 3.9 per cent for pub sales and 4 per cent for cans sold in supermarkets. The packaging was also changed as the size of can was changed from 440 to 500 ml. These

changes were instituted to address the changes in consumer tastes in the product's target market.

4 *Total repositioning*: This option involves both a change of target market and accompanying product modifications. Skoda has managed under Volkswagen's ownership, to totally reposition itself. The product quality and design has changed significantly and the brand now has credibility with new more affluent consumers. This has also allowed the brand to expand its sales outside its Eastern European heartland.

Raising a brand's profitability. If a brand is in a static or declining market and a company judges that the brand has finite potential, then it may be prudent to force the maximum profitability out of the product. This can be achieved by:

- *Raising prices*: Although this may lead to a drop in sales it is likely to dramatically improve margins. In a declining market competitors may be dropping out of the market, restricting consumer choice. Thus consumers who still purchase the product may have little choice but to accept the higher price.
- *Cut costs*: This action will obviously be a matter of management judgement as it will obviously mean ceasing to invest in the brand and it may hasten its decline.
- *Cut the brands product range*: Rationalising the range of marginal product lines will save additional costs whilst having a limited impact on overall sales.

■ Brand extinction

Inevitably, over a period of time, brands die. They may last for decades or even in some cases centuries but even well-established brands can falter. This can happen for a number of reasons:

- *Intense brand competition*: Weak brands face increasing competition from both overseas brand entering domestic markets and the growth of retailers own label brands. This leads to poor profitability for brands with small market share and in the end withdrawal from the market.
- *Acquisition and mergers*: Companies that acquire brand names or undergo a merger often rationalise the portfolio of brand names owned by the new organisation. Since acquisition, Nestle has over time replaced the Rowntree brand name on its products.
- *Rationalisation*: Organisations periodically review their brand portfolio and may decide that in relation to their promotional budgets they cannot sustain the range of brand names that they have propagated. The now deceased Rover Group over a 40-year period terminated the production of a stable of famous brand names including Triumph, Austin, Morris, Riley and Wolsey. The Jaguar and MG brands have been lucky to escape this cull having been transferred to different owners who saw value in the heritage of the respective brand names. Jaguar is now

owned by Ford and MG by the Chinese company Nanjing Automotive. Ford recently also exercised its right to purchase the Rover brand name rather than let either Shanghai Automotive or Nanjing Automotive gain access to the brand name. Ford obviously felt that the Rover brand still had value in the market and decided not to let that potential value fall into a competitor's hands. The aquisition of the Rover brand also protected the value of the Land Rover brand which Ford had previously bought from previous owners of the Rover group.

- *Globalisation*: In order to create global brands, companies have also rationalised domestic brands in particular markets. Mars changed the name of Marathon chocolate bars in the UK to the Snickers brand name in order to create a consistent brand image internationally.
- *Weak brand management*: Brands also falter through mediocre marketing, uncompetitive production costs or poor quality. It is an ignominious end for what should be the key asset of any organisation.

■ Summary

Targeting aims to align an organisation's assets and competencies to attractive market segments. Once these market segments have been identified an organisation has to decide how it will position its product in the market, relative to the competition. One key aspect of this positioning process is branding.

An organisation's assets and competencies can be used to create new products and services, to unlock the potential in market segments that are not currently served, either by the company in question, or by companies in general. Product development and innovation are critical issues to any organisation and they are discussed in detail in Chapter 6.

■ References

Aaker, D., *Managing Brand Equity*, Free Press, New York, 1991.

Aaker, D., *Strategic Market Management*, 4th edn, Wiley, New York, 1995.

Buckley, A., *The Essence of Services Marketing*, Prentice Hall, Hemel Hempstead, 1993.

Brown, L. and McDonald, M., *Competitive Marketing Strategy for Europe*, Kogan Page, London, 1994.

Davidson, H., *Even More Offensive Marketing*, Penguin Books, London, 1997.

Hooley, G. H., Saunders, J. A. and Piercy, N. F., *Marketing Strategy and Competitive Positioning*, 2nd edn, Prentice Hall, Hemel Hempstead, 1998.

Jobber, D., *Principles and Practice of Marketing*, McGraw Hill, Maidenhead, 1995.

Kapferer, J., *Strategic Brand Management*, 2nd edn, Kogan Page, London, 1997.

Kotler, P., Armstrong, G., Saunders, J. and Wong, V., *Principles of Marketing: The European Edition*, Prentice Hall, Hemel Hempstead, 1996.

Murphy, J. M., *Branding: A Key Marketing Tool*, 2nd edn, MacMillan, New York, 1991.

Ries, A. and Trout, J., *Positioning: The Battle for Your Mind*, McGraw-Hill, New York, 1981.

Shell Chemical Company, *The Directional Policy Matrix: A New Aid to Corporate Planning*, Shell, UK, 1975.

■ Further reading

Davidson, H., *Even More Offensive Marketing*, Chapters 9, 10, Penguin, London, 1997.

Doyle, P., *Marketing Management and Strategy*, Chapter 6, Prentice Hall, Hemel Hempstead, 1994.

Kapferer, J., *Strategic Brand Management*, 2nd edn, Chapters 6, 7 and 11, Kogan Page, London, 1997.

CHAPTER 10

Product development and innovation

About this chapter

Product development is a strategic necessity. In terms of product development, organisations can modify, imitate or innovate. A rigorous NPD process is essential to avoid marketing failures. Additionally, managers must address the concept of innovation across the entire organisation.

■ The strategic agenda

It is essential that all organisations develop products. Product development and innovation are the 'life blood' of any business. By definition, development and innovation are strategic activities that shape the future. The creation of an acceptable product offering involves many strategic decisions. For example, building on core competencies, matching resources to market opportunity and co-ordinating activities across functional boundaries are all accepted strategic activities which normally determine the success or failure of our products. Given that many organisations now face difficult commercial conditions – static/declining demand and intense competition – innovation and product development should top the agenda of today's (and tomorrow's) successful organisations. In essence, all organisations must evolve or they will perish. Product development and innovation allow organisations to evolve.

It is important to define 'product' in its broadest sense. What counts is the total product offering – this provides benefits to the customer. Hence, the process of product development involves not only innovation of the core product, but innovation in areas such as support services and production processes. Business cannot afford to view innovation in the narrow sense of technical/scientific development, but rather as a management process. Such a process focuses creative effort with the intention of developing products perceived as delivering superior benefits. Innovative projects require the right balance of creative, technical and managerial skills. Blending these factors together fosters an organisational culture that embraces innovation, product development and strategic success.

■ The nature of products and product development

As stated above, products must be considered in terms of the total product offering. Remember, the term 'product' covers goods, services, ideas and information. In reality, most products are combinations of these items. Service-based products tend to be intangible in nature. Above all, products must meet needs and deliver benefits to the user.

Kotler et al. (1999) defines a product as having three levels. Firstly, a *core product* defines the fundamental need being meet. Fundamental needs are generic in nature (e.g. transportation, data storage or self-esteem). Secondly, the *actual product* is the specific offering aimed at meeting a core need. This includes attributes such as; styling, branding, performance features and packaging. Finally, the *augmented product*, which enhances the actual product by offering additional services and benefits, making the product a more attractive proposition to the consumer. Examples include factors such as after-sales support, maintenance and affordable finance.

It is important to consider product development at each of the above levels. Organisations must fully understand their core product(s) – what need does it meet? Then develop actual and augmented product offerings that are attractive to specific customers groups. As an illustration, consider Orange PLC:

Core	Actual	Augmented
● Communications	● Mobile phone network	● Voice mail
	● Handset	● Insurance against lost
	● Brand image	

One 'school-of-thought' suggest that in certain markets, advances in quality management, manufacturing systems and information technology, will tend to generate competitive products indistinguishable from each other. Therefore, the only way to differentiate products is at an augmented level – who offers the best service and support? Indeed, the augmentation may become such a vital part of the product offering, that it is absorbed into the actual product. It becomes an integral, essential part of the product. For example when buying a new car, the warranty package is an integral part of the product offering.

Illustrative Example 10.1

Clarks footwear

Clarks dates back to 1825, when Cyrus Clark started tanning sheepskin rugs. He was joined by his brother in 1830, who introduced sheepskin slippers. Production was boasted in 1856 with the advent of the Singer sewing machine. An early marketing success was William Clark's introduction of the 'Hygienic line', a range which followed the natural shape and line of the foot and established Clarks reputation for producing foot-friendly shoes. Clarks expanded rapidly during the early twentieth century. They introduced new technologies and materials, took full advantage of the economies of mass production, and responded to changing fashions and the emergence of the female ankle by putting much more emphasis on the development of women's shoes.

(Continued)

Illustrative Example 10.1 (Continued)

The end of the Second World War saw dramatic expansion for Clarks as they moved into world markets.

In the early 1950s Nathan Clark introduced what was to become a Clarks classic – the 'Desert Boot'. Modelled on the simple comfortable boots worn by army officers, the boot had attitude, and quickly gained popularity.

The 1960s saw a huge success for Clarks children's shoes as their unique fitting properties set standards for comfort and fit.

Today the company has global turnover of £921 million and sells almost 41 million pairs of shoes each year. Clark's success is founded on a commitment to comfort and performance. This involves incorporating the latest comfort technology in their footwear. For example, the company's 'Active Air' system incorporates a network of air chambers in the sole, allowing air to circulate, provide impact absorption and provide an 'energy return' effect with each step.

Source: www.clark.co.uk, Accessed 5/2/07.

Fundamentally, a product delivers a set of benefits to a customer, in order to meet a need. Organisations must strive to fully understand this process and be certain their product offering best matches not only need, but also customer expectation.

Product development strategy

There is much debate relating to product development strategies. For example, how is the term 'new product' defined? The reality is that few products are 'new in the sense of being innovative, unique or novel. Most 'new' products are updates and revamp of existing goods and services. Jain (1997) views new product strategy in terms of three categories (see Figure 10.1).

1 *Product improvement/modification*: Unless products are to be replaced by completely new entities, they must be upgraded and enhanced as a matter of necessity. The process can have two possible aims; (i) maintaining the competitive position in an existing market and/or (ii) adapting the product in order to appeal to other market segments. Major changes may result in the need to reposition product offering within a given

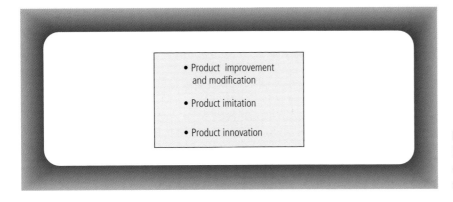

- Product improvement and modification
- Product imitation
- Product innovation

Figure 10.1
Product development strategy

market. Conversely, organisations may only make minor changes aimed at ensuring the products remain up-to-date.

2 *Product imitation*: This strategy involves capitalising on the initiatives of others and suits organisations that are risk averse and/or have limited funds to invest. Clearly, there are potential ethical and legal problems with this option and organisations must define the line between imitation and copying. The strategy is most effective when the 'new' version of the product brings some additional dimension of added value.

3 *Product innovation*: This involves bringing new and novel ideas to the market place. Product innovation may be aimed at: (i) replacing existing products with new approaches and items which enhance customer satisfaction or (ii) providing diversification in order to target opportunities in new markets. Clearly, organisations should expect a correlation between risk and diversification.

Booz, Allen and Hamilton (1982) classified 'new' products using the categories shown in Table 10.1. Again this demonstrates that truly original, innovative products represent only a small proportion of total development.

Table 10.1 Type of 'new' product

Type of product development	Nature
1 New world	Often scientific or technical development. High risk/return activities which can revolutionise or create markets.
2 New product lines or line additions	Such products can be: (i) new to the provider as opposed to the market place or (ii) be additions to the product ranges already on offer.
3 Product revision	Replacements and upgrades of existing products. This category is likely to cover the largest single number of NPDs. Additionally this may cover changes aimed at generating *cost reductions* – no perceived change in performance but more economic product/provision of the product.
4 Reposition	Aiming to diversify away from existing markets by uncovering new applications, uses or market segments for current products.

New product development process

Regardless of whether we are developing a 'new to world' product, a new product line or simply aiming to reduce cost, we need a new product development (NPD) process. All organisations require some mechanism, or process, which enables ideas to be evaluated and, when appropriate, translated into commercial products. Such a process provides a vital ingredient in the fight for commercial success. Indeed, Davidson (1997) sites lack of rigorous process as a factor commonly contributing to the failure of new products.

NPD processes take many shapes and forms. It is vital that any process is driven by an overall NPD strategy, otherwise development activities will lack co-ordination and focus. This concept is expanded upon later in the chapter.

Stages commonly found in an NPD process include:

1 *Idea generation*

New product ideas have to come from somewhere. This may be through a formalised technical research and development process or from systems that scan the business environment, enabling the organisation to identify trends, customer requests and competitors' intentions. Market research certainly has a role to play in this process. Equally, management needs to encourage staff to suggest product development ideas and have systems to enable and reward such activity.

2 *Idea evaluation*

Next, ideas must be screened in order to establish what is feasible and where opportunities exist. Ideally, ideas are screened against strategic objectives by demonstrating how they are likely to contribute to such objectives. It is important to establish criteria against which all ideas are evaluated. This provides a consistent approach to decision making and the safeguard of rigorous testing. Evaluation is likely to include marketing and operational/production criteria.

3 *Concept development*

Having passed through a screen process, ideas are developed into product concepts. This stage involves initial technical and marketing evaluations. Having established the technical/operational feasibility and resource requirements, marketing (often using secondary data – general industry trends, key competitor profiles, etc.) evaluates the potential for the product. A marketing strategy needs to be outlined – target segment(s), product positioning and marketing goals, such as market share.

4 *Business evaluation*

The aim is to evaluate commercial potential and investment requirements. Sales volume, revenue and cost projections will establish the viability of the project. Clearly, this is more difficult when dealing with diversification or highly innovative products. Often organisations have predetermined returns on investment, which projects must demonstrate they will meet.

5 *Product development*

This stage turns the concept into an actual product. The stage tends to be dominated by technical and operational development. There is a need to examine both the development of the product (e.g. styling, features, performance, branding, etc.) and the means of its production/delivery (e.g. manufacturing, administration, after-sales support, etc.). The stage may see the building of a prototype and the use of market research to establish the final product offering. To gauge market place reaction, products may be test marketed with groups of actual consumers.

6 *Product launch*

Using the knowledge and targets generated in the previous processes, a final plan is developed. This includes all the other elements of the marketing mix. For example, a final price is set, a promotion campaign is designed and the buildup of stock begins within the distribution channels. It is vital that the product has the correct marketing, operational and logistical support to make it a success. Competitor and customer reaction should be monitored and the product offering 'fine-tuned' if required. Where resources are limited, or where high degrees of uncertainty exist, the product may be introduced using a 'roll-out' strategy. This entails a phased launch, gradually building market coverage.

Given the importance of NPD, managers must endeavour to make the process as rigorous and objective as possible. Only in this way, can organisations maximise the likelihood of success and minimise the chances of progressing with poor ideas. However, there is a dilemma, while a robust development process has its advantages. There is increasing commercial pressure to do things quickly. This may result in 'corners being cut' and ultimately mistakes being made in the NPD process. So, the reality of business life means management has to develop the right products in increasingly shorter time frame. How can we enable this? Adhering to the following principles should optimise the entire process:

1 *Multi-functional teams*

There is much evidence to suggest that projects go more smoothly when a multi-functional team is in control. By taking people from different functional backgrounds (e.g. production, marketing, design and finance) a balanced viewpoint is obtained. For example, problems relating to the manufacture/provision of the product are addressed early in the project. Additionally, the multi-functional approach promotes 'ownership' of the project and staff can be more committed and motivated.

2 *Completeness and evaluation*

NPD can be viewed as a six stage process (see above). The simple process of completing all these steps can increase the likelihood of product success. Undertaking each stage in a systematic manner and building an on-going evaluation into the process, may not guarantee success, but it will reduce the chances of failure. So-called 'evaluation gates' at the end of each stage can review the potential product and whether the NPD process has been properly conducted.

3 *Customer involvement*

Often market research is used to evaluate possible ideas and to review products after launch. It may be advisable to integrate the 'voice of the customer' into the entire project. This is possible by having an on-going process of market research that takes place during each development stage or by having customer representation on the multi-functional team.

4 *Parallel processing*

Traditionally, NPD has been viewed as a sequential process – activities follow each other in sequence. It may be possible to conduct some activities co-currently. In other words, undertaking a process of parallel development. Encouraging functional areas, department and individual to work more closely has a number of advantages. Firstly, this overlapping, parallel approach reduces overall development time. Secondly, as activities are being undertaken at the same time, they can share information and a more interactive approach can be taken. This can improve the overall quality of the process. To illustrate, a technical and marketing feasibility assessment could be conducted as one process, generating a more vigorous product/market specification.

5 *Strategic direction*
NPD requires a strategic focus and clear links must be established between overall corporate strategy and the NPD process. As previously stated, strategic objectives can be used as a template against which new product ideas are evaluated.

Additionally, the process of strategic analysis and audit should provide valuable information (external and internal) relating to the development of product offerings. The aim is to integrate: (i) technical development – improving the technical capability of the product, (ii) process development – improving the provision/production of products and services and (iii) marketing strategy into one coherent framework (Figure 10.2).

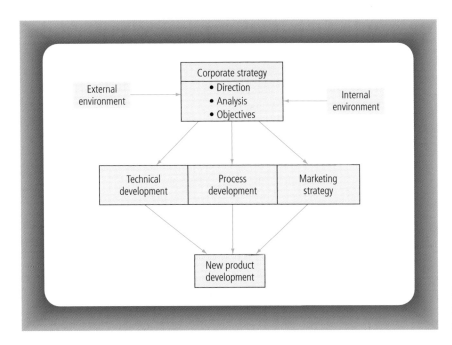

Figure 10.2
Strategic direction of NPD

6 *Knowledge management*
This concept is closely related to strategic direction. Increasingly, organisations are developing knowledge management strategies. Mobilising and managing the knowledge base of the organisation is rapidly becoming a management priority. The collective experience and accumulated

learning within the organisation can be vital to successful NPD. The organisation needs to facilitate the development of, and access to, information. Enabling technologies and methods include: benchmarking, brainstorming, computer networks, 'groupware' – software products enabling work and knowledge to be shared (e.g. Lotus Notes) and data warehousing. O'Connor and Galvin (1997) define data warehousing as constructing a high-level database of all operating and customer data, and making such a database available to support decision making.

■ Why do products fail?

It is reasonable to suggest that an understanding of the pitfalls of product development can help us to avoid them. When addressing this question, managers need to consider the nature and background to NPD, as some types of development activity are inherently more risky than others. Additionally, the organisation attitude to risk and investment has a baring on the situation. Common reasons for failure can be summarised as follows:

1 *Under investment*, where the project is short of funds and lacks the investment required to establish/sustain it in the market place.
2 The product fails to deliver any *customer benefit*. This can happen with technical or scientific advance. While the technology may be innovative, it must be perceived as innovative by the market place, otherwise it is unlikely to be adopted. Additionally, the product must perform to the required performance parameters. Remember, quality is defined as 'fit for purpose'. There needs to be a clear definition of market segment and how the product offering is positioned.
3 *Forecasting* is a common source of failure. It was once said ' ... *forecasting is difficult, especially if you're forecasting the future'*. This is certainly true! Often, forecasting errors relate to over optimistic forecasts of demand and/or under estimates of costs. Managers need to examine the assumptions supporting forecasts as well as the forecasting techniques used. Also, time scales for planned development have to be realistic.
4 *Internal politics*, trade-offs and compromise can result in problems. The project may lack the support and commitment of staff and vested interests may conspire against its success. Equally, trade-offs, and other such factors, may result in the project drifting from its original target, as internal conflict distracts management. Internal conflict has been the graveyard of many good product ideas.
5 *Industry response* is vital. For example, success may be completely dependent on retailers stocking products or on the response of competitors – what happens if they drastically cut price? Such factors are less controllable, but good quality market research and competitor intelligence can lessen the negative effects.

While some factors are unpredictable, and projects are a 'hostage to fortune', most issues are simply a matter of management and marketing.

Applying a sound structured approach to NPD and having effective project management should move the odds in your favour. Products need a product champion – a leader/manager who gets things done. In turn, this leader needs the support of the organisation.

■ Managing innovation

The term 'innovation' means different things to different people, with common definitions relating to scientific advance and the development of high-technology products. However, the reality is that innovation is a far broader activity. Essentially, innovation is about changing established products, processes and practices. Innovation must blend creativity, clear thinking and the ability to get things done into one process. Ultimately, the market place will judge innovation. New ideas need support, commitment and resources, if they are to be effectively implemented.

Illustrative Example 10.2

Dasani: The 'Del Boy' effect

The growing importance of the bottled water market is recognised by many beverage providers. Coca-Cola acknowledged this by launching 'Dasani'. However, the company faced a negative reaction in the UK, when newspaper articles revealed that the UK product was essentially tap water which had been treated, bottled and marketed under the 'Dasani' label. Adverse public reaction was fuelled by parallels to the BBC's popular situation comedy 'Only Fools and Horses', where the central character 'Del Boy' attempts to sell bottled tap water.

Organisations cannot remain focused on the past. The static organisation that believes the 'old ways are the best' will flounder. Innovation means change. Such changes are not normally single events, but are complex combinations of actions and functional activity. Note, innovation and invention are not one and the same, as innovation is concerned with the commercial application of ideas.

Senior management should address the issue of innovation and create a culture and infrastructure to support the process. After all, organisations that continue to learn and effectively translate this learning into product offerings are the ones who will prosper.

Innovation creates the environment for successful product development. Product improvement and modification, product imitation and product innovation (where the product is truly new or novel – see Figure 10.1) all stem from the overall process of innovation.

Having established the importance of innovation, how do organisations facilitate the process? Figure 10.3 summarises common enablers. *Teamwork* is vital, as successful innovation requires a combination of skills and functional activity (e.g. marketing, research and design, etc.). Innovation tends to flourish where frequent contact and good working relationships exist among groups. The *exchange of information* and ideas should be encouraged, as this not only facilitates innovation but also enhances teamwork. Information flow and effective communication contribute greatly to creativity. However, it is important to recognise that more information is not necessarily better – information overload should be avoided. There is a need to be focused on the external environment. *External inputs* relating to market trends, customer perception, technological development and competitor activities are vital inputs into the overall process. The organisation must be receptive to new ideas/change and have the capacity to evaluate such concepts. Clearly, *senior management* has a role to play in the process. They need to develop appropriate strategies and act as facilitators to the process. This normally involves taking calculated risks and allocating required resources (see section on Risk and the innovation dilemma). Consequently, senior managers need to be committed to long-term growth as opposed to short-term profit. If it is to work properly, innovation requires the correct systems and support. Frequently, this relates to organisational culture. Creating the right organisational climate is important, as the wish is to challenge existing practice and generate creativity. *Systems*, such as communications networks, computer-aided design and project management structures need to be in place. The organisation must foster and exploit innovation.

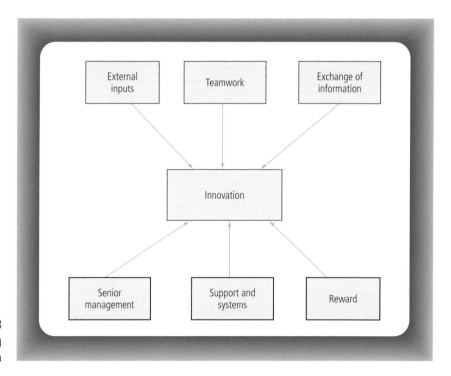

Figure 10.3
Generating
innovation

Group and individual motivation are important. *Reward* and recognition for innovation helps to generate ideas and foster a collaborative atmosphere. Additionally, the role of the individual must not be neglected in the discussion of innovation. While the organisation can facilitate and foster innovation, individuals have to take ownership. People need to have the courage, skill and motivation to make things better. Only this type of commitment will see the process to completion.

■ Risk and the innovation dilemma

Inevitably, conflict between innovation and operational efficiency will occur. All organisations need to develop new ideas and translate such ideas into new products, if they are to remain competitive. Equally, organisations require stable and efficient day-to-day operations in order to accomplish basic tasks effectively. Indeed, many views of management, and management techniques, tend to focus on eliminating waste, reducing cost and optimising the use of assets. Figure 10.4 illustrates the principle.

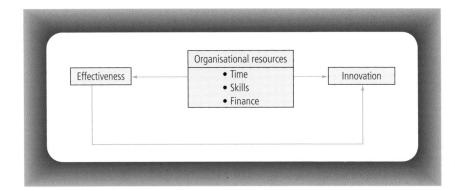

Figure 10.4
The innovation dilemma

Illustrative Example 10.3

Dell computers: product recall

Product recalls can easily turn into a crisis which can damage an entire brand. However, with careful handling and appropriate responses the effect of recalls can be minimised.

Dell faced a product recall in 2006, when it announced the voluntary recall of over 4 million Dell branded batteries. The batteries were sold as part of/in support of the company's notebook computer range. Although very rare, the product posed a potential fire risk. This was dramatically illustrated by media coverage of a notebook product busting into flames.

Consider, how an organisation can reduce the negative aspects of product recall, and what role does the Internet play in product recall?

So, should management focus resources on generating innovation or ensuring optimal efficiency? This is a dilemma, to which there is no easy answer. The answer may be a hybrid solution attempting to balance innovation with operational effectiveness. A key maxim is that innovation should be fostered, but never allowed to disrupt activities. Clearly, the nature of the industry and/or product life cycle is important. So called 'sunrise' industries which are research and design lead (e.g. telecommunication, biotechnology, etc.) will have a different innovation profile from more mature industries, or service sector industries. Such industries tend to be affected more by process and customer service-based innovations.

Innovation and operational effectiveness cannot be seen as mutually exclusive. They are inter-linked, with one supporting the other. Given these factors, innovation should lead to operational effectiveness – however this is defined. Remember, innovation is invention plus commercial exploitation, and there is little point in pursuing innovations that do not lead to operational effectiveness. The question is not should we innovate, but rather how we support and resource the process, given other often more immediate demands.

Assuming organisations have the right factors in place (as outlined in section Managing innovation) it can be argued that innovation will eventually pay for itself several times over. However, in order to stimulate the process, forward looking organisations allocate funds to such activities. A number of methods are commonly used for this purpose:

- Gap analysis is used to establish the difference between desired and projected future revenue requirements. Management then examines how much of the 'gap' can be closed by innovation. This provides an 'innovation target'. Resources can then be allocated to the NPD areas and innovations most likely to close this gap.
- An alternative is to allocate a percentage of sales revenue to an 'innovation fund' and request internal bids for this money. These bids are then evaluated and screened, with funding being given to the strongest.
- Additionally, we can seek collaborative ventures, partnerships and external funding (e.g. government grants, venture capital, etc.).

Organisations, and individuals, need to balance the risk associated in innovation with the potential return. Higher-risk projects invariably need to demonstrate greater potential returns. Pearson (1991) developed the concept of an uncertainty map. This helps to understand the concept of risk and uncertainty in innovative projects. Pearson identifies two key variables. Firstly, uncertainty about the endpoint – what is the project is likely to result in? Secondly, uncertainty about process or approach – how will the endpoint will be achieved. The model is adapted (see Figure 10.5) to reflect the importance marketers attach to market reaction and product development issues. High degrees of uncertainty relating to market reaction tend to exist when organisations are dealing with: (i) Innovative new technologies, with the potential to create markets or (ii) Diversifying away from core customers/markets in order to find new applications/markets for our existing products. In terms of product development it is important to consider product development issues and the infrastructure required to deliver the product (e.g. distribution, after-sales support, etc.)

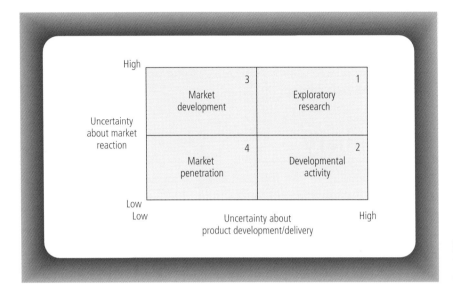

Figure 10.5
Marketing
uncertainty map

This gives us four possible situations with varying degrees of uncertainty and helps management convert ideas and concepts into workable solutions.

1 *Quadrant 1 Exploratory research*: Here there is much uncertainty. Innovation needs to be nurtured overtime and immediate commercial gain cannot be expected. Typically, this involves state-of-the-art technical research and development of new technologies. Risk relates to two factors: (i) The work may be resource intense and divert resources away from more commercial activities and (ii) No actual exploitable benefits may be generated. While activities in this area may require to be shielded from commercial pressure, this cannot be done indefinitely. Such activities require to be evaluated and either further developed or dropped. This requires a clear focus in terms of likely commercial outcomes and overall strategic goals. Given the right management structures risks can be kept to acceptable levels.

2 *Quadrant 2 Developmental activity*: This situation sees clear marketing goals and a well-defined market reaction, but uncertainty as to how such outcomes can be achieved. Many NPD projects fall into this category. For example, marketing has defined a specific need, but there is a debate as to the means of satisfying such needs. Given the high degrees of uncertainty over how to achieve outcomes plus a requirement to commit (often substantial) resources, risk factors can be high.

3 *Quadrant 3 Market development*: The method and technologies are proven and well understood and uncertainty of outcome relates to applying such methods to new opportunities. The process of market development aims to find new applications and target new markets or market

segments. As businesses move away from core markets, uncertainty will increase. Innovation revolves around the creative use of market information, creative segmentation and positioning.

4 *Quadrant 4 Market penetration*: The uncertainty pertaining to outcomes and method is low, and there appears to be an immediate opportunity. The organisation needs to align its assets and competencies in order to capitalise on this. The problem is often one of speed of response. Here, innovation relates to flexibility, recognising opportunity and adaptation of product offering.

■ Summary

Product development and innovation are strategic activities. Given the increasing competitiveness of the business world, organisations and their product offering must evolve to survive. It is vital that management understand the true nature of their core, actual and augmented products. It is often the augmentation – enhancing the actual product through additional services – that generates commercial success.

Product development falls into three categories: product improvement/modification, product imitation and product innovation. It is product innovation that brings new and novel ideas to the market place. Regardless of the degree of innovation, an NPD process is required. Essentially, this is a six stage process covering: (1) idea generation, (2) idea evaluation, (3) concept development, (4) business evaluation, (5) product development and (6) product launch. The NPD process can be enhanced by using factors such as multi-functional teams and customer involvement to instil a market focus and ensure operational problems are resolved in advance of launch. Additionally, it is important that all product development has a strategic direction, with the process integrated into overall business strategy. To successfully develop products we must understand the pitfalls of NPD. Such pitfalls relate to factors like: investment, failing to deliver customer benefit, forecasting errors, internal conflict and competitor response.

Innovation is effectively a management process aiming to bring together creative thought, technical/process development and commercial exploitation. Organisations need the right climate to promote innovation. They need to encourage teamwork and the on-going exchange of information, coupled to support and reward systems. In this way, it is possible to innovate across their entire field of business operations. Managers need to consider the risks and returns associated with such activity.

■ References

Booz, Allen and Hamiltion, *New Product Management for the 1980s*, Booz, Allen and Hamilton Inc., New York, 1982.

Davidson, H., *Even More Offensive Marketing*, Penguin Books, London, 1997.

Jain, S., *Marketing Planning and Strategy*, 5th edn, South-Western, Ohio, 1997.

Kotler, P., Armstrong, G., Saunders, J. and Wong, V., *Principles of Marketing*, 2nd European edition, Prentice Hall, New Jersey, 1999.

O'Connor, J. and Galvin, E., *Marketing and Information Technology*, Pitman, London, 1997.

Pearson, A., *Managing Innovation*, Henry, J. and Walker, D. (eds), Open University/ Sage Publications, London, 1991.

■ Further reading

Davidson, H., *Even More Offensive Marketing*, Chapter 11, Penguin Books, London, 1997.

CHAPTER 11

Alliances and relationships

About this chapter

Increasingly businesses recognised the importance of alliances and joint ventures to future success. In marketing, vertical marketing systems (VMS) demonstrate the benefits co-operation can bring. Additionally, organisations need to build relationships with range of 'markets'. Therefore, a broader definition of marketing is required.

■ Introduction

The saying *'no man is an island'* could easily be adapted to *'no business is an island'*! No organisation can exist in isolation. All organisations depend on establishing and developing relationships. In short, they must develop relationships with other organisations (e.g. suppliers, distributors, etc.) and, even more critically, with customers. Indeed, this latter relationship provides the fundamental basis of all marketing activity.

Alliances, joint ventures and other co-operative strategies are now widely recognised as effective strategic solutions to the challenges of the commercial world. Many commentators predict the future of many organisations depends on their ability to successfully enter, and manage collaborative ventures. The coming decade will be one of strategic collaboration.

Marketers readily acknowledge the importance of building relationships with customers. We have seen the emphasis move from transaction marketing (focusing on single sales) to relationship marketing (focusing on customer retention and building meaningful customer relationships).

When considering inter-organisational relationships, or relationships with customer, increasingly there are moves away from conflict and towards collaborative-based strategies and philosophies. In this chapter, we examine the role of alliances within marketing strategy and principles of relationship marketing.

■ Alliances

At a strategic level, managers aim to 'add value' by ensuring the organisation has the optimal level of assets and competencies. Increasingly, strategic thinking recognises that it is neither wise, nor feasible, to attempt to exclusively provide/own this optimal level of assets and competencies. Rather than do everything ourselves, it may be more feasible to enter into partnership arrangements with other organisations. For example, two manufacturers could set up a joint distribution system and both benefit from economies-of-scale. Telecommunications and computer manufacturers could combine their technical expertise to produce a range of integrated

Illustrative Example 11.1

McKean Foods: Haggis maker needs US alliance

The Internet has opened up global opportunities to Glasgow-based food manufacture McKean Foods. Their website attracts interest from all over the world, with a 40 per cent increase in sales of haggis through online operations. Popular products include the 500 grams 'Warrior' haggis and the larger 'Chieftain' haggis – A big favourite on Burns's night. Around 80 per cent of website hits originate from North America. Such interest is pleasing, but also frustrating as United States Department of Agriculture restrictions mean the company is unable to export its product to the US. Despite the UK having some of the world's most stringent hygiene regulations and the company achieving the highest level of European food safety accreditation. They are unable to service this growing demand due to US import regulations. McKean is looking at the possibility of a partnership with a US-based manufacturer. Thus enabling the company to meet demand in North America.

products. While the concept of alliances is now more common, it is hardly new. The history of business is littered with good, and bad, examples of collaborative ventures.

What motivates an alliance? There is no single answer to this question. Any number of factors can initiate such action. Common factors include:

- *Globalisation*: Businesses are increasingly able, or indeed compelled, to competing on a world scale. Alliances and joint ventures are a means of responding to this challenge. Shortening product life cycles, the globalisation of technology, and political change means the world is becoming a smaller place with more opportunity/necessity for collaboration. For example, parts and components can be sourced worldwide, or organisations can now more readily seek partners to distribute their products in previously inaccessible markets. Joint initiatives give access to expertise and contacts in local markets and greatly help the process of market entry. It should be noted that while world markets are increasingly open, some less-developed economies (e.g. China, etc.) may insist on joint venture agreements as a condition of market entry, thus ensuring inward investment.

- *Assets and competencies*: As previously stated, there is a recognition that organisations can not be truly effective at all activities. The move towards 'down-sizing' has seen organisations concentrate on core activities and contract out non-essential activity. Additionally, the cost (plus shortages of skills) associated with product development may facilitate joint activity. This allows market opportunities and new technologies to be developed at a relatively lower cost. Complementary activities and/or management skills can lead to inter-organisational synergy – the combined effect of two, or more, organisations working together is greater than their individual effect. To illustrate synergy, consider the following example. 'In-House Cuisine', provides a restaurant delivery service – customers' order, through 'In-House Cuisine', from a directory of top restaurants and In-House's uniformed waiters collect the meal and deliver it to the customer. The scheme has now been extended to hotels, with the Scottish Tourist Board allowing hotels, with limited restaurant services, to retain their three star status by using 'In-House Cuisine' as a form of room service.

- *Risk*: Collaboration is often born from the need to reduce risk. The sheer financial commitment may be so great that a consortium approach is required to spread the financial risk across a number of participants. A 'go-it-alone' strategy may incur other risks. Co-operative ventures can promote industry standards and common practice. For example, JVC's alliance with Sharp and Toshiba helped to establish VHS as the industry standard for video recorders. Thus, 'go-it-alone' firms risk being isolated from accepted industry practice and technical standards. Additionally, joint activity can reduce the time taken to develop products, thereby reducing the risk associated with launching products.

- *Learning and innovation*: Collaborative ventures are great opportunities to learn and innovate. Technology and skills transfer are often essential in generating meaningful commercial benefits. Indeed, Morrison and Mezentseff (1997) attribute sustainable competitive advantage (generated through collaborative ventures) directly to learning and knowledge transfer. Consider the alliance between Rover and Honda. When active, this collaboration enhanced Rover's expertise in total quality management. The expertise and skills gained during the venture proved more durable than the alliance.

When examining the concept of alliances, it is important to consider the various forms such ventures may take. The scope of alliance ranges from highly formalised agreements involving ownership, to informal co-operation based on little more than a handshake. Johnson and Scholes (1999) summarise alliances in terms of four main categories. Firstly, *acquisition and mergers* involve taking formalised ownership. This includes co-operative or hostile takeovers. Commonly, this is driven by: (i) possible efficiency gains which lead to lower operating costing in areas of activity: procurement, transaction processing and operational scale and (ii) synergy effects, where combined activity leads to greater 'added value' than the two organisations could hope to generate separately. Acquisition strategies normally look to benefit from eliminating duplicated activities. For example, the merger of the Leeds and Halifax Building Society (subsequently converted into a Bank) has seen the rationalisation of the branch network. Secondly, *consortia and joint venture* activities involve independent organisations entering into specific project agreements or setting up jointly owned ventures. Consortia are groups of companies in partnership, normally to develop large-scale projects. For example, the 'Euro-fighter' project brings together a European-wide consortium of defence, electronic and aerospace companies developing the next generation of military aircraft. Thirdly, *Contract and licensing* agreement are legal, contractual agreements whereby the right to a product/activity is assigned to an independent operator.

Common forms include sub-contracting and franchising arrangements. Such agreement can allow organisations to focus on core activities, while contracting-out work to specialist operators. For instance, the prison service has experimented with contract-out transportation and custodial services to 'Group-4' – a private security firm. Finally, *networks* are informal agreements of co-operation built on working relationships and mutual benefit, as opposed to contractual agreement or ownership. Networks can also take the form of opportunistic alliances that, while informal, focus on specific opportunities. For example, a group of independent local retailers may join together and launch a customer loyalty card, as a response to increased competition from national retail chains.

For any alliance to stand the test of time, there needs to be strategic and cultural fit. *Strategic fit* essentially means that the core assets/competencies of the partners are configured in such a way as to complement each other and offer more effective pathways to strategic goals than generic internal development. As previously stated, strategic fit relates to efficiency, synergy and, on occasions, legal necessity. Strategic fit need to be clearly defined and must offer sustainable competitive advantage. *Cultural fit* is vital if organisations are going to work together. For any partnership to be successful there is a need for the partners to have similar aspirations, goals and attitudes. For example, joint ventures between a fast moving entrepreneurial company and highly risk averse conservative organisation could be difficult to achieve. The question of cultural fit is pivotal in the selection of a partner and type of alliance.

A marketing perspective on alliances can be illustrated by examining the development of *vertical marketing systems* (VMS). A VMS approach offers an alternative to the traditional view of distribution channels. Traditional distribution channels involve a chain of independent companies, each pursuing individual goals. Each channel member aims to optimise its position, normally at the expense of other channel members. The resultant tension and conflict between the buying/selling organisations, within the channel, tends to lead to distrust, erosion of margins, higher costs and other lingering problems. A VMS approach aims to integrate channel members into one cohesive unit, with common objectives and distribution being actively managed across all channel members. Such an approach has the advantages of: (i) reducing overall cost by avoiding repetition and reducing administration and (ii) enhance quality and effectiveness by means of joint problem solving and shared expertise. Figure 11.1 illustrates both activities.

VMS ventures tend to operate in one of the following ways. They can be *corporate* – all parties in the VMS having common ownership. Alternatively, it is possible to have an *administrative* VMS – independent organisations agree to conform to common standards and compatible interlinked systems, normally determined by the dominant partner. For example Ford car dealerships, although independent, conform to service, stock holding and marketing criteria set by the Ford Motor Company. Finally, there are contractual VMS agreements which have legally binding obligations. For example, the 'SPAR' retail chain is a group of independent retailers who sign-up to a centralised buying agreement.

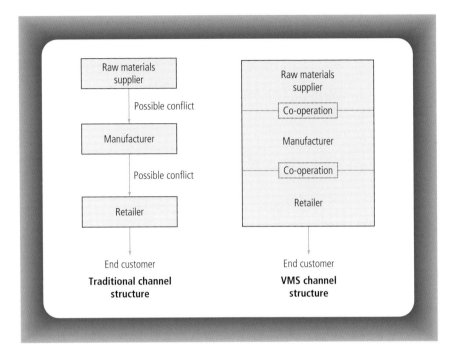

Figure 11.1
Traditional and VMS
marketing channels

To examine a practical VMS example, consider Marks & Spencer. M&S has remained at the forefront of British retailing for longer than most commentators can remember. Although the mighty M&S has recently experienced troubled times, its enduring appeal and acknowledged strengths flows from its relationships with suppliers. Over decades, it has developed innovative and mutually beneficial supplier partnerships. Close working relationships enable the company to effectively manage the entire supply chain. Indeed, supply chain management will prove increasingly vital as M&S faces future challenges.

■ Relationship marketing

The concept of relationship marketing takes marketing back to basic principles. It recognises the fundamental importance of sustaining customer relationships in order to generate customer loyalty and repeat business. Additionally, relationship marketing acknowledges a broader view of marketing, and defines a number of 'markets' which must be addressed in order to optimise customer relationships. Christopher et al. (1994) identify a six 'market' model relating to the organisations' relationships (see Figure 11.2).

Undoubtedly, customer markets should be the primary focus of any organisation. Previously, marketing has tended to focus on finding new customer and winning new business. Modern marketing practice (relationship marketing) now recognises the importance of retaining customers and generating repeat business. Relationship approaches aim to

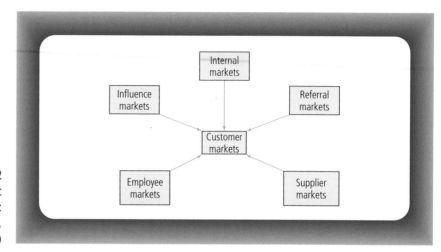

Figure 11.2
The six market
model (*Source*:
Christopher et al.,
1994, p. 21)

develop customer alliances, whereby the customer not only sees the organisation as their preferred provider, but actively recommends others to use their products and services. This 'elevated status' is more achievable when a broader view of marketing is taken. Such a view recognises the role of 'markets', other than the direct customer, in developing customer relationships (see Figure 11.2).

Supplier markets are important, as strong supplier links and joint innovation enable the overall supply chain to be optimised. This leads to reduced cost and potentially enhances the overall quality of the customer experience. *Employee markets* – recognise the importance of recruiting and retaining the right staff. Ultimately, it is staff who, directly or indirectly, delivers the desired levels of customer satisfaction. Closely related to the employee market is the concept of *internal markets*. The idea of internal markets and internal marketing is examined in Chapter 12. The concept uses marketing principles (segmentation, targeting and the 'mix') internally. By treating employees, departments or functions as customers, we can deliver internal services and support more effectively. Thus motivating staff, improving effectiveness and ultimately enhancing the external customer experience. External groups can have a significant influence on the organisation and its customer base. Marketing strategies may need to consider such *influence markets*. For example, management may need to build relationships with financial analysts, the media, local communities and campaign groups. Finally, *referral markets* lead to new business. Organisations that deliver high degrees of customer services are well placed to receive customer referrals. Additionally, referrals may come through other parties (e.g. trade groups, distributors, etc.) and relationship marketers must strive to establish a wide referral network.

The process of relationship marketing is summarised by Kotler et al. (1999) in terms of creating and further developing *'value laden'* relationships with stakeholders.

■ Developing relationships

There is a strong body of evidence supporting the economic case for relationship marketing. For example, Reichheld and Sasser (1990) illustrate that relatively minor improvements in customer defections can generate significant improvements in profit. As relationships are built on mutual benefit, what benefits does relationship marketing bring to customers? The approach typically benefits customersthrough: (i) requires marketers to have a much closer understanding of customer needs and therefore provide more appropriate solutions to customer problems, (ii) may result in schemes rewarding customer loyalty and (iii) fuses together all aspects of the business, making the entire entity more customer focused and responsive to customer need.

Having clearly established the benefits of a relationship approach organisations must consider, how they can move from transaction-based marketing (focusing on single sales) to sustainable relationship-based strategies? Common principles of relationship marketing are:

● *Appropriate use*: Like any technique, relationship marketing works better in certain situations. Not all transactions are relational in nature. For example, impulse buys or one-off purchases generally do not require, or offer, scope to develop relationships. Indeed, attempts to install a relationship approach in such circumstances may simply agitate potential customers. Relationship strategies work well in high-involvement purchases categorised by: (i) complex decision making, (ii) a degree of risk associated with purchase, (iii) a requirement for on-going support and/or (iv) regular purchase. To be worthwhile, the additional revenue generated needs to exceed the cost of any relationship programme. Organisations may well prioritise customers in terms of relationship potential, with higher priority being given to certain segments or type of customer.

Illustrative Example 11.2

Costa Coffee: strategic relationships

Coffee has now become a hot market! Driven by changing lifestyle patterns and the popularity of US TV shows featuring coffee houses (e.g. Friends, Frazer, etc.). The coffee market is emerging as one of the fastest growing retail sectors.

The UK market leader Costa, owned by Whitbread, has embarked on programme of rapid expansion. Strategic relationships with other parts of the Whitbread group are vital to building the chain. David Thomas, Managing Director of Whitbread Restaurants and Leisure states, 'In addition to stand alone coffee retail outlets, we are developing opportunities for the brand in our existing retail and leisure businesses' (e.g. Marriott Hotels). Additionally, outlets are opening in airports and railway stations. By building working relationships with other outlets, Costa is well placed to extend its brand and develop long-term relationships with the consumers.

- *Establish relationship drivers*: If a relationship strategy is feasible, what are the key components driving success? Market research techniques facilitate an understanding of what is important to building/maintaining relationships. By identifying how customer expectations are set and evaluated, organisations are more able to generate positive interactions. For example, if it is found that key customer service attributes are; accurate order processing and delivery time as per agreed schedule, it is possible to allocate resources to ensure such expectations are met (or hopefully exceeded).

- *Build customer value*: Businesses need to adopt a value-building approach to relationships. There are three basic approaches to generating customer value. Firstly there are *financial benefits*, where the relationship has some economic benefit to the customer. For example, Tesco was the first major supermarket chain to introduce a customer loyalty scheme. 'Tesco Clubcard' points can be exchanged for goods or discounts. The firm now plans to enhance the scheme by creating three classes of loyalty points – gold, silver and bronze – with higher spending customers receiving bigger awards. Secondly, there are *social benefits*. Here, relationships are based on social contact, belonging, support and personal interaction. For example, friendly relationships with clients may provide the basis of a hair-dressing business. Brand loyalty may also be based on this concept. In the fashion market, people adopt brands as a symbol of lifestyle and group identity. Thirdly, *structural benefits* stem from close operational association. For instance, manufactures and retailers could implement automated stock control/replenishment to facilate a 'just-in-time' approach to inventory management.

- *Retention*: It is a normal fact of business life that long-established customers tend to be more profitable than new or occasional customers. They tend to be larger, more frequent consumers and major sources of referral business. Therefore, organisations need to not only measure retention, but also to guarantee all employees are aware of its importance. The ideas outlined above all have a role to play in retaining customers, but organisations must actively seek to strengthen on-going business relationships. Common methods include: corporate hospitality, sending referral business to customers and briefing clients on new developments. A key step in many retention programmes is to establish a relationship management structure within the organisation. This involves: (i) identifying which customers (or customer groups) merit special attention, (ii) assigning account/relationship managers to develop and implement a relationship plan. Such a plan requires specific objectives and strategies aimed at enhancing the organisation's business position with that target group.

'Amazon' – the Internet book shop – offers a practical illustration of relationship marketing. Obviously, as a virtual book shop Amazon has no direct, face-to-face contact with its customers. However, its website allows customers to write book reviews, read what others thought of a given text and track the progress of individual orders. The process engenders a feeling of belonging – a social benefit.

■ Summary

Increasingly, businesses need to recognise the importance of alliances and joint ventures. A collaborative approach has much to commend it, and is being driven by factors such as globalisation, risk reduction and the need to share learning and generate innovation.

Alliances can range from acquisition and merger, through to networks based on informal co-operation. To be successful, organisations need to seek partnerships where strategic fit exists. Strategic fit relates to factors like: (i) economy-of-scale, (ii) synergy benefits resulting from complementary assets/competencies and on occasion (iii) legal necessity. Cultural fit is also important as it sustains relationships.

Relationship marketing is a vital component of business success. To be truly effective, organisations must recognise that they serve a range of 'markets'. They need to consider a broader definition of marketing, one that embraces 'markets' such as employees, suppliers, internal function, referral sources and influences. However, relationship marketing is not applicable in all cases. When applicable, organisation must strive to identify the key relationship drivers, build customer value and do everything reasonable to retain customers.

■ References

Christopher, M., Payne, A. and Ballantyne, D., *Relationship Marketing,* Butterworth-Heinnemann, London, 1994.

Johnson, G. and Scholes, K., *Exploring Corporate Strategy*, 5th edn, Prentice Hall, London, 1999.

Kotler, P., Armstrong, A., Saunder, J. and Wong, V., *Principles of Marketing*, 2nd edn, Prentice Hall, London, 1999.

Morrison, M. and Mezentseff, L., Learning alliances: a new dimension in strategic alliances, *Management Decision*, **35**(5/6), May/June, 1997, 351–357.

Reichheld, F. and Sasser, W., Zero defections: quality comes to services, *Harvard Business Review*, September/October, 1990, 115–111.

■ Further reading

Hooley, J., Saunder, J. and Piercy, N., *Marketing Strategy and Competitive Positioning*, 2nd edn, Prentice Hall, London, 1998.

CHAPTER 12

The strategic marketing plan

Planning is an integrative, co-ordinating activity that gives focus. Strategic and tactical decisions are made at corporate and functional levels. Addressing the analytical, behavioural and organisational aspects of planning can help overcome the many barriers to success. While the format and presentation of marketing plans may vary, a common purpose exists – to identify, select and implement appropriate marketing activities.

■ Corporate and marketing plans

Marketing managers plan in order to complete tasks on time and without exceeding pre-set resource limits. It is likely that objectives, targets and budget will be set as part of the overall corporate planning and budgeting process. The task is to translate these factors into a workable marketing plan.

When developing a plan, the process involves choosing certain courses of action and ruling out other possible options. Planning should be systematic, structured and involves three key components:

1 Objectives – what has to be achieved.
2 Strategy (or actions) – defining how the objectives are to be achieved.
3 Resource implications – the resources required to implement the strategy.

Clearly, it is important to understand the interface between marketing and corporate strategy. This is best illustrated by considering the hierarchical structure of an organisation. Senior management formulates objectives and strategy for the entire organisation (or a strategic business unit – SBU). Managers in various functional areas, such as marketing, contribute to the process by developing specific functional strategies and ultimately tactics to achieve these corporate objectives. Effectively, the process involves a hierarchy of plans, with strategy at one level becoming the objective(s) at the next. Additionally, this process provides feedback on the success/failure of any strategy. Figure 12.1 illustrates the concept.

■ Corporate planning

The corporate plan will define objectives for the entire business and should co-ordinate the various functional strategies (e.g. marketing, operations, human resource management, finance, etc.) to deliver the overall corporate objectives. It is important that functional strategies are inter-related (see Figure 12.1). For example, if the marketing strategy focused on developing high levels of customer service in order to retain key customer groups, both the operations and human resource management

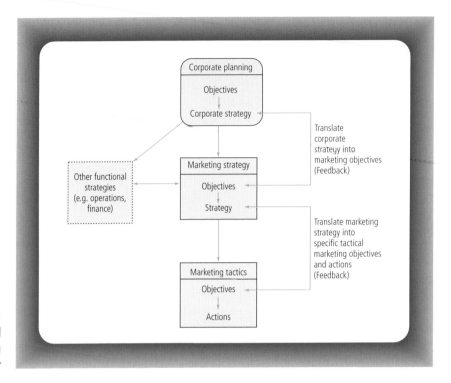

Figure 12.1
Corporate and
marketing planning
hierarchy

functions would have a role to play in delivering this. Corporate strategy can be summarised as being:

- *Integrative*: The process *co-ordinates functional activity* towards a common goal and takes 'whole organisation' view of the corporation. By defining corporate targets, normally in financial terms, collective targets are set for the functional groups.
- *Provide focus*: Strategy defines the scope of the business – general nature of activities and markets served. This *strategic direction* allows functional areas to develop appropriate strategies and tactics.
- *Importance*: By its very nature, corporate strategy is the process of making major business decisions. It defines business direction over the *long term* and is critical in setting the overall resource profile available to the organisation.
- *Matching*: There is a need to match the organisations activities and resource base to the current and future business environment.

A useful summation of corporate strategy management is provided in Figure 12.2. This model takes a top-down view of the overall strategy process. It identifies the five components vital in achieving corporate success:

1 *Vision*: Senior management and other stakeholders must establish an overall vision of what the corporation should be. This defines the basic need they fulfil and establishes the generic direction of the business.

2 *Corporate objectives and strategy*: Collective goals and strategy define the 'benchmarks' for success, and ways of achieving success. This level co-ordinates corporate activity and initiate activities to achieve desired results.

3 *SBU/functional objectives and strategy*: Corporate strategy translates into objectives and plans for individual elements of the business. This may take the form of SBUs' (divisions within a company) or functional activities. For example, a hotel chain could divide its business into three SBUs – accommodation, food and beverage and conferences and leisure.

4 *Resources*: For a given strategy, the need exists to match resources to strategic intent. This process normally involves annual budgeting.

5 *Structure*: Management must develop the appropriate organisational and staffing structures to facilitate success.

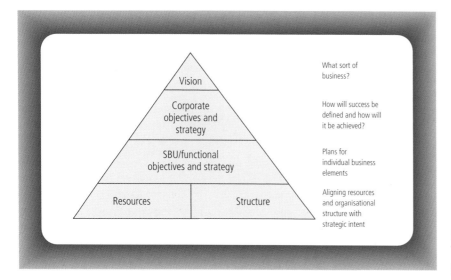

Figure 12.2
The strategic process

Successful businesses ensure these factors are aligned in order to turn strategic intent into business reality.

■ Marketing plans: strategy or tactics?

There are two types of marketing plan – strategic and tactical. This distinction generates much confusion and debate; is it a strategy or a tactic? This question may be academic when faced with the reality of the business world, as the distinction between the two will vary from organisation to organisation and manager to manager. However, much of the confusion can be removed if characteristics common to strategic plans and tactical plans can be identified.

- *Strategic marketing*: Takes a longer-term time frame and broadly defines the organisation's marketing activities. The process seeks to develop effective responses to a changing business environment by analysing markets, segmentation and evaluating competitors' offerings. Strategy focuses on defining market segments and positioning products in order to establish a competitive stance. Marketing strategy tends to embrace all of the mix, or significant components of the mix (e.g. distribution strategy, communications strategy, etc.). Problems in this area tend to be unstructured and require external, often speculative, data.
- *Tactical marketing*: This takes a shorter-term time frame and concerns day-to-day marketing activities. It translates strategy into specific actions and represents the on-going operational dimension of marketing strategy. Tactical marketing tends to deal with individual components of the marketing mix elements (e.g. sales promotion, advertising, etc.). Problems are often repetitive and well structured with data being internally generated.

Table 12.1 examines the differences between strategic and tactical marketing.

Table 12.1 Strategic and tactical marketing

	Strategic marketing	Tactical marketing
Time frame	Long term	Short term
Focus	Broad	Narrow
Key task(s)	Defining market and competitive position	Day-to-day marketing activity
Information and problem solving	Unstructured, external, speculative	Structured, internal, repetitive
Example	New product development	Price discounting

■ Why does planning matter?

The organisation needs a strategic marketing plan in order to adapt to a changing business environment. Given the basic business premise of – *success through effectively meeting customer needs* – it is clear organisations must continually adapt and develop to remain successful. Strategic marketing facilitates this process and provides robust solutions in an increasingly competitive world. Essentially, the plan should provide a systematic framework with which to analyse the market place and supply a well-defined way to pursue strategic goals.

However, the truly successful plan goes further than the simple process of planning. It is a vehicle to communicate, motivate and involve staff in fundamental business activities. Too often planning is viewed as a restrictive process based on programming events and generating paperwork. Remember, plans need employee commitment and 'ownership' to achieve results.

The key reasons for planning are summarised as follows:

- *Adapting to change*: Planning provides an opportunity to examine how changes in the business environment have/will affect the organisation. It enables management to focus on strategic issues as opposed to day-to-day operational problems.
- *Resource allocation*: Planning allows us to deploy resources to effectively meet opportunities and threats. No plan can succeed without appropriate resources. When a strategic perspective is taken, organisations are better placed to marshal the resources required to meet strategic 'windows of opportunity'. Doyle (1994) defines strategic windows of opportunity as changes that have a major impact in the market place. Strategic windows include factors such as: (i) new technology, (ii) new market segments, (iii) new channels of distribution, (iv) market redefinition – where the nature of demand changes, (v) legislative changes and (vi) environmental shocks – sudden unexpected economic or political change. Essentially, the process involves aligning marketing activities with opportunities in order to generate competitive advantage.
- *Consistency*: By providing a common base to work from (e.g. techniques and assumptions) the overall decision-making process can be enhanced. Additionally, common methods and formats should improve internal communication.
- *Integration*: As a strategic process, planning should facilitate the integration and co-ordination of the marketing mix. By providing a strategic focus it should be possible to generate synergy from the individual elements of the marketing mix.
- *Communication and motivation*: The plan should clearly communicate strategic intent to employees and other stakeholders. Clear objectives and an understanding of the individual, or group, contribution to the process serves to generate 'ownership' and motivation.
- *Control*: All control activities are based on some predetermined plan. The planning process should set meaningful targets, thus defining the criteria by which success is measured.

■ Barrier to successful planning

Few would argue with the concept of planning. In any activity, a plan provides a fundamental basis for success. Marketing plans should offer exactly what is required – optimising the use of marketing techniques and resources in order to make the most of marketing opportunities. However, even the most charitable of marketing managers would view this statement as naive and unlikely to be fully achieved. If mangers view planning as 'fine in theory' but failing, in practice, to deliver its full potential – where does it go wrong?

Clearly, barriers must exist to successful planning. Often, these barriers are more to do with the human aspects of the business management. They involve people, politics, skills and culture, to a greater degree, than formal systems, methodology and data.

Common barriers to successful planning are:

- *Culture*: The prevailing culture may not be amenable to marketing plans. If the fundamental principles of marketing are not accepted by the organisation, any move towards being market led and customer orientated could be dismissed as 'not the way we do it'. Often we see considerable resistance to change and gradual regression back to old work practices.
- *Power and politics*: All organisations are subject to internal politics. The development of strategic planning becomes a battlefield where vested interests fight each others proposals and squabble over status and resources. This process absorbs much management time and can result in ill-advised compromise and unnecessary delay.
- *Analysis not action*: Much time and energy can be wasted by the process of analysing data and developing rationales for action, as opposed to simply acting. While a rigorous process is commendable, it should not displace action. This 'paralysis-by-analysis' barrier tends to substitute information gathering and processing for decision making. Perhaps surprisingly, many planning systems do not promote action and are more concerned with reviewing progress and controlling activity, rather than tackling strategic issues.
- *Resource issues*: In any planning situation, the potential exists to negotiate over resources. Indeed, a major aspect of the process is to match resources to strategic aims. Managers must take a realistic view of the resource position and endeavour to ensure resources are not over-committed or needlessly withheld.
- *Skills*: In some instances, managers do not have the skills (e.g. project management, forecasting, etc.) required to make the best use of the planning process. Here, planning takes on a ritual nature – a meaningless but 'must-do' annual task. Often, planning is reduced to incremental increases/decreases in annual budget and fails to examine opportunities for business development.

Many of these barriers relate to the implementation of plans rather than the planning process itself. Chapter 12 deals with the issue of implementation in detail. However, the sound management practice would advocate the inclusion of implementation as part of the planning process. Indeed, Piercy (1997) suggests a multidimensional model of planning. This considers the analytical dimension, the behavioural dimension and the organisational dimension of any plan. Figure 12.3 summarises the model.

- *Analytical dimension*: Analytical tools, techniques and models are important, as they provide a framework to tackle issues and identify/solve problems. While formalised planning systems have the advantage of offering a common (corporate wide) systematic approach, to be truly effective they must address behavioural and organisational issues.
- *Behavioural dimension*: Here we focus on the people aspects of the planning process. Plans only become successful because of the support, participation, motivation and commitment of people. There is a need to understand and fully communicate the strategic assumptions underpinning the strategy. Plans must address behavioural factors in order to gain the support so vital to smooth implementation.
- *Organisational dimension*: Strategic planning takes place within the context of a given organisation. Therefore, it will be influenced by organisational factors, such as culture and style of management. Remember, organisational structures determine the flow of information, as well as defining responsibilities and reporting lines. Major strategic initiatives may require radical organisational changes.

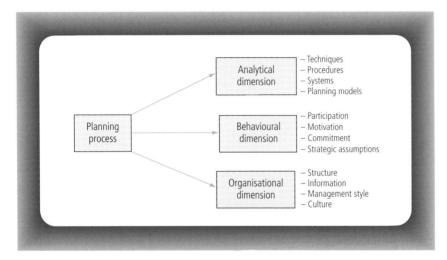

Figure 12.3
A multidimensional model of marketing planning (*Source*: Piercy, 1997, p. 436)

By taking this 'multidimensional' approach to planning and actively considering behavioural and organisational issues within the planning process, it is possible to enhance the overall likelihood of success.

■ The structure of a strategic marketing plan

What does a strategic marketing plan look like? While the answer to this question will vary from organisation to organisation (in terms of structure

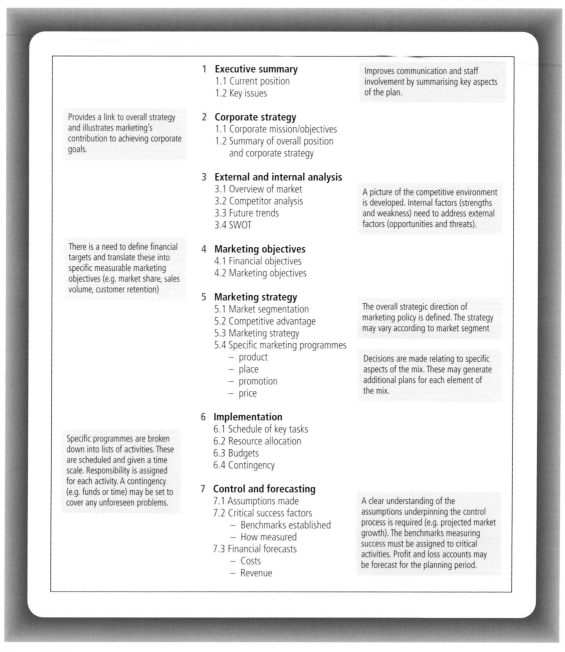

Provides a link to overall strategy and illustrates marketing's contribution to achieving corporate goals.

There is a need to define financial targets and translate these into specific measurable marketing objectives (e.g. market share, sales volume, customer retention)

Specific programmes are broken down into lists of activities. These are scheduled and given a time scale. Responsibility is assigned for each activity. A contingency (e.g. funds or time) may be set to cover any unforeseen problems.

1 **Executive summary**
   1.1 Current position
   1.2 Key issues

Improves communication and staff involvement by summarising key aspects of the plan.

2 **Corporate strategy**
   1.1 Corporate mission/objectives
   1.2 Summary of overall position
       and corporate strategy

3 **External and internal analysis**
   3.1 Overview of market
   3.2 Competitor analysis
   3.3 Future trends
   3.4 SWOT

A picture of the competitive environment is developed. Internal factors (strengths and weakness) need to address external factors (opportunities and threats).

4 **Marketing objectives**
   4.1 Financial objectives
   4.2 Marketing objectives

5 **Marketing strategy**
   5.1 Market segmentation
   5.2 Competitive advantage
   5.3 Marketing strategy
   5.4 Specific marketing programmes
       – product
       – place
       – promotion
       – price

The overall strategic direction of marketing policy is defined. The strategy may vary according to market segment

Decisions are made relating to specific aspects of the mix. These may generate additional plans for each element of the mix.

6 **Implementation**
   6.1 Schedule of key tasks
   6.2 Resource allocation
   6.3 Budgets
   6.4 Contingency

7 **Control and forecasting**
   7.1 Assumptions made
   7.2 Critical success factors
       – Benchmarks established
       – How measured
   7.3 Financial forecasts
       – Costs
       – Revenue

A clear understanding of the assumptions underpinning the control process is required (e.g. projected market growth). The benchmarks measuring success must be assigned to critical activities. Profit and loss accounts may be forecast for the planning period.

Figure 12.4
Illustrative example of a strategic marketing plan

and presentation), marketing plans perform a common function and have common components. Indeed, McDonald (1999) views marketing planning as a systematic way of identifying, selecting, scheduling and costing activities in order to achieve objectives. Such definitions focus on the purpose, as opposed to the structure, of planning.

Regardless of precedent and planning formats, strategic plans tend to have common elements. Marketing managers would expect a strategic plan to cover: (i) industry analysis, (ii) internal analysis, (iii) opportunity identification, (iv) objective setting, (v) formulation of strategy, (vi) proposed marketing programmes and actions and (vii) implementation and control – including financial forecasts.

Figure 12.4 presents an annotated example of a strategic marketing plan. *Note*: Figure 12.4 does not attempt to portray the definitive marketing plan. It merely illustrates the component parts common to such plans.

Strategic marketing plans take on many different guises. The content, structure and complexity of a plan will vary. While planning formats and conventions are largely a matter of historic precedent within the organisation, the key imperative is to generate action. Plans should address critical issues in a way that is relevant to the organisation. For example, promoting decisive marketing initiatives within a limited time scale.

■ Approaches to marketing planning

The development of a marketing plan is a significant and time consuming activity. All planning is essentially objective driven – objectives are translated into actions. A number of 'schools of thought' exist as to how the task is best approached. The standard approaches to planning are:

- *Top-down*: Senior managers develop objectives and strategy. Managers at an operational level are then required to implement these strategies. This approach is said to encourage professionalism and promote a corporate strategic view of marketing activity.
- *Bottom-up*: Here, authority and responsibility for formulation and implementation of strategy is devolved. Senior marketing managers approve, and then monitor, agreed objectives. It can be claimed that this approach encourages ownership and commitment.

Hybrid systems are also common, where objectives are 'top-down' and responsibility for the formulation/implementation of strategy is devolved.

■ Summary

Strategic planning offers a systematic and structured approach to choosing and implementing certain courses of action. Corporate plans define overall business objectives, while providing focus and co-ordinating functional activities. Such plans need to align the stakeholders' vision to the objectives, strategy, resources and structure of the SBUs.

There is a need to differentiate between marketing strategy and marketing tactics. Essentially, strategic marketing focuses on defining segments, establishing competitive positions and co-ordinating all the elements of the mix. Tactics translate strategies into action and deal with day-to-day marketing transactions.

Planning allows organisations to adapt to a changing business environment and provides a framework for resource allocation. Additionally, sound planning promotes a consistency of approach and facilitates: integration of activity, communication, motivation and control of activities. In order to achieve these benefits, we must overcome the numerous barriers to successful planning. These include: culture, internal politics or lacking the requisite skills to make planning a successful activity. Truly successful plans make use of analytical techniques but also address the behavioural and organisational dimensions of the process.

The structure and content of a strategic marketing plan will vary. However, plans tend to have common elements – industry analysis, internal analysis, opportunity identification, formulation of strategy, marketing programmes/actions and implementation/control.

Formulating marketing plans can take a top-down, bottom-up or hybrid approach.

■ References

Doyle, P., *Marketing Management and Strategy*, 2nd edn, Prentice Hall, London, 1994.

McDonald, M., *Marketing Plans*, 4th edn, Butterworth-Heinemann, Oxford, 1999.

Piercy, N., *Market-Led Strategic Change*, 2nd edn, Butterworth-Heinemann, Oxford, 1997.

■ Further reading

Aaker, D., *Strategic Market Management*, 4th edn, Chapter 17, Wiley, Chichester, 1995.

Piercy, N., *Market-Led Strategic Change*, 2nd edn, Chapter 12, Butterworth-Heinemann, Oxford, 1997.

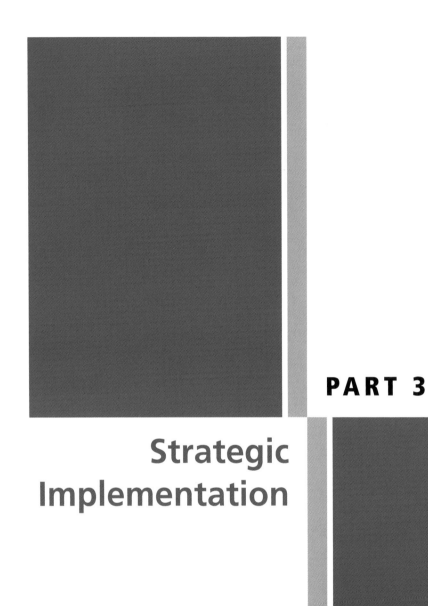

PART 3

Strategic
Implementation

■ Implementation

■ Control

Part 3 examines issues relating to implementation and control. Any strategic activity must address two basic issues – selecting a competitive strategy and putting it into practice. Implementation and control address the second issue. Managers should never underestimate the importance, or indeed complexity, of 'putting in into practice'.

Chapter 13 assesses the general issues pertaining to implementation and how to build effective implementation approaches within the context of marketing projects. Chapter 14 is concerned with the application of financial measures, performance appraisal and benchmarking as control mechanisms. The concept of control loops applied to marketing is also examined.

CHAPTER 13

Strategic implementation

Implementation is critical to the success or failure of any venture. Basic generic management principles (e.g. leadership, team building and delegation) contribute to the process. Marketing managers must evaluate the easy, or otherwise, of implementation and deploy project management techniques to achieve desired goals. Additionally, 'internal marketing' can ease the process of implementation.

■ Implementation: stressing the importance

A key maxim in business is: never acquire a business you do not understand how to run. Equally, it would be true to say – never adopt a strategy you do not understand how to implement.

It can be said that, in terms of strategy, planning is the easy part. With a basic grounding in marketing, most managers could sit down with a blank sheet of paper and develop an outline marketing plan. This plan may contain all the correct 'buzz-words.' Ideas relating to – market penetration, segmentation, globalization and competitive advantage would fill the page and a clear concise way forward formulated. However, it is not that simple. While many managers could produce such an outline – how many could implement it? Without implementation, the plan remains some ideas on a piece of paper.

In the context of marketing the goal will be to achieve and/or maintain a marketing orientation: success *by a process of understanding and meeting customer need.* It is doubtful if a marketing strategy can be implemented where this orientation does not exist. Achieving such a view is dependent on the quality of management and their understanding of marketing as a business philosophy.

It is reasonable to suggest that implementation is often a key determinant in the success or failure of any strategic activity. Therefore, it should be an integral part of any marketing strategy. This view is supported by examining the history of corporate strategy. Recent times have seen a move away from corporate planning to the concept of strategic management. The main difference is that strategic management addresses the issue of implementation.

■ Success versus failure

Two dimensions determine the success of a strategy: the strategy itself and our ability to implement it. A useful starting point in considering success or failure is outlined in Figure 13.1. Bonoma (1984) examines the appropriateness of the strategy and the effectiveness of execution skills thus establishing four general positions.

1 *Success*: The ideal situation, an appropriate strategy and a strong ability to execute such a strategy. This should present little or no problem.
2 *Chance*: Here the strategy is poor, perhaps lacking detailed analysis or not building on existing strengths. However it may be saved by effective execution. This may be such that we can adopt and adapt from a weak opening basis and, with luck, do what is required. Clearly, the degree of 'inappropriateness' is highly significant. Is the strategy saveable? Notwithstanding this question, this position always brings a high degree of risk.
3 *Problem*: We are doing the right things badly. The strength of strategic planning is dissipated by poor execution. Often the true value of the strategy is not fully recognised and it is dismissed as being inappropriate.
4 *Failure*: A no-win situation. With failure on all levels there is a danger of struggling on with implementation and simply 'throwing good money after bad'. Organisations should try to learn from such situations. Do not make the same mistake twice.

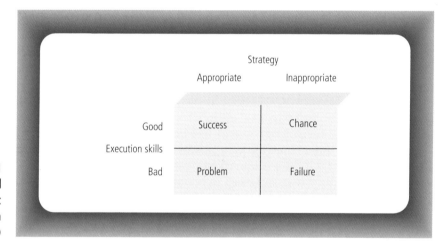

Figure 13.1
Strategy and
execution (*Source*:
Adapted from
Bonoma, 1984, p. 72)

Clearly, there is an issue of subjectivity within defining good/bad and appropriate/inappropriate and it is all too easy to be wise after the event. It is simple to classify a strategy as inappropriate after it is deemed to have failed. The key quest is to ensure strategies fall into the 'success' category. Formulating an appropriate strategy has been dealt with in the preceding chapters of this text and we will now focus on the execution of strategy – in other words implementation.

Effective implementation can be viewed in terms of:

1 Understanding the fundamental principles of implementation.
2 Assessing the ease, or otherwise, of implementing individual projects.
3 Applying project management techniques.

■ Fundamental principles

Having stressed the importance of implementation we turn to the issue of what factors are required for success. These are summarised in Table 13.1.

Illustrative Example 13.1

Kall Kwik: implementing a national marketing strategy

Kall Kwik operates a UK wide chain of outlets, offering design, print and copy services to business. The organisation faces the challenge of implementing clients' marketing strategies across a distributed, geographically dispersed, network. Kall Kwik Centre owners provide local service, while adhering to centrally set quality, pricing and production time standards. The network of local Kall Kwik Centres allow multi-site client organisations (e.g. retailers) to implement marketing campaigns without incurring the high-distribution costs normally associated with centralised print purchasing.

Table 13.1 Key elements in implementations

• Leadership	• Control
• Culture	• Skills
• Resources	• Strategy
• Structure	• Systems

Any successful strategy must be supported by each of the components shown below. These cover the human aspects of business and a more objective process approach to management (Table 13.1). *Note*: These factors can either have a positive or negative effect on a given project. Each is considered in turn.

● *Leadership*
The role of the leader is to get the best out of people and deal with the unexpected. They should be viewed as facilitators. This is achieved by creating an environment where actions can take place. Leaders require effective people skills such as negotiation and delegation. Often leaders acquire their leadership position by means of technical expertise. This can be dangerous, remember their primary function is to facilitate rather than undertake the work themselves. The leader needs transferable management skills in addition to technical and marketing competence. Adair (1984) summarises leadership as (Figure 13.2):

1 *Task needs*: Aiming to complete the project.
2 *Group needs*: Developing team spirit and morale.
3 *Individual needs*: Harmonising the above with the needs of the individual.

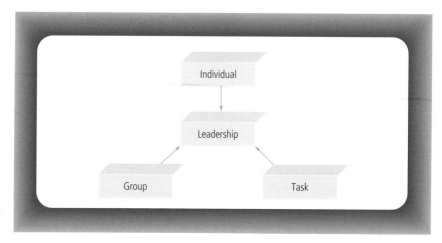

Figure 13.2
Leadership

Depending on circumstances, the leader will emphasis task, group or individual needs.

Leaders need to adopt an appropriate *style* of management. If a crisis looms then a more direct autocratic style may be called for. However, under different circumstances a participative style may be best suited. Hence leaders can move from task, individual or group orientation depending on the circumstances.

● *Culture*

Much management theory relates to corporate culture. Culture can be defined as a combination of *shared values* and beliefs. These are commonly reinforced with corporate symbols and symbolic behaviour. For example, a company may wish to pursue a culture of openness and accessibility. The symbol of this may be to encourage all staff to dress informally on a Friday, to promote a more relaxed atmosphere.

Great care must be taken when implementing strategy. If the strategy goes against the dominant culture it is likely to fail unless a major effort is made to develop and maintain support. This could be achieved through staff training, appraisal and restructuring. The strategist needs be sensitive to the *shared values* that exist within the organisation. Normally it is best to work with, as opposed to against, such values.

● *Structure*

The structure of any organisation, or project, has two primary functions. Firstly, it defines lines of authority denoting levels of responsibility. Current management thinking promotes a move towards flatter structures with more devolved authority. Secondly, structure is a basis for communication. Structures can filter out information making senior management remote from the customer. In the area of implementation consideration should be given to how communication occurs.

In relation to developing marketing strategy, it can be advisable to have multi-functional teams. A group with a diverse range of backgrounds can promote ownership of projects, identify operational problems in advance and enhance overall quality.

- *Resources*

  Any project needs to be properly resourced. Leaders have the role of obtaining and making optimum use of resources. The resourcing of projects is often more to do with internal politics than actual need. In many organisations there needs to be a more objective process of resource allocation. Resource will ultimately relate to finance and staff.

  Resourcing is normally budget driven. However, there is now a recognition of the importance of being time focused. For example, a 3-month time delay is likely to be more serious than a minor budgetary overspend. The concept of 'time-to-market' is dealt with in a later section.

  Remember, implementation never takes place in a vacuum – things change and it is important to be flexible and build in an acceptable degree of contingency (additional resource to be called on) within any implementation strategy.

- *Control*

  Control is simply a way of making sure what is supposed to happen actually happens. The term itself – 'control' often appears to have negative connotations and is seen as limiting and coercive in nature. This should not be the case. Astute management can develop effective control systems.

  The basic approach is a simple feedback loop. You measure progress, compare against some pre-set standard and if required take action. Given the importance of control the concept is expanded upon in the next chapter.

- *Skills*

  The appropriate skills mix is required in order to achieve any aim or goal. Within the context of implementing marketing strategy 'softer' human resource management (HRM) skills can be lacking. It should be remembered that project management is a skill in its own right. To summarise, successful implementation requires skills such as:

  ○ Technical/marketing skills for example, design, market research, industry analysis.
  ○ HRM skills for example, delegation, performance appraisal, training.
  ○ Project management skills for example, budgeting, resourcing, forecasting.

- *Strategy*

  To state the obvious, there must be a strategy to implement. However the fact that a strategy exists may not be apparent to everyone. Additionally, the strategy may not be seen as appropriate by all staff. The project leader must ensure people are aware of the strategy, the reason for it and their role in making it work.

  Potential strategy should be screened to ensure that it is appropriate to current circumstances. For example, what is the basis of competitive advantage? What organisational changes need to take place?

The development of strategy is an on-going activity. During and after the implementation phase, management should review and adapt policy as required. While the overall objectives remain intact – there may be changes in how we set about achieving such targets (Figure 13.3).

- *Systems*
  Several systems are important in the implementation process and fall into two general groups: reporting and forecasting. It is necessary to have systems which aid management decision making. *Note*: These are aids to decision making and not replacements for decision making. Such systems will cover areas such as finance and budgeting, project evaluation/refinement and market research. The key factor is often the interpretation of information rather than the system itself.

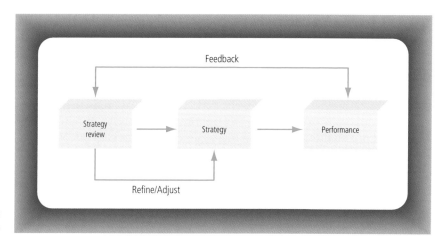

Figure 13.3
Reviewing strategy

The seven S's

The McKinsey and Company's 'Seven-S' model provides a useful summation of these ideas. The model can be adapted as seen in Figure 13.4 and split into: (i) HRM – dealing with the people-based aspects of implementation and (ii) process – the policy, procedures, reporting and systems aspects of implementation.

■ Assessing ease of implementation

It is now possible to test and evaluate the likely ease of implementation. Firstly, strategic fit – how easily will the strategy fit into current activities? Unsurprisingly, the easier the fit the less likely implementation problems are to occur. *Note*: It must be recognised that an 'easy fit' does not guarantee success. The strategy must be right for the business environment.

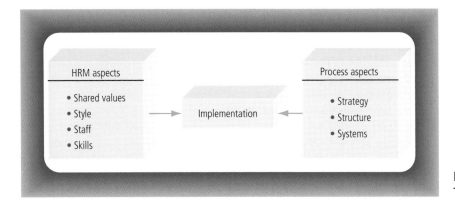

Figure 13.4
The seven S's

   Primarily, the concern is with the level of change associated with the implementation. The greater the change, the greater the management challenge and the perceived benefit of the change needs to be. Hence there is a need to consider the potential pay-off and the amount of change required to achieve this. Figure 13.5 illustrates the relationship between change and importance.

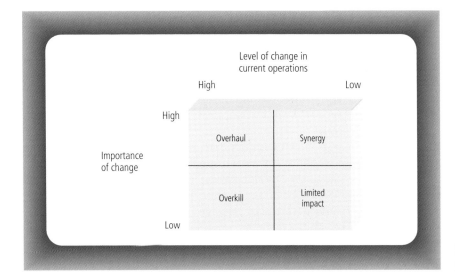

Figure 13.5
Strategic fit

● *Overhaul*: Here implementation will have a significant impact and face significant challenges. Given that a high degree of change is likely, one must expect increasing levels of resistance and risk as the strategy has only a limited fit with current activity. There needs to be compelling strategic reasons and significant support for this strategy's implementation. Such activities are likely to involve factors such as restructuring, downsizing, mergers and overhauling business culture.

- *Synergy*: The word can be defined as 'working together'. The combined effect of high importance and relatively limited change offers a potentially 'easy ride'. Problems should be limited and risk of failure is reduced. However, great problems occur when a strategy is deemed to fall into this category, only to find it is not the case and far more change is required. Be doubly sure you have the required synergy before embarking down this route.
- *Limited impact*: Low levels of change affecting relatively unimportant areas of activity. Often a series of such activities can yield incremental change. This could represent a stage-by-stage approach to change, where relatively minor changes are introduced over a period of time. This option of incremental activity can be used where resources are limited or a phased-consolidated approach is deemed more appropriate.
- *Overkill*: Has high risk and limited impact importance. Questions have to be asked. Why are we doing this and what is the pay-off? Care is needed in order not to alienate staff and disrupt activity. Such projects often occur as a result of political manoeuvring and compromise.

Successful management requires an appreciation of the nature of change and its subsequent impact on the organisation and individual. The process starts with an awareness of the need to change, then progresses to a transition phase and finally reaches some predetermined state. Normally, the transition stage is the most critical as it is fraught with risk and uncertainty.

Management must assess the level of change associated with a project and deploy strategies relating to the management of change. For example:

- *Justification*: Have supportive evidence in the form of facts and quantitative/statistical data. Hard data often proves a powerful ally.
- *Commitment*: Try to involve others through group problem solving, participation and communication. Such factors tend to generate commitment to change.
- *Learning*: Change is often difficult to achieve and mistakes will be made. Learning from mistakes is important. Remember, experience is the name we like to give our mistakes.
- *Incrementalise*: It may be better to have an overall strategy that can be broken down into a series of smaller on-going changes, as per the 'limited impact' strategy.
- *Operations*: Ensure that change is reflected in operational activities through the appropriate systems, structures, policies and monitoring. In this way, change becomes a permanent feature and the organisation avoids slipping back into old practice.

■ People, power and politics

When addressing the issue of implementation there are no panaceas. However, not all staff will be equally supportive of a given marketing strategy. Hence it is wise to consider the likely levels of support and resistance that may exist relative to a given project. Piercy (1997, p. 591) sets out general categories into which staff can fall (see Figure 13.6).

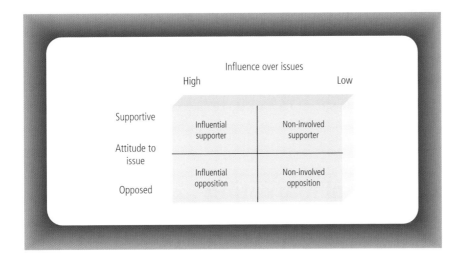

Figure 13.6
Key players matrix

Those with influence, often the appropriate decision-making unit (DMU), need careful consideration. Common tactics include:

● Converting or isolating opposition.
● Upgrading the status of influential supporters.
● Recruiting the active involvement of non-involved supporters.
● Negotiation and trade-off with vested interest.

In short, the success of any programme requires sufficient influence and support. This becomes more complex when the project generates high levels of change.

The issue of supporters and their influence tends to relate to the dreaded, but vital concept of internal office politics. Within the organisation, political behaviour can be either desirable or undesirable. Often this depends on your perspective. Good strategies can flounder on the rocks of political self-interest and behaviour.

Kakabadse (1983) identifies seven common approaches to playing the political game. They are as follows:

1   Establish who the interested parties are – the stakeholders.
2   Consider their comfort zones. What do they value, fear or tolerate?
3   Work within these comfort zones.
4   Use networks – those interested or influential.
5   Identify 'gatekeepers' and adhere to the norms of the network.
6   Make deals for mutual benefit.
7   Withhold and withdraw. Consider withholding information and know when to withdraw from areas of conflict and dispute.

Arguably, political behaviour is an essential part of strategy implementation. This view requires management to identify key players and consider their potential reaction to strategic initiatives. Remember, the art of politics is about influencing people when you cannot rely on direct authority. By considering the political dimension related to the project it is possible to gauge resistance and support, develop justification and counter argument in advance of critical decisions.

Additionally, you may be able to develop influence through various power bases. For example, controlling resources, having access to people and controlling the flow of information. These can all assist in playing the political game.

■ Internal marketing

No discussion relating to the ease, or otherwise, of implementation would be complete without considering the potential use of internal marketing. Internal marketing focuses on the relationship between the organisations and its employees. Berry and Parasuraman (1991) define the process in terms of viewing employees (or groups of employees) as internal customers.

Definitions of this type encompass the work traditionally within the remit of personnel/HRM function (e.g. recruitment, training, motivation, etc.). Few would argue with the importance of staff in relation to implementation. Therefore, can marketing techniques be used to motivate employees and ease the path of project implementation?

By applying the marketing concept internally, it may be possible to enhance the likely success of a project. Factors such as internal segmentation and application of the 'mix' may well have a role to play. Consider the following:

- *Segmentation*: The process of dividing groups into sub-groups with similar characteristics. This is perfectly feasible within any organisation. For example senior managers may have different training needs from other staff. By grouping like types together more effective training and communication is possible.
- *Product*: This may well be the strategy and accompanying process of change. Equally, the individuals' job or function could be viewed as an 'internal product'. The internal product, service or task is a component in delivering the overall strategy.
- *Promotion*: Clear communication has a vital role to play in establishing success. The project manager could design a 'promotional campaign' stressing the benefits of a new strategy. In all cases, communication is an issue that must be considered when planning implementation.
- *Place*: How to get the 'product' to the internal customer. Channels of distribution for information, services and training can be developed and optimised. These could include team briefings, seminars and day-to-day business interactions.

- *Price*: It is a complex issue. While it is relatively easy to cost factors like training, communications vehicles and other associated tangible costs, it is worth remembering a price is also paid by the group and/or individual. This 'psychological' price is difficult to measure, but important. It takes the form of uncertainty, loss of status, stress and loss (hopefully short term) of operational efficiency.

In its simplest form internal marketing offers a framework (the four P's) which can lay the foundations of successful policy implementation. It offers the marketing concept as a way to achieve specific strategic goals. Figure 13.7 illustrates how the concept could be applied to an organisation. Here we segment by level of support. However, other criteria (e.g. department or management level) could be applied.

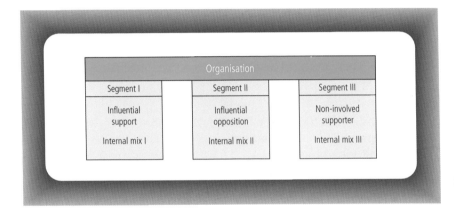

Figure 13.7
Internal marketing

■ Applying project management techniques

The ability to manage a project is a skill in its own right. Such skills are 'transferable' and can be applied to any situation. Therefore, they adhere to general principles which can be learned by the marketing strategist.

Essentially, project management involves achieving unity of purpose and setting achievable goals within given resource and time scale parameters. Efforts tend to focus on integrating activity, building teamwork and monitoring progress. Marketing projects are rarely simple and often have to be achieved while overcoming unforeseen problems and barriers. Effective project management deals with such problems as and when they arise.

Table 13.2 summarises common tasks in project management. Each task is reviewed in turn.

- *Objective setting*
  An overall strategic objective will be broken down into a series of 'sub-objectives'. It is important that these are clear, concise, understood and

Table 13.2 Project management

• Objective setting	• Team building
• Planning	• Crisis
• Delegation	• Management

accepted by team members. A useful acronym is to develop **SMART** objectives. These add focus and relate to the task(s) required.

S – Specific. They should be clear and task orientated.
M – Measurable. Objectives must be measured in order to establish progress.
A – Action. They should be task related and promote activity.
R – Resourced. A realistic resource base has to be allocated to enable progress.
T – Time. There is a need to make the objective time focused. How long will it take?

● *Planning*
Having established what is to be achieved. Planning breaks an activity into a series of structured manageable tasks, co-ordinates these tasks and monitoring progress.

Tasks can happen in series or parallel. So-called 'parallel processing' – running several tasks simultaneously, has several advantages. Namely, it can reduce the overall time scale for the project and reduce the risk of a delay in one task delaying the entire project (Figure 13.8).

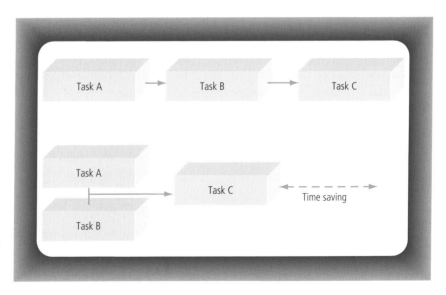

Figure 13.8
Serial versus parallel
processing

Increasingly there is an awareness of being time focused. Business is now adopting a Time-to-Market (T-t-M) philosophy. This T-t-M approach advocates the importance of reducing the overall time taken to implement a project. Consider the potential benefits of reducing implementation time. Firstly, a commercial return is produced sooner. Secondly, by being early into the market the opportunity exists to gain a price premium and/or market share. The T-t-M focus is achieved by parallel processing and, conversely, spending more time developing a robust planning specification.

- *Delegation*
  Effective managers realise they cannot do everything themselves, they know that management is the art of delegation. The art is often to balance the degree of delegation with the appropriate span of control. The manager needs to understand the strength, weakness and group dynamics of the team members.

Illustrative Example 13.2

Ericsson: time-to-market

The mobile phone industry provides an illustration of how critical T-t-M cycles can be. Although the market is booming, it is characterised by intense competition and rapid technological development. Ericsson – the manufacturer on mobile phone handsets – has recently seen its market share drop within this growing market. These difficulties are largely attributed to the delay in launching a key product (The T28). The company is quoted as stating that the T28 was nearly a year late and that they had to cancel the T36 because it had only a short market life. Such delays caused Ericsson to miss out on demand for low-cost handsets aimed at the expanding pre-pay mobile phone market.

Many managers have a problem with letting go. Remember that delegation extends the capacity to manage and frees the leader from the mundane. Additionally, if staff are encouraged to take decisions, overall decision making can be improved. The people 'on the spot' are more likely to have a fuller grasp of the situation and be able to make effective decisions.

Key principles of delegation include:

- Focus on the objective. Be crystal clear about what has to be achieved but flexible in how it is to be achieved.
- Delegate authority not just responsibility. Empower people to make decisions and manage resources.
- Test people on smaller and less important tasks and gradually give the more able employee greater scope.
- Explain how tasks are monitored and define circumstances in which they should refer back to senior management.
- Refrain from undue interference but be watchful.

- *Team building*

  Clearly there is a need to use the skills and capacity of the team to the optimal level. It is important to have a core goal as this gives the team a focal point. Each team member must understand their contribution to this collective goal. As Wickens (1997) states teamwork does not depend on people working together but upon working to obtain the same objective.

  A winning team has the right combination of skills. These should blend and complement each other. The environment should be positive and supportive but not complacent or overly relaxed.

  Basic team building principles, which can be applied to a marketing project, are:

  ○ Encourage a positive supportive environment. It is okay to make a mistake but ensure you learn from them.
  ○ Show and encourage respect for each other. Encourage constructive criticism as opposed to personal attack.
  ○ Link individual reward to group performance.
  ○ Disagreement and discussion should not be suppressed and ideas should be listened to. However this should not detract from effective decision making.

- *Crisis management*

  There will be times when things go dramatically wrong and a crisis point is reached. The basic premise of crisis management is to take urgent action in response to unexpected events. By definition, the process is reactive in nature and invariably is a turning point. However, it does not negate prior planning. Management can develop a series of scenarios and have appropriate responses available as a contingency. This scenario planning allows a crisis management approach to be developed in advance.

  Additionally, we may be given prior warning of a pending problem. Often there is a gradual worsening of events until the point of crisis is attained. If these signals are picked up early enough decisive action can be taken before the problem becomes a crisis.

  A key idea is to maintain confidence and for management to be clearly in control. Basic techniques include:

  ○ Assess the situation coolly and establish the facts before taking any rash action.
  ○ Draw up a plan of action and establish a management structure.
  ○ Set up a communications system to receive and disseminate information.
  ○ Separate the trivial from the important and prioritise tasks.
  ○ Be decisive and take responsibility.

■ Summary

Do not downplay the importance of implementation. Organisations need to consider not only the development of strategy, but address issues that turn strategy into reality.

The key to successful implementation is the application of basic management principles – leadership, systems, and resourcing are all important. Such factors must be taken within the context of the organisational culture and business environment that exists.

Prior to implementation, it is wise to consider how easy the task(s) are likely to be. This relates to the importance of the task and the level of associated change. The attitude and influence of interested parties will also have a significant impact on the ease, or otherwise, of implementation.

Internal marketing techniques and the deployment of standard project management principles, such as objective setting, planning and delegation, facilitate a workable framework for the implementation of strategy.

■ References

Adair, J., *Action Centred Leadership*, McGraw-Hill, New York, 1984.

Berry, L. and Parasuraman, A., *Marketing Services: Competing Through Quality*, New York Free Press, New York, 1991.

Bonoma, T., Making your marketing strategies work, *Harvard Business Review*, **62**(2), March–April, 1984, 68–76.

Kakabadse, A., *The Politics of Management*, Gower, Aldershot, 1983.

Piercy, N., *Market-Led Strategic Change*, 2nd edn, Butterworth-Heinemann, Oxford, 1997.

Wickens, P., *The Road to Nissan*, Macmillan, London, 1997.

CHAPTER 14

Control

Control mechanisms aim to translate strategic plans into specific actions. The purpose is to ensure behaviour, systems and operations conform to corporate objectives/policy. Marketing managers need to be aware of a range of control variables; financial measures, budgets, performance appraisal and benchmarking.

■ Introduction

The term 'control' has received a bad press. The phrase smacks of coercive action, limiting freedom and keeping costs to an absolute minimum. The reality is somewhat different and managers should consider the control process as simply a mechanism to protect your strategic plans during implementation. Murphy's Law states that – *'if anything can go wrong, it will go wrong'*. Hence a control system detecting and pre-empting the inevitable problems that accompany implementation is a valuable asset.

Control can be defined as attempting to guarantee behaviour and systems conform to, and support, predetermined corporate objectives and policies. Such 'hard edged' views illustrate the importance of linking behaviour to overall strategic direction. This is a fundamental reason for having control systems.

■ Control: the basic principles

The basis of control is the ability to measure. In essence it compares what should happen with what actually happened or is likely to happen. Given the importance of measurement, a tendency exists to measure what is easy to quantify rather than what is important. Project managers must guard against this and focus on the key areas. Good control systems often detect and rectify problems before they become significant and managers should remember that prevention is better than cure. Try to be proactive rather than reactive.

The process is broken down into a series of simple steps. Firstly, a target is set. Ideally, this is integrated into overall strategic planning. Secondly, a method of measurement has to be determined and implemented. Finally, measured results are compared with the predetermined target(s) and corrective action, if required, is undertaken.

There are two sides to the control equation – inputs and outputs. If only output is considered then the system is one of inspection as opposed to control. Correctly addressing both sides of the equation allows management to optimise the process and take a strategic view. Typical inputs include:

● *Finance*: Investment, working capital and cash.
● *Operations*: Capacity, usage, efficiency and application of machines, systems and other assets.
● *People*: Numbers, quality and skills of staff.

Output is measured in terms of overall system performance. Performance is derived from a combination of efficiency and effectiveness.

● *Efficiency*: How well utilised are the inputs? Do we make maximum use of finance, minimise cost and operate at optimal levels of capacity?
● *Effectiveness*: Are we doing the right things? This relates to actual performance and will include sales revenue, profit, market share and measures of customer satisfaction.

Remember, it is better to pursue effectiveness. For example, a company may be a very efficient producer (low cost, high volume, etc.) but relatively ineffective at finding buyers for its goods.

Control systems can operate as simple feedback loops. Figure 14.1 illustrates the concept. However more sophisticated systems of *feed forward control* are possible.

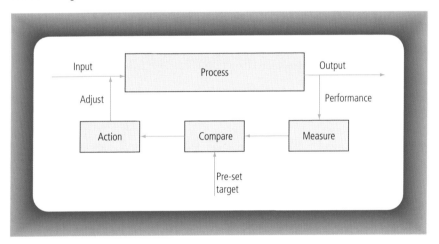

Figure 14.1
Feedback control

Such systems try to pre-empt problems by anticipating the effect of input(s) on overall performance. However, such systems are more complex and consequently more difficult to set up.

Figure 14.2 illustrates the application of a basic control loop to the marketing management process. Here marketing objectives, such as increasing market share, are translated into performance targets. These targets define a specific measurable basis against which managers will be judged. The objective of increasing market share would be quantified. For example, we may aim at a 7 per cent increase over 12 months. Responsibility for achieving the target is assigned and actual performance is evaluated against planned performance. The adjustment of the process is achieved

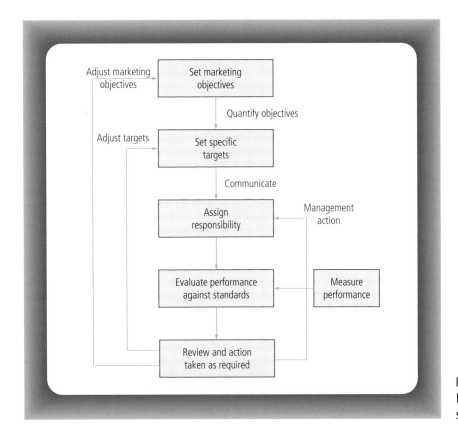

Figure 14.2
Marketing control systems

by management action and/or altering the objectives or standards within the system. In this way, the system becomes flexible and can react to changes in performance and the business environment.

■ What makes an effective control system?

Control systems require careful design. Generic principles exist which are common to all effective control mechanisms. As with management processes, it is important to retain a degree of flexibility and common sense. The project manager can deploy the following principles to ensure effective control.

● *Involvement*: It is achieved by encouraging participation in the process. Management can achieve desired results through consultation. For example, staff could contribute towards setting targets. Their own staff development needs could be considered along with the required tasks. Correctly applied, the process enhances morale, promotes ownership and develops the skill's base of employees.

● *Target setting*: There are two important factors. Firstly, the target criteria should be objective and measurable. How this is assessed needs to be communicated and agreed in advance. Secondly, it needs to be achievable but challenging.

● *Focus*: It recognises the difference between the symptoms and the source of a problem. While it may be expedient to treat the symptoms, tackling the source of the problem should eliminate it once and for all.

● *Effectiveness*: The tendency exists to measure efficiency as opposed to effectiveness. Efficiency is the usage and productivity of assets. Effectiveness is about doing the right things. Ideally, we want measures of efficiency applied to areas of effectiveness. In reality we tend to apply efficiency measures to areas easiest to measure. Be careful to measure what is important, not what is easy to quantify. Additionally, measurement should be accurate, valid and consistent.

● *Management by exception*: Management attention is directed to areas of need. Identifying what constitutes an exception to the norm is a useful exercise in its own right. The process involves setting tolerances and benchmarks for normal operation. Management action only becomes a priority when pre-set limits are breached. Figure 14.3 shows a simple tolerance control chart. This is based on planned sales revenue plus or minus a tolerance of 5 per cent. If the levels are broken, or in a proactive system appear as if they may be breached, management will begin to take an interest in the process.

● *Action*: Good control systems promote action. Such systems do not just detect problems; they solve problems. Basically, actions adjust the inputs to the process. For example, extra resources could be made available to deal with a backlog or we could redesign a process or procedure to make it more effective.

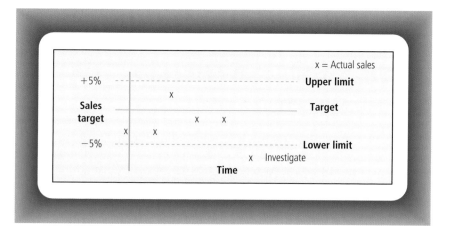

Figure 14.3
Tolerance control
chart

Problems of control

A good control system is not easy to develop. The project manager requires an awareness of the general problems associated with control systems. Remember, no system is perfect and no control system offers 100 per cent accuracy. Often, the concern is keeping operations and plans within acceptable limits.

Three problems are commonly associated with control systems. Firstly, such systems can be *costly*. Here the benefits of control and subsequent improvements are outweighed by the cost of the control mechanism. This often relates to large bureaucratic systems – layer upon layer of administration is built upon each other. This is self-serving rather than customer focused, often absorbing resources that would be more effectively deployed in core activities. Secondly, control systems *stifle effort and creativity*. Such systems promote uniformity and conformance to pre-set targets. They become barriers to innovation. Thirdly, control promotes a view of *inspection as opposed to development*. Systems often deal with the symptom rather than the root of the problem. Here, we tend to be constantly 'fire fighting' and looking for the quick fix as opposed to developing a better overall method of operation. The effect is to filter and/or suppress information from those with the power to radically overhaul a poor system.

■ Management control

Having reviewed the basic concept of control, we can now focus on the key aspect of management control. Management control takes place at a number of different levels within the organisation (see Figure 14.4). Control criteria apply to strategic, operational and tactical levels. The control variables at one level become targets for the next level down. Effectively, this means that a 'cascade' system of control is in operation. Senior/strategic levels use fewer, more critical, control variables. These are predominantly financial in nature and focus on divisional or strategic

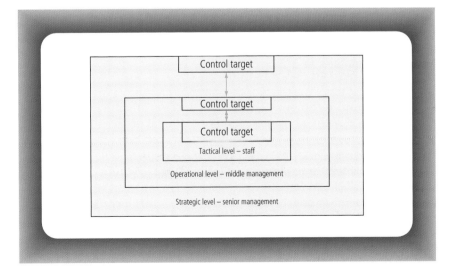

Figure 14.4
Cascade control

business unit (SBU) targets. The operational level relates to project or departmental activities and encompasses financial and non-financial information. The tactical level relates to group or individual performance and focus is on productivity.

Good performance means that employees (at all levels) have a clear view of what the priorities are, what they should be doing currently, how their area of responsibility contributes to overall performance and what levels of achievement are acceptable.

Management control will focus on: *finance, performance appraisal* and *benchmarking*. The relative importance of each may vary with level of management.

Financial measures will give both short- and long-term control data and are fundamental to decision making. Performance appraisal examines the personnel and human resource aspects of management. Finally, benchmarking is a means of comparison and identification of best practice. As Figure 14.5 illustrates, management control is applied to marketing in order to establish marketing performance. Remember, performance is a function of efficiency and effectiveness.

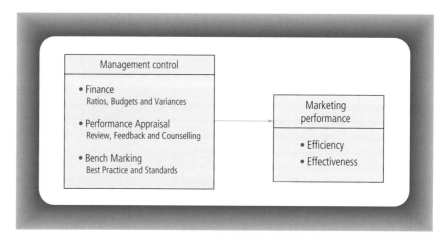

Figure 14.5
Management
control related to
marketing

■ Financial control

Financial control techniques are vital to successful strategy. Such techniques apply to both the planning and operational phases of projects. We will focus on three main financial control activities: ratios, budgeting and variance analysis.

A basic understanding of financial terminology is required. Remember, ultimately all business activities are measured in financial terms and managers require a grasp of accounting terms. Key terms include:

● *Assets*: Items that have value to the business. Assets are sub-divided into two categories: (i) *Fixed assets* – retained by the business, in the long term, for continual use. Typical examples include buildings, machinery, vehicles and long-term investments. (ii) *Current assets* – items that are readily convertible into cash or cash itself. Such assets are to be used in the short term. Examples included: stock, cash and debtors (those owning us money).

● *Liabilities*: Financial obligations owed to others. *Current liabilities* are those debts which must be paid in the near future. Therefore cash will be required to meet current liabilities. Additionally, *capital* invested by the owner can be classified as a liability as it is technically owed to the owners.

Ratios

A simple and effective control technique is to express performance in terms of ratios. Ratios should not be used in isolation. Trends and comparisons with planned or standards ratios should be considered. Remember, they are no more than indicators and rarely identify the source of a problem. However, managers can identify key ratios for their areas of responsibility. These ratios provide a quick and effective way to establish performance and highlight areas warranting more detailed analysis. Figure 14.6 outlines the uses of ratios.

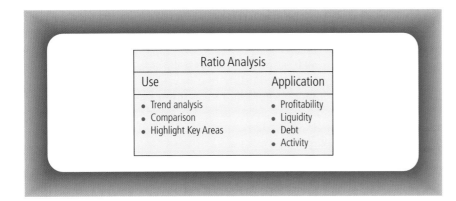

Figure 14.6
Use and application of ratios

Ratios represent a snap shot of the firm's financial/productivity position and fall into four general categories (see Figure 14.6): profitability, liquidity, debt and activity. Remember, when calculating ratios it is important to be consistent with the terms used. For example, how is profit defined – before or after tax?

Profitability ratios
Here, effectiveness is measured by evaluating the organisation's ability to produce profit. Profit margin is expressed in terms of a ratio of profit to sales. The profit margin is a key trading concern. Clearly, the profit margin can be enhanced by raising selling price and/or reducing costs.

Return On Capital Employed (ROCE) is expressed as net profit as a percentage of capital. It examines to what extent an investment is paying off. It can be applied to an entire business or to specific projects requiring capital investment. ROCE is used to indicate the extent to which an investment is justified or to compare investment opportunities.

Examples

$$\text{Gross profit margin} = \frac{\text{Profit}}{\text{Sales revenue}} \qquad \text{Profit} = \text{Revenue} - \text{Cost}$$

$$\text{Net profit margin} = \frac{\text{Profit after tax}}{\text{Sales revenue}}$$

$$\text{ROCE} = \frac{\text{Net profit}}{\text{Capital employed}}$$

Liquidity ratios

Ratios evaluate the ability to remain solvent and meet current liabilities. The firm needs to be able to convert assets into cash in order to meet payment demands. If the current ratio is more than one, sufficient assets exist to meet current liabilities. The quick (or acid test) ratio gives a stricter appraisal of solvency as it assumes stock is not automatically convertible into cash. Ideally, this ratio should be one to one. However, many businesses operate with lower acceptable ratios. If the ratio is too high it may suggest that the organisation does not make optimal use of its financial assets (e.g. holding too much cash).

Examples

$$\text{Current ratio} = \frac{\text{Current assets}}{\text{Current liabilities}}$$

$$\text{Quick ratio} = \frac{\text{Current assets} - \text{Inventory}}{\text{Current liabilities}}$$

Debt ratios

These ratios help to determine the company's ability to handle debt and meet scheduled repayments. They examine the extent to which borrowed funds finance business operations. If creditors begin to outweigh debtors this may signify overtrading – unable to collect money owed.

Examples

$$\text{Debt to assets ratio} = \frac{\text{Total liabilities}}{\text{Total assets}}$$

$$\text{Debt to credit ratio} = \frac{\text{Debtors}}{\text{Creditors}}$$

Activity ratios

These ratios determine how effective the organisation is at generating activity, such as sales from assets. These activities often relate to business cycles or processes, such as the time taken to turnover stock or collect debts. For example, the greater the stock turnover the better for the organisation. An additional example, common in retailing, is sales per unit of floor space. This gives a measure of retail effectiveness.

Essentially, such ratios measure the relationship between inputs to outputs.

Examples

$$\text{Inventory turnover} = \frac{\text{Sales}}{\text{Inventory}}$$

$$\text{Sales per square foot} = \frac{\text{Sales}}{\text{Floor space}}$$

$$\text{Productivity} = \frac{\text{Units Produced}}{\text{Number of Employers}}$$

Budgeting

The processes of strategic development and budgeting are intrinsically linked. To be blunt; no budget equals no strategy! The budgeting process translates marketing strategy into financial terms which, whether we like it or not, are the way all plans are expressed, evaluated and controlled.

Budgeting is the single most common control mechanism. It serves not only to quantify plans but also to co-ordination activities, highlight areas of critical importance and assign responsibility.

Many industry practitioners would agree with Piercy (1997). He talks about the *'hassle factor'* – difficulty, time, negotiation, paperwork, etc. – associated with budgeting.

This serves to highlight two points. Firstly, budgeting is about resource allocation. Secondly, budgeting is a political process (negotiate, bargaining, etc.) necessary to obtain required resources.

Before managers can prepare a budget certain fundamental requirements exist:

- *Budget guidelines*: The organisation's policy and procedure relating to budget formulation must be understood. These set out assumptions, method and presentational requirements.
- *Cost behaviour*: Management must understand what drives costs within their area of responsibility. Additionally, it is important to be clear on how costs are allocated. For example, what is the basis of overhead cost allocation?
- *Time scale*: A specific time period needs to be set. This could be for a fixed budgetary period, such as a financial year or alternatively a *'rolling budget'* could be prepared. Here, the budget is split into manageable time periods, and outline forecasts are updated at regular intervals. New periods are added as the budget progresses.
- *Establish objectives*: Specifically, what are we aiming to achieve and how is it being assessed? Corporate or departmental goals should be translated into resource and subsequent budgetary requirements.

Approaches to budgeting

Many approaches exist to formulating a budget. Most organisations have developed a historic way of approaching the task. Recent times have seen a move towards greater objectivity and the need to justify assumptions and requirements. Common methods of budgeting are:

- *Historic*: Traditionally the main determinant of a future budget is previous expenditure. Organisations simply base the budget on previous financial data. Adjustments are made for factors like inflation and level of activity. The model is basically incremental in nature; last year, plus or minus some factor, with managers concentrating on justifying or challenging changes.
- *Zero based*: Budgets are systematically re-evaluated and senior management establishes priority within the context of overall financial constraints. The process involves examining activities and deriving the cost and resulting benefit from these activities. Alternative methods of achieving objectives are simultaneously considered and there is often a trade-off between activities. The method relates to analysing objectives and tasks and is highly 'political' in nature.
- *Activity related*: Here budgets are based on often crude measures of activity. Simple calculations rules such as percentage of sales, or average industry spend are used as precursors to determining available funds.

Variance analysis

Finally, in this section on financial control, variance analysis is reviewed. Basically, this examines the variation between actual and planned results and is a concept applicable to a range of activities. It is commonly used along with budgetary control. We compare the actual results with budgeted forecasts and then examine the variance in order to determine the reason for the difference. Variance analysis allows us to identify the main areas of concern and break problems down into component parts. For example, in marketing, variance analysis is often applied to sales price and sales volume. Standard formulae are useful in calculating the effect of these variables on overall revenue.

- Variance in sales revenue = Actual revenue − Planned revenue
- Variance due to price = Actual volume × (Planned price − Actual price)
- Variance due to volume = Planned price × (Actual volume − Planned volume)

Consider the following example. We plan to sell 4200 units at £25 per unit. However, due to market conditions, we actually sell 3850 units at £16 per unit. Hence the variance in sales revenue is:

$$\text{Variance in sales revenue} = (3850 \times 16) - (4200 \times 25) = -43\,400$$

Variance analysis can be used to determine whether the loss of sales revenue is predominantly due to the lower than expected volume or failure to maintain planned price.

Variance due to price	$= 3850 \times (16 - 25)$	$= -34\,650$	80%
Variance due to volume =	$25 \times (3850 - 4200) =$	-8750	20%
		$-43\,400$	100%

Therefore, we can see that 80 per cent of the failure to achieve planned revenue is due to the lower unit price. Management could then investigate why we failed to achieve the planned unit price.

Note: Variance analysis is not limited to price and volume calculations. A wide range of factors can be analysed in this fashion (e.g. profit, cost and market size).

■ Performance appraisal

Performance appraisal concerns achieving better results from groups and individuals. A performance appraisal framework is based on: planned objectives, levels of achievement and competence. The focus is on the control and development of staff, and is critical to project implementation. Effective performance appraisal requires managers to have good people skills and appraisal should be constructive in nature. It is about doing a better job. Three key skills are involved: reviewing performance, giving feedback and counselling.

1 *Reviewing*: The performance of individuals, or groups, should be reviewed continuously as part of normal management activity. Additionally, there may be a formal review which summarises activity. Try to use objective criteria as a basis of review. Such criteria should be communicated and agreed in advance. Work and personal development plans should be considered in tandem with set criteria.
2 *Feedback*: Feedback, relating to performance, is based on actual results, or observed behaviour. Do not just focus on the negative but try to give credit where it is due. When giving feedback, be specific and describe rather than judge results. By reference to specific actions and behaviours, managers can more readily focus on key aspects of improvement.
3 *Counselling*: Performance appraisal should be positive in nature. In order to build on strengths and overcome weaknesses, management may well have to counsel staff. This is particularly relevant to areas of underperformance. Counselling needs to consider performance, not personality, and invite a degree of self-appraisal. Aim to identify and agree problems then choose required actions.

■ Benchmarking

In order to be 'the-best-you-can-be', it pays to compare yourself with leading performers. Benchmarking provides a method of enabling such comparisons to take place.

Benchmarking is defined as:

> A systematic and on-going process of measuring and comparing an organisation's business processes and achievements against acknowledged process leaders and/or key competitors, to facilitate improved performance.

However benchmarking is more than just copying. The process is about continuous improvement and becoming a learning organisation. The credo is one of adaptation rather than adoption. Ideas, practices and methods have to be screened and adapted to specific business situations. Benchmarking falls into three general areas:

1 *Competitive analysis*: Reviewing competitor's activities, strategy and operations so we can improve our performance.
2 *Best practice*: Determining the best way of undertaking an activity. This could involve examining activities in unrelated areas of business or industries. For example, a computer manufacturer could benchmark a mail-order retail company in order to improve its stock control system. Equally, best internal practice could be identified and spread to other units or departments within the organisation.
3 *Performance standards*: Benchmarks can be performance standards. Performance indicators become targets to be met or surpassed. As way of illustration – if the average industry conversion of enquiries into

sales was 1 in 20 and we achieve 1 in 25, what does this say about our sales process?

The process of benchmarking

Benchmarking comprises a four-stage approach. This is illustrated using the 'Deming Cycle' (Watson, 1993): plan, do, check and act (see Figure 14.7). The planning stage involves identifying what to study and who or what should act as the benchmark. Common areas to benchmark are: customer service levels, logistic and distribution methods, product quality and 'time-to-market' cycles. Organisations will benchmark against competitors, acknowledged leaders or successful internal activities. Next, conduct research. This may involve co-operation and direct contact with the benchmark. Alternatively, secondary data may be used to establish standards and actions. The data is then analysed. This involves establishing the extent of performance gaps and identifying assignable causes for such gaps. Finally, the lessons learned are adapted, as appropriate, and applied in order to generate improvement in performance.

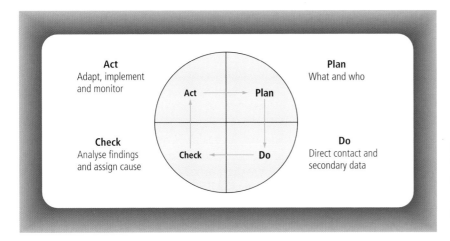

Figure 14.7
The Deming Cycle applied to benchmarking (*Source*: Watson, 1993, p. 4)

■ Controlling marketing performance

In contrast to mechanical systems, marketing activities are inherently more volatile. This is due to a constantly changing business environment driven by the needs and wants of the market. Measuring marketing performance is a process of determining appropriate criteria by which to judge activity. Kotler (1997) identifies four main areas associated with the control of marketing activity (see Figure 14.8).

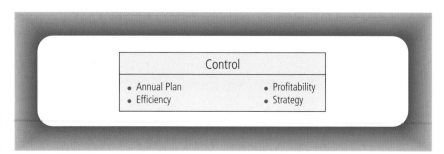

Figure 14.8
Control of
marketing activities

Illustrative Example 14.1

British Airways – measuring marketing success

Organisations spend a great deal of time and money marketing their products, therefore they require objective measures relating to the effectiveness of such expenditure. British Airways is reported to evaluate marketing success through measurement of awareness, feedback on customer satisfaction and market share data. Additionally, a more focused approach is applied to specific promotions. These measure factors such as repeat business and level of sales.

1   *Annual planning*: This has the purpose of evaluating the extent to which marketing efforts, over the year, have been successful. Evaluation will focus on analysing: sales, market share, expenses and customer perception. Commonly, sales performance is a major element of this analysis. All other factors provide explanation of any variance in sales performance.

2   *Profitability*: All marketing managers are concerned with controlling their profit levels. Examining the profitability of products, or activities, it is possible to make decisions relating to the expansion, reduction or elimination of product offerings. Additionally, it is common to break distribution channels and segments down in terms of profitability. Remember, it is important to have a systematic basis for allocating cost and defining profit.

3   *Efficiency control*: Efficiency is concerned with gaining optimum value from the marketing assets. Managers are looking to obtain value for money in relation to marketing activity. The promotional aspects of marketing (sales, advertising, direct marketing, etc.) are commonly subject to such controls. Figure 14.9 displays examples.

4   *Strategic control*: There is a need to ensure that marketing activities are being directed towards strategic goals and that marketing is an integral part of the overall process of delivering value. A strategic review will aim to assess that marketing strategy, and subsequent implementation, is appropriate to the marketplace. A review of this nature will take the form of a marketing audit – a comprehensive examination of all marketing activity to assess effectiveness and improve marketing performance.

The aforementioned areas of marketing control are general in nature and specific measures of marketing performance are required. Performance measures and standards will vary by organisation and market conditions. A representative sample of the type of data required to successfully control marketing activities is shown in Figure 14.9. The aim is to break the general areas (annual, plan, profitability, efficiency and strategy) into measurable component parts to which responsibility can be assigned.

Remember, in the context of marketing a balanced view is required. No one variable should dominate the control process. For example, marketing strategists have been guilty of following a credo of 'market share at any cost'. While such a variable is important, it is not a panacea and consideration needs to be given to other factors such as profitability. Additionally, marketing control should measure only dimensions over which the organisation has control. Rewards, sanctions and management actions only make sense where influence can be exerted. Control systems should be sensitive to local market conditions and levels of competition. For instance, developing market and mature markets may require different control mechanisms.

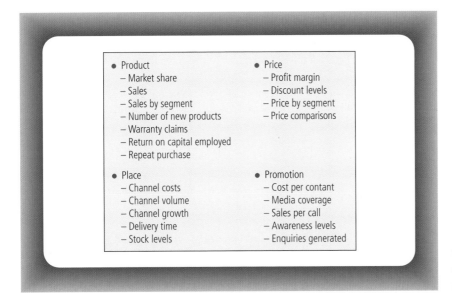

Figure 14.9
Control of
marketing mix

■ Summary

The basic essence of control is the ability to measure and take action. Control systems are concerned with efficiency and effectiveness and often operate as simple feedback loops. In marketing terms, control ensures what is supposed to happen actually happen and is a mechanism to protect strategic plans when they become operational.

Effective control systems have focus, involve people and promote action. Management control extends to cover finance, performance appraisal and establishing and maintaining performance benchmarks. Marketing managers are concerned with the following control mechanisms; annual plans, profitability, efficiency of marketing and strategic control.

■ References

Kotler, P., *Marketing Management*, 9th edn, Prentice Hall, New Jersey, 1997.
Piercy, N., *Market-Led Strategic Change*, 2nd edn, Butterworth-Heinemann, Oxford, 1997.
Watson, G., *Strategic Benchmarking*, Wiley, New York, 1993.

■ Further reading

Piercy, N., *Market-Led Strategic Change*, 2nd edn, Chapter 12, Butterworth-Heinemann, Oxford, 1997.

PART 4

Contemporary
Issues in
Strategic
Marketing

- Customer Relationship Management (CRM)
- Ethical issues and strategy

The process of strategic marketing and its associated research is continually evolving. This text highlights two current, or contemporary, issues which have and will continue to greatly influence marketing at a strategic level. While the issues of CRM and ethics are corporate wide in nature, they will impact significantly on marketing-based business strategies.

Two key areas are considered. Firstly, Chapter 15 examines the role of CRM. CRM is commonly IT driven, but such technical associations should not detract from its key function; retaining customers. Given customer relationships and retention are vital marketing functions; CRM is likely to be increasingly driven from a strategic perspective. Secondly, Chapter 16 considers the ethical dimension associated with marketing. Increasing levels of legislation and consumerism has placed ethics and social responsibility firmly on the corporate agenda.

CHAPTER 15

Customer relationship management

This chapter examines the concept of customer relationship management (CRM), primarily from a strategic perspective. The chapter defines the concept and highlights the importance of CRM being seen as an integrative process which is supported by technology, as opposed to being lead by it. Issues relating to service and lifetime customer value are also examined.

■ Introduction

Most business people are familiar with the term CRM, or to give it its full title – **C**ustomer **R**elationship **M**anagement. However, while there is a degree of familiarity there is no general consensus in relation to what CRM actually entails. In short, CRM differs from organisation to organisation in terms of both definition, application and process. While no universal definition of CRM exists, few would decry the growing importance of the concept. All definitions/versions of CRM have a core guiding principle relating to the effective development and management of relationships with customers. Ultimately, such relationships sustain the key drivers of business success (e.g. customer loyalty). Moreover, the rapid expansion of technology and Internet applications has greatly enhanced the potential of CRM to operate at both strategic and operational levels.

Lets consider some definitions:

.... a comprehensive strategy and process of acquiring, retaining and partnering with selected customers to create superior value for the company and the customer.

(Parvatiyar and Sheth, 2001)

.... strategic use of information, processes, technology and people to manage the customer's relationship with your company across the whole customer life cycle.

(Kincaid, 2003)

... a term for methodologies, technologies and e-commerce capabilities used to manage customer relationships.

(Foss and Stone, 2001)

When the above definitions are amalgamated they provide an overview of CRM. This emphasises that CRM needs to be seen from a strategic perspective and impacts on all aspects of customer interaction, it must generate value and is often IT based.

Kotler (2003) suggests that delivering increasing levels of customer satisfaction is the key to retaining customers. Clearly, organisations would wish to retain their customer base and view CRM as a significant tool to achieve this. Therefore, CRM has a role in the strategic marketing process.

Illustrative Example 15.1

Customer management activities

Football clubs benefit from brand loyalty in a way other businesses could only dream about. The already strong relationship with a club's fan base can be further strengthened via CRM applications. CRM suppliers have been busy developing systems specifically for football clubs. For example, Carnegie Information Systems has supplied CRM to Glasgow Rangers, Tottenham Hotspur and Feyenoord.

CRM systems offer the potential to develop on-line ticket sales and merchandising. Additionally, benefits can include access control via wireless cards, reward schemes and the ability to re-sell tickets.

Source: Financial Times, 2004.

Regardless of the technical issues associated with the process, organisations are likely to undertake the following customer management activities:

1 *Targeting*: Identifying and communicating with potential customers and moving these prospects to becoming actual customers.
2 *Response handling*: Handling sales leads and customer enquiries effectively is fundamental. This normally involves an element of qualifying – determine the nature/likelihood of enquiry becoming a firmer commitment.
3 *Customer induction*: This covers the initial relationship building process with the customer and aims to make them feel valued.
4 *Customer development*: Involves developing the relationship with customers and may involve upgrades, loyalty incentives and analysis of buyer behaviour.
5 *Complaint handling*: Things will, from time-to-time go wrong. Therefore procedures must be in place in relation to problem resolution. Many systems focus on openness and aim to provide a satisfactory resolution.
6 *Retaining customers*: Retaining customers is vital and a basic tenant of relationship marketing. The process aims to establish the reasons for customer loss, plus win back customers who are ready to defect to rivals.

The organisation needs a system (often IT based) which combines the above factors into one integrated system. Having a successful CRM system involves being customer focused across the entire organisation. Ideally, customer service staff should have a single source of customer data which is continually updated, thus avoiding the need for customers to repeatedly provide data. CRM requires senior management support and needs to be 'championed' at board level. Additionally, customer service/marketing staff need to be actively involved in the design of the system. It is not simply an IT project!

Given that the above principles are adhered to, it is possible to develop a system which achieves three major goals. Firstly, reduced marketing can be achieved by making marketing more effective. Retaining existing customers and/or converting a higher degree of prospects into customers is nearly always more efficient than trying to find new customers. Secondly, CRM promotes a better understanding of customer behaviour and motivation. This understanding can translate into loyalty and sales. Finally, it highlights the organisation's internal problems, bottlenecks and weaknesses. For example, management can analyse customer complaints to identify where improvements can be made.

Buttle (2004) provides an interesting perspective in relation to the confusion and misunderstanding surrounding CRM:

- *Misunderstanding 1 CRM is database marketing*
  Jobber (2004) defines database marketing as '... *using individually addressable marketing media and channels to provide information to a target audience, stimulating demand and staying close to customers'*. Given this definition it is clear that CRM has a wider remit.
- *Misunderstanding 2 CRM is a marketing process*
  Leaving CRM to the marketing department would be a mistake. The process requires numerous inputs and should be an integrative vehicle (e.g. production, sales and distribution combined into one seamless customer process) not a functional activity.
- *Misunderstanding 3 CRM is an IT issue*
  Most CRM systems are highly IT dependent, but technology should be viewed as something that enables service delivery and the creation of customer value. The key is how it is used. Buttle (2004) makes the comment; '... *to say that CRM is about IT is like saying gardening is about the spade'*.
- *Misunderstanding 4 CRM is about loyalty schemes*
  While loyalty is very important CRM is bigger than a loyalty scheme. CRM may provide the basis for a scheme (e.g. customer databases) but is more multifaceted.
  Misunderstanding 5 CRM can be implemented by any organisation
  CRM often requires an analytical element (e.g. statistical analysis of data) if the organisation lacks the data and/or request skills to interpret such data, then CRM is unlikely to be successfully implemented. Firstly, an infrastructure needs to be built.

The above points show that CRM is a combination of processes/factors which can be summarised in Figure 15.1.

The combination of databases, marketing information and IT applications permits the development of increasingly sophisticated CRM systems.

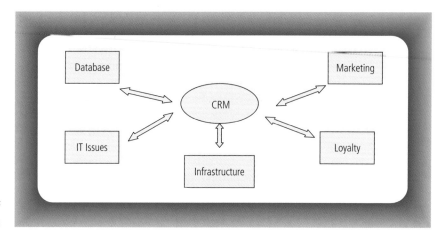

Figure 15.1
Component parts of
a CRM System

These deploy artificial intelligence (AI) as a means to enhance the customer experience. Two such examples are:

1 *Case-based reasoning*
   Case-based reasoning contains a library of past cases. Each contains a problem description and a solution and/or outcome. This knowledge provides an 'expert source' of information relating to customer problems, complaints or inquires. The current problem is matched against similar passed cases. For example, a helpdesk could use this to diagnose problems.
2 *Rule-based expert systems*
   Expert systems attempt to classify knowledge as a series of rules which generates a course of action. This can be simple true/false logic or apply more sophisticated 'fuzzy logic', which considers uncertainty and probability.

Illustrative Example 15.2

Beer and nappies: an urban legend

Allegedly, a major supermarket chain undertook a data mining analysis of customers' buying habits and established a statistically significant link between purchases of beer and purchases of nappies. Speculation suggests that this was due to the fact that fathers buying babies nappies were also likely to purchase beer, as they were going to be spending more time at home as opposed to going to the pub! Subsequently, the retailer placed nappies and beer closer together, generating increased sales of both.

There is no confirmation that this story is true but it has been recounted so many times it has become an urban legend.

Source: Wikipedia.org, 2006.

Database mining has become an important CRM tool. It involves sorting through large amounts of data and picking out relevant information. Data mining has been defined as 'the nontrivial extraction of implicit, previously unknown, and potentially useful information from data' (Frawley et al., 1992) and 'the science of extracting useful information from large data sets or databases' (Hand et al., 2001). Data mining gives information that would not be available otherwise. However, given that the collected data stores and manipulates actual live data relating to individuals, questions relating to privacy, legality and ethics exist.

■ Strategic versus operational CRM

CRM can be conceived as operating on two levels. Firstly, strategic CRM aims to contribute to making the business more market orientated. Essentially, market orientation means understanding and meeting customer needs, with the customer being the focal point of the business. This is an all-embracing process involving corporate culture, staff development and major infrastructure investment (e.g. IT systems). CRM has a key part to play in developing relationships with, and retaining, customers. It is a business philosophy more than a process. Secondly, at an operational level CRM is essentially a process of automating activities and the providing of assistance to customer-facing activities (e.g. a helpdesk) using the technology described above. For example, customers who have not used a service for a while could be e-mailed with a discount offer to encourage use.

Illustrative Example 15.3

Finding customer value

SPSS is a major supplier of statistical and predictive analytical software. Colin Shearer, a Vice President at SPSS states: *'Most companies have always dealt with their customers en masse. You need to identify the small percentage of very high-value customers that are generating 80 to 90 percent of value in the company. You are also interested in the trends, such as customers who are dropping out of the top to become less valuable and take their business elsewhere'.*

Source: Financial Times, 2004.

■ What makes a strong relationship?

The heart of any CRM programme is relationship building. Relationship marketing is a commonly held marketing principle. The process aims to build and enhance strong relationships with customers and other related groups (e.g. suppliers). Subsequently, CRM should assist this fundamental process. From a marketing perspective a relationship has several key drivers, these are summarised in Figure 15.2.

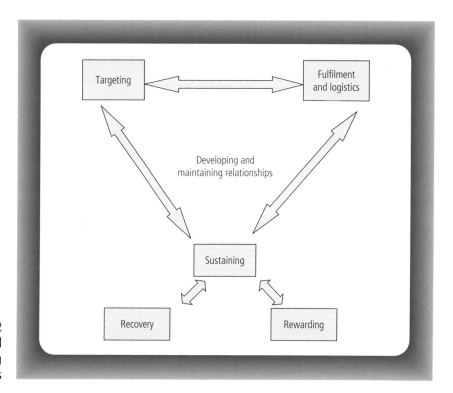

Figure 15.2
Developing and
maintaining
relationships

The above diagram summarises the key elements associated with developing and maintaining customer relationships. CRM needs firstly to target potential customers. *Note*: Not all customers merit attempts to build relationships. The customer may simply be a brand-switcher who continually changes supplier or who generates insufficient revenue to make relationship efforts worthwhile. The basis of targeting is segmentation, with the organisation needing to identify high value, frequent use customers and those most likely to convert from enquiry to purchase. Fulfilment and logistics concerns the meeting of customer expectations, and is often seen as a pillar of relationship marketing. It is important to manage expectations (e.g. do not set unrealistic delivery dates to get an order). Commitments made to customers should be credible and achievable. There is an old saying in sales management – '*Under promise and over deliver!*' It should be noted that fulfilment is the responsibility of the entire organisation, not just customer service staff. Sustaining a relationship is about building trust with a customer. Hence, it is important to have an open, two-way method of communication. For example, customers should be surveyed regularly and encouraged to report problems and errors. Sustainability can be supported by reward schemes, which endeavour to provide added value and encourage customer loyalty. Things will from time-to-time go wrong and it is important to have a recovery scheme. This aims to resolve problems and should have the goals of openness (e.g. Admit an error) and problem resolution. Customer contact staff need to be empowered to resolve issues fairly and effectively.

■ Lifetime customer value

The term lifetime customer value is an important marketing concept. It is used to differentiate between customers and identify those an organisation should concentrate on. Peppers and Rogers (1997) state *'some customers are more equal than others'* and organisations need to learn to *'capitalise on customer differences'*. Customer lifetime value takes into account the potential revenues generated over a specific period of time by a customer. Economic models can be used to establish the value of various customer groups and allocate marketing resources accordingly. Marketers need to predict future purchasing behaviour based on general trends and customer profiles. For example, in the banking sector, banks may be willing to sustain losses on operating children's accounts on the basis that the child may well continue to bank with the provider for their entire lifetime.

■ Summary

CRM is widely used as a means to develop and maintain customer relationships. Its key aim is to manage customer interactions effectively across the entire customer life cycle. Increasingly, it is IT based but should not be IT lead. Technology needs to be a means to deliver factors such as: customer loyalty and service recovery. A CRM system 'bonds' together the organisation and acts as an integrative vehicle. Strong relationships are maintained through: targeting, fulfilment, sustainability, service recovery and reward.

■ References

Buttle, F., *Customer Relationship Management*, Elsevier, Oxford, 2004.

Foss, B. and Stone, M., *Successful Customer Relationship Marketing*, Kogan Page, London, 2001.

Frawley, W., Piatetsky-Shapiro, G. and Matheus, C., Knowledge discovery in databases: an overview. *AI Magazine*, Fall, 1992, 213–228.

Hand, D., Mannila, H. and Smyth, P., *Principles of Data Mining*. MIT Press, Cambridge, MA, 2001.

Jobber, D., *Principles and Practice of Marketing*, 4th edn, McGraw-Hill, London, 2004.

Kincaid, J. W., *Customer Relationship Management: Getting it right!*, Prentice Hall, New Jersey, 2003.

Kotler, P., *Marketing Management*, 11th edn, Prentice-Hall, New Jersey, 2003.

Newing, R. and Shearer, C., Reaping the benefits of customer insight tools, *Financial Times*, 9 June, 2004, 5.

Parvatiyar, A. and Sheth, J. N., Customer relationship management: emerging practice, process and discipline, *Journal of Economic and Social Research*, **3**(2), 2001, 1–34.

Peppers, D. and Rogers, M., *Enterprise One to One: Tools for Competing in the Interactive Age*, Doubleday, New York, 1997.

CHAPTER 16

Marketing ethics and strategic marketing decision making

The ethical stance an organisation takes on an increasingly wide range of activities has been coming under greater and greater scrutiny over the last 20 years. This chapter explores some of the ethical frameworks that can be employed to inform the strategic marketing decisions taken by an organisation. The chapter also explores the way that individuals in an organisation actually go about judging what is a moral decision and highlights some of the problems this poses for companies.

■ Introduction

Marketing practitioners have to take decisions not only based on their individual values and beliefs but also within both the values and beliefs present within their organisation and the wider community. Complex strategic marketing decisions about priorities, values and standards are unlikely to be straightforward. Many of the dilemmas they create are ethical in nature.

The impact of considering any ethical dimensions in making strategic marketing decisions generates a wide spectrum of issues. To some extent an individual's perceptions of the ethical issues involved in a decision are informed by their wider political beliefs about the nature of the market.

■ Political philosophy and ethical decision making

Capitalism can be summarised as being an economic system consisting of privately owned institutions that produce goods and services in competition to each other with the aim of making profits. Milton Friedman was a proponent of a laissez-faire form of capitalism. This proposes an unfettered capitalist system where there is little government intervention on the activities of the organisations in the market. Within this ideological perspective Friedman argued that (1970) 'The social responsibility of business is to increase its profits'. Friedman claimed that the only responsibility an individual had as a corporate manager was to the owners of the organisation. Although he did allow for the fact that some institutions, such as hospitals and schools, may have charitable aims he still advocated that the managers of those institutions only have a responsibility to deliver against that organisation's charitable objectives. However even within this argument Friedman did suggest there are some limited ethical boundaries in that competition should be without deception or fraud (1962).

At the other extreme from Friedman's position is the view that it is unethical for an individual or an organisation to make profits at the expense of another individual's needs. The contention is that the idea that all activities should be based on the concept of a market is based on a capitalist ideology that has only become a dominant perspective since the end of the cold war. In fact some would claim that marketing itself is the manifestation of a capitalist ideology that is ethically challengeable. At one end of the spectrum the argument would be made that nothing should be exchanged on a market basis as it is unethical to distribute products and services on an individual's ability to pay rather than on the basis of their needs. Karl Marx believed that resources should be allocated according to the principle of 'From each according to his ability, to each according to his needs' (1875). Even those who would not hold this unqualified view would have reservations as to whether services, such as, health and education provision should be allocated to individuals on the basis of their ability to pay.

The philosophical stance an individual holds about the nature of the market will influence their perspective as to the ethical issues that have to be considered when making decisions within an organisational context. However some would argue that even within a capitalist perspective of the market there is no ethical conflict for those making decisions in the marketing arena as practicing 'good ethics' should produce 'good business results' in the long term. A former chairman of L'Oreal, Lindsay Owen-Jones stated 'Business ethics are not a restraint that companies impose on themselves for simply moral reasons. Doing business honestly is also the most efficient way to do business long-term' (1989).

This perspective that good ethics is good business stems from the realisation that companies have interactions with a much wider range of stakeholders other than just their shareholders. That even at the basic level of making profits companies have to satisfy such groups as consumers, employees, investors, suppliers, local politicians and others (see Figure 16.1).

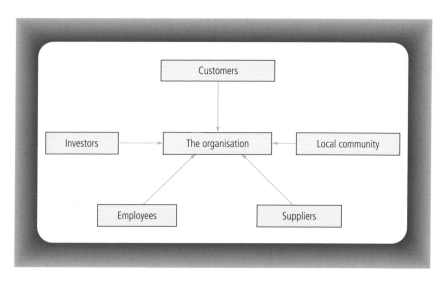

Figure 16.1
Example of
stakeholder groups

It is everyday interactions with these wider groups that create positive brand and corporate images and therefore the profitability of an organisation's activities. There are occasions when the interests of different stakeholder groups diverge and these tensions can become the seedbed of problematic ethical issues for managers to resolve. For instance, consumers may wish to have 24-hour availability 365 days of the year for a product or service that an organisation offers. However, employees may feel that the anti-social work practice that responding to this demand may induce is severely detrimental to their quality of life.

Ideas of corporate social responsibility (CSR) are consistent with a stakeholder perspective on an organisation's activities and the growth of the CSR agenda has acted as a catalyst in making organisations focus on ethics of their marketing decisions.

There are a number of other political philosophies, such as, feminism environmentalism, that inform the ethical perspectives an individual may form on an issue. These may also provide a wider set of stakeholder perspectives surrounding an organisation's activities. Whatever the political philosophy held by an individual they are likely to face ethical dilemmas in their working lives. Certain professions, such as medicine, have always had a very strong ethical dimension to their training and practice. Many have ethical guidelines to which members of the professional group have to adhere. In business and management this tradition of ethical training and standards has been much weaker although in recent times the emphasis on an ethical dimension to degree programmes has been growing in many business schools. The marketing profession has also set some standards but only in limited areas of its activities.

Managers and marketing practitioners are likely to face many ethical dilemmas in the course of their career. How can they start to evaluate how best to make decisions that would withstand scrutiny on ethical grounds. A number of frameworks are available to individuals to employ to assess the issues facing them.

■ Ethical frameworks

Teleological or consequentialist ethical frameworks

Goal-related approaches to ethical decision making are often referred to as teleological approaches. This is derived from the Greek word telos which means 'end', 'purpose' or 'goal'. When considering the ethical stance that should be taken on an issue teleological approaches focus on the end result of an action. Thus it is the final consequences that are the focus of any judgements that are made rather than any of the actions that have been undertaken to achieve ends or goals that have been set. Although there are a number of teleological theories the one that has had the greatest impact is the utilitarianism theory. The basic tenants of this theory where proposed by Jeremy Bentham who suggested that 'The greatest happiness of the greatest number is the foundation of morals and legislation' (1843, p. 142). Applying this theoretical approach would mean that marketing practitioners would need to identify all the beneficial and harmful consequences to each group of stakeholders associated with all the potential alternative actions that it is considering for possible implementation. If there are more beneficiaries than sufferers as a result of a decision then utilitarian theory would suggest that there is justification for considering that decision ethical. One common tool that has developed out of utilitarian theory is cost benefit analysis.

Cost benefit analysis

Cost benefit analysis is a tool which attempts to quantify the value of the costs associated with a project against the value of the benefits created. Thus a new road development would have an economic cost and a value in terms of the economic impact in terms of growth of the local economy that might come about as the result of the new transport route. Cost benefit models would also try to cost other issues such as environmental impacts or road safety.

Cost benefit analysis as a tool highlights two difficulties associated with teleological approaches to ethical decision making. Firstly, both Bentham and John Stuart Mill, who actually coined the term utilitarianism, were writing about individual not organisational actions. The actions that an organisation can undertake are likely to have a significantly wider impact on a far wider group of stakeholders than an individual acting on their own. Of course, organisations are made up of individuals whose actions should be informed by ethical considerations. Nevertheless the complexity of the decisions made by corporations can make it extremely difficult for them to forecast all the potential consequences on all the possible affected parties of a proposed course of action.

The second difficulty with the utilitarian approach is what about the minority groups who have been disadvantaged for the benefits of the majority? In contemporary society many would assert that these minority groups have rights that are being ignored. However the idea of rights does not flow out of teleological theories of ethics but out of deontological theories which will be discussed in the next section. To summarize teleological theories of ethics are entirely focused on outcomes and any other considerations carry no weight.

Deontological ethical frameworks

The term deontological is derived from the Greek word deon which means 'duty'. From a deontological perspective the judgements that have to be made in deciding whether an action is ethical focuses on the individuals duty in a situation not on the consequences of the decision itself. Duty-based ethical frameworks focus on broad abstract principles such as honesty, fairness, compassion, justice, respect and rights. Therefore a decision may be ethical if the individual has acted honestly even if a majority of stake-holders are adversely affected by the outcome. A key concept that has developed out of this theoretical approach is the idea of rights. The concept of rights has its origins in the classical Greek idea of 'natural rights' that develop out of the concept of 'natural law'.

Rights can be both positive or negative in nature. A positive right would be a right to health and safety at work. Negative rights would be exemplified by limitations on organisations' activities due to an individual's right to privacy. Rights of different groups can come into conflict with each other. The rights of a company to pursue profit could clash with the rights of the individual to live in a healthy environment. Rights and duties are also related. When the rights of one group are given pre-eminence by society it tends to result in other groups having a duty to respect those rights. Employees are deemed to have a right to experience a safe and healthy work environment therefore organisations have a duty to protect their workers from hazardous situations.

Given that there are many different and potentially competing rights how does an individual decide which right or duty is the correct one to follow? According to Kant one duty took precedence over all others. Kant called this the 'categorical imperative' which means the 'unconditional principle'. Kant proposed 'unconditional principle' is that individuals should 'Act as if the maxim of thy action were to become by thy will a universal law of nature' (1785).

According to Kant an individuals actions are acceptable only if they could be judged to be adopted as a universal principle that everyone should follow. On this basis breaking one's word to someone else would only be acceptable if it was accepted as a universal principle that everyone could follow. If this was deemed to be an acceptable universal principle then obviously giving one's word to someone would no longer have any value.

There are a number of issues that arise from deontological approaches. Firstly, they do not take into account the consequences of an action. Kant himself actually made the argument that truth telling should be regarded as a universal principle to be followed even if this meant an innocent person might die as a result. Secondly, which right, duty or principle takes precedence in any particular situation? Many current ethical debates are centred on this issue. The debate surrounding abortion is centred on which should have precedence; the rights of the woman or the rights of the unborn child.

Virtue ethical frameworks

Virtue ethics are concerned with integrity of the individual making a decision rather than the decision itself. This approach to ethical thinking is associated with Aristotle. Virtue according to Aristotle is exhibited in an individual's behaviour as judged by the wider community in which they live. The aim should be for the individual to live a virtuous life as judged by his peers.

This approach is focused on the individual and it is concerned with what you are, not about what you do, its about being not doing. Aristotle saw virtues as means by which an individual could reach the goal of achieving their full potential. Therefore although there is a goal it is an internal goal. The consequences to the individual of not acting ethically are that they will have failed in achieving the goal of having lived a virtuous life. This is unlike the teleological approaches to ethics which focus on external goals. Aristotle agreed with Plato's proposition of four virtues, wisdom, courage, self-control in physical pleasures and justice. However, Aristotle saw these as being virtues associated with a good life and suggested additional virtues that were associated with a civilised life. These were concepts of patience, amiability, sincerity, right ambition, magnanimity, wittiness, liberality and munificence. All these virtues were judged as being at the mean between two vices at the two extreme ends of the scale. For instance courage would be judged to be found at the mean between the vice of cowardice at one end and rashness at the other. Aristotle sees justice as a pre-eminent virtue although his definition of justice is rather vague. He states that 'to do injustice is to have more than one ought, and to suffer it is to have less than one ought and justice is the mean between injustice and suffering it' (1976, p. 78).

Aristotle's proposed virtues have to be seen as growing out of the peer group that would make a judgement as to an individual's character. They are a product of the male dominated society and of the wealthy elite within which Aristotle circulated. It would therefore be difficult for women or the poor to achieve the ideal character as proposed by Aristotle.

However in the last 15 years writers have suggested that a virtue-based approach to ethics may offer an alternative to the teleological and deontological approaches for considering ethical behaviour within organisations. Soloman (1993) suggests that an alternative is to focus on the character of the individuals working within an organisation. He goes on to suggest that honesty, fairness, trust and toughness are the key virtues for managers in contemporary organisations. Soloman envisages toughness in terms of having the robustness to have a strategy and seeing through its implementation.

The implication of Gilligan's (1982) research is that a virtue based on care could also be considered. This would have care/wisdom as the mean between the two vices of inflexibly following rules and appeasement (see next section on moral reasoning for more detail on the concept of care).

Illustrative Example 16.1

UK clothing retailers

In 2005 Ethical Consumer magazine released the results of a survey it had undertaken on UK clothing retailers. They rated companies based on an evaluation of workers rights and whether they traded with countries that were judged to have oppressive regimes. At that time, the findings were that none of the UK's top 27 clothing retailers could be recommended as places in which someone who wished themselves to be regarded as an undeniably ethical consumer could shop.

■ Moral reasoning

There are, therefore, a number of frameworks that individuals and organisations could employ to help ensure that the strategic marketing decisions they are concerned with are ethical. However, it is the way individuals think about ethics and decision making that will actually affect whether organisations make ethical decisions rather than the availability of theoretical frameworks that could be employed. Kohlberg (1976) decided to study how individuals actually decide what is morally right and developed a moral reasoning theory that has profound implications for aspects of strategic marketing decisions. Kohlberg undertook a longitudinal study of 58 American boys between the ages of 10 to 16 years interviewing them every 3 years over a 12-year period. As a result of this study Kohlberg proposed that there were three stages that an individual could possibly progress through in terms of their cognitive moral development and within each of these stages were two sub-divisions. These stages and sub-divisions are as follows:

1 *The pre-conventional stage*: At this stage an individual perceives rules to be external in nature and imposed by an external force. Decisions are therefore made in terms of the rewards or punishments that the individual may receive as a result. Within this stage there are two sub-divisions:
   ● *Obedience and punishment orientation*: At this level an individual will abide by the normal standards of behaviour in order to avoid punishment. An individual at this level will therefore comply with management instructions without question.
   ● *Instrumental purpose and exchange*: An individual at this level of moral development will make decisions based on rewards that might come to them as a result. In organisational terms they will make decisions based on what the possible gain to them might be in terms of potential increases in salary, promotion or other aspects of status.
2 *The conventional stage*: At this stage an individual will act in accordance with the norms and expectations of society or particular social groups to which they belong. Within this stage there are two sub-divisions:
   ● *Interpersonal accord, conformity, mutual expectations*: Individuals at this level will act in accordance with the norms and expectations of those social groups close to them, such as, family, friends or work colleagues. This is done in order to be socially accepted by the group not because they perceive the group norms and expectations as ethically correct. In this situation an individual may decide not to contradict managers in their organisation because they may loose the social approval of their superior and other colleagues.
   ● *Social accord and system maintenance*: At this level the individual perspective takes into consideration wider society. Moral decisions are seen in terms of abiding by rules and regulations because this is of benefit to both themselves and the wider society. At an organisational level individuals at this stage could follow the company's rules and

procedures but they may also refer to their professional body's code of practice or the wider society's institutional laws and regulations.

3 *The post-conventional stage*: At this stage individuals will reflect upon and question the moral principles to which they adhere. Within this stage there are two sub-divisions:

- *Social contract and individual rights*: At this level an individual while generally following the social rules and regulations of society, may begin to challenge aspects of them and consider whether laws should be changed to the benefit of everyone. Within an organisational context individuals at this level may begin to challenge and suggest changes to the company's policies and decisions.
- *Universal ethical principles*: At this level an individual makes moral decisions based on universal principles. They will see their individual responsibility to be beyond wider social standards and are likely to take a principled stand on an issue, mainly seen in terms of justice, where they feel an unethical decision has been made in the face of potentially adverse social consequences to them as an individual.

Kohlberg argued that individuals could move up through these stages and their sub-divisions one level at a time. Individuals move a level when they see a contradiction between their current reasoning level and the one above.

This theory is focused on the reasoning that the individual undertakes not the decision that is made or its final outcome. What is important about this theory is that only those individuals at post-conventional stage are likely to think in terms of universal principles or theory discussed early in this chapter. Kohlberg, however, suggested that most American adults' moral reasoning was at the conventional level. That is, it is highly influenced by the immediate and wider social environment within which they find themselves.

Gilligan (1982) criticised Kohlberg's theory on the basis that his study had concentrated purely on boys but generalised the findings to all adults. In her research Gilligan's findings supported Kohlberg's focus on justice at the post-conventional stage for males but found these were not fully reflected in females who focused on issues both in terms of justice and in terms of care. This concept of care came out of females' socialisation in the family where mothers in particular take on a role encouraging children to seek compromises that keep all members of the family happy. Her contention is that females tend to wish to resolve conflict in a way that leaves long-term relationships intact rather than creating fractured relationships through the one-off implementation of a decision based on a concept of justice.

The implications of Kohlberg's theory for organisations are quite profound. The majority of staff in an organisation are going to be primarily influenced by internal and external social factors in judging the ethics of a decision. In Chapter 6 we have already explored groupthink, one type of problem relating to the internal social environment in an organisation, and its impact on futures forecasting. Here the social dynamic within an organisation can impinge on the ability of individuals to evaluate the ethics of a course of action. If the senior management of an organisation does not consciously try and develop a company culture that encourages open ethical debate then the majority of staff will go along with decisions without challenging them. Thus decisions will be implemented that could be challenged if seen from the perspective of someone from outside the immediate social situation within the company. Even more difficult for organisations is that if staff are given training in ethics then the individuals concerned may just adhere to whatever stance is advocated by that training rather than being prepared to challenge any dominate perspective.

One way to try and ensure that strategic marketing decisions are not made that are intrinsically poor, as well as potentially commercially damaging, is to put in place formal mechanisms to consider those decisions from the perspective of each of the organisation's wider stakeholder groups.

■ References

Aristotle, *The Ethics of Aristotle*, translated by J. A. K. Thompson, Penguin, New York, 1976.

Bentham, J., Extracts from Bentham's Commonplace Book, in *The Works of Jeremy Bentham*, published under the superintendence of John Bowring, Vol. X, Tait, Edinburgh, 1843, p. 142.

Gilligan, C., *In a Different Voice: Psychological Theory and Women's Development*, Harvard University Press, Cambridge, MA, 1982.

Friedman, M., *Capitalism and Freedom*, University of Chicago Press, Chicago, 1962.

Friedman, M., The social responsibility of business is to increase profits, *The New York Times Magazine*, 13 September, 1970.

Kant, I., *Fundamental Principles of the Metaphysic of Morals*, translated by Thomas Kingsmill Abbott, 1785.

Kohlberg, L., Moral Stages and Moralization: The Cognitive-Development approach, in Lickona, T. (ed.), *Moral Development and Behaviour: Theory, Research and Social Issues*, Holt, Rhinehart and Winston, New York, 1976.

Marx, K., *Critique of the Gotha Programme*, Marginal notes to the program of the German Worker's Party, April–May, 1875.

Owen-Jones, L., Interview with Lindsay Owen-Jones, *The Mckinsey Quarterly*, Autumn, 1989, p. 41.

Soloman, R. C., *Ethics and Excellence: Cooperation and Integrity in Business*, Oxford University Press, Oxford, 1993.

■ Further reading

Fisher, C. and Lovell, A., *Business Ethics and Values*, Prentice Hall, London, 2003.

Trevino, L. K. and Nelson, A. N., *Managing Business Ethics*, 3rd edn, Wiley, New York, 2004.

PART 5

Teaching
Strategic
Marketing

Many approaches exist in relation to teaching marketing from a strategic perspective. No one method offers a panacea, all have strengths and weakness. Tutors, students and practitioners all have many and varied ways of addressing issues related to teaching and learning. The author offers a problem-based learning (PBL) approach as one perspective. Experience suggests that this lends itself to teaching strategic marketing. PBL allows students to develop the correct balance of academic analysis and transferable skills, such as teamwork. Tutors should note that the companion website to this book will provide additional examples and support in relation to PBL as a teaching strategy.

CHAPTER 17

Problem-based learning

This chapter examines how problem-based learning (PLB) can provide a unique approach to teaching strategic marketing. As a teaching/learning vehicle PLB enables the learner to acquire critical subject knowledge whilst developing problem-solving proficiencies, becoming a self-directed learner and fostering team working skills. Problems act as a stimulus or focus for gaining and synthesising knowledge. It is felt, the nature of PBL-based work closely resembles, in both nature and structure, the work undertaken by industry professionals engaged in strategic marketing projects. Subsequently, PBL is considered to be a highly appropriate teaching mechanism.

This chapter introduces the PBL concept, outlines its advantages and provides a generalised approach to its application in relation to strategic marketing teaching. It can be thought of as an alternative to the traditional 'case study'-based approaches advocated by many marketing texts.

■ What is problem-based learning?

Numerous definitions of problem-based learning (PBL) abound. Bould and Feletti (1991) define PBL as: *'a way of constructing and teaching courses using problems as the stimulus and focus for student activity'*. The process is essentially simple – students work in groups to solve unstructured problems relevant to their field of study. They are required to define the problem, identify, synthesis and analyse information and generate solutions. The process is not simply adding problem-related tutorials to otherwise traditionally taught material. Tutors replace traditional lectures with problem-based scenarios supplemented with advice, supplementary reading and the development of generic problem-solving skills. The process means both tutor and students perceive the subject/curriculum as focused on problems relating to professional practice. Bligh (1995) summarises the process as a curriculum-based approach where learning unfolds through the application of knowledge and skills to the solution of real world problems.

The characteristics of PBL can be summarised as follows:

1 Students work in small groups with the lecturer acting as a facilitator, who presents a problem to solve as opposed to more traditional direct teaching.
2 The problem(s) presented are unstructured and complex in nature, require group co-operation to resolve and typically have any number of correct answers.
3 Learning is student centred and structured around both the problem and the process of problem resolution.

Table 17.1 summarises PBL in comparison to traditional teaching strategies.

Table 17.1 PBL versus traditional lecturing

Traditional lecturing	Problem-based learning
Teacher or expert centred	Student/learner centred
Teaching as transmission	Teaching as facilitating
Learning as receiving	Learning as constructing
Highly structured approach	Unstructured/flexible approach

Source: Samford University (2003)

Table 17.1 shows the PBL approach advocates moving from learning being centred around the lecturer as an expert transmitting information for learners to receive, to a learner focused environment where students are required to source, evaluate and apply information within the context of a specific problem. The benefits claimed for PBL are:

1 Given that PBL is essentially a form of experiential learning (Savin-Baden, 2000) it has advantages over more passive forms of learning (such as listening to lectures) in as much as it engages the learner and promotes the active use of the knowledge acquired.

2 PBL promotes the development of 'transferable' skills such as team-work, communication and data acquisition.

3 Students are motivated through the real life problems used in the learning.

4 Research (Smith, 2005) suggests that PBL learners display greater knowledge retention and recall.

However, PBL is not a panacea. The process does have some acknowledged limitations, such as: (i) it denotes a significant culture shift, both for tutors and students, (ii) the development and restructuring of courses is time consuming and (iii) it is more difficult to implement in certain types/level of programme.

In summary, PBL takes the following format. Working in small groups, students are presented with a problem (e.g. scenario, news item or video). It is important that the students do not have sufficient prior knowledge to resolve the problem immediately. The groups, with tutor support, are required to define the problem, identify their information/data requirements and propose/evaluate solutions. Tasks are normally assigned to group members, with the group reconvening to present a solution which encompasses the new knowledge they have learned. Clearly, problem design/selection is critical to the success of the process (see later).

The question is often asked: Is not PBL just the same as using case study-based teaching? It is acknowledged the methods are similar, but they differ in respect to the presentation of the problem. Case study approaches normally present the participants with specific questions (e.g. Apply the Ansoff matrix to …) which guide the learner. Additionally, cases are likely to contain relevant resource material (e.g. financial information, sales trends, customer feedback) whereas PBL provides only the problem, with participants required to identify the key questions and resources needed to generate a solution. *Note*: A general brief containing 'open' questions is often given to guide the learner. In other words the learner(s) must define the problem. It should be noted that PBL represents a continuum as opposed to stand-alone strategy. It could be blended into a programme of study and used to teach specific parts of the curriculum or provide the basis for an entire course of study.

■ Applicability of PBL to strategic marketing

The authors feel that PBL is particularly suited to teaching a strategic marketing curriculum for a number of reasons. Firstly, the process emulates the work typically undertaken by marketing managers in industry. For example, they are required to work with incomplete data, define problems and communication solutions. Therefore, the process contributes to the development of professional marketers. Secondly, participants are normally required to assimilate knowledge from a variety of disciplines and sources (e.g. financial, production) into an integrated solution. Such actions are strategic in nature. Thirdly, as stated above, the PBL process promotes the acquisition of transferable skills applicable to both marketing and general business tasks. Finally, marketing as a subject discipline, offers a wealth of problems and scenarios readily converted into appropriate teaching material. *Note*: Examples are given in the support material available with this text.

■ Writing effective PBL problems

The entire learning process hangs on the ability of the tutor to develop an effective problem. It goes without saying that PBL requires the tutor to make numerous changes to their delivery approach, but without giving careful thought to how a problem is devised the entire venture is likely to fail. So, what makes a problem suitable for a PBL approach? Duch (2001) highlights five traits commonly associated with effective PBL problems:

1 The scenario should engage the learner and relate to 'real world' situations. This will develop the learner's interest and maintain motivation.
2 Problems promote the ability to make decisions based on rational, informed judgement supported by learning resources such as theory and data. Ideally, the problems should generate multiple hypotheses.
3 Problem resolution requires team effort.
4 The initial problem needs to be open-ended, incorporate a diverse range of elements and build on previous knowledge.
5 The process should develop higher order skills (e.g. synthesis and evaluation) and incorporate programme objectives.

PBL requires that learners work in groups, learn from/support other group members and benefits from diverse perceptions and shared knowledge. Hence, the problem must be challenging, complex and lend itself to multiple solutions. An example is given later in this chapter, with additional materials available in tutor support materials. A well-designed PBL task encourages learners to become information seekers as opposed to the tutor being the information provider.

■ PBL tasks in the classroom

Normally, PBL requires the class to be organised into groups of 4 or 5. These groups work independently of other groups, with students assuming responsibility for acquiring and synthesising the information required to resolve the given problem. The group must engage in collaborative learning with support from a tutor. The tutor operates as facilitator as opposed to being the 'expert'. Typically, the tutor answers questions, suggests possible approaches (e.g. brainstorming) to the problem and clarifies issues. A cyclical process is advocated as a means for groups to analyse and resolve the given problem (see Figure 17.1). Firstly, the problem is presented to the students. The group then meets to discuss the issues, identify required tasks, information needs, etc. and allocate assignments to individuals. During the research phase, individuals undertake their assigned tasks, which may include summarising journal articles, obtaining/tabulating data, conducting Internet searches. Group members then report back to assimilate and review their findings. The process is then repeated until the group is satisfied a feasible solution has been found. Findings are then presented to the tutor. This may/may not form the basis of an assessment. Sherwood (2004) suggests that tutors consider PBL from both a social and physical dimension. The social aspects involve considering exactly who will participate and how relationships will develop within the working group. The physical dimension consists of items such as workspace and technological support.

■ Example of PBL for strategic marketing

The following example provides an illustration of how a PBL problem can be framed. Support material related to this problem is provided in the instructors resource pack available from the publisher.

PBL example: Burberry

Burberry, the UK-based designer brand manufacturing clothing and other apparel, recently celebrated its 150 year anniversary. The history of the company dates back to 1856, when Thomas Burberry, a former apprentice

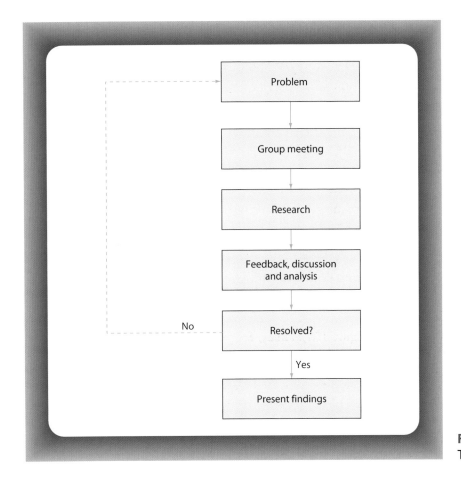

Figure 17.1
The PBL process

Draper, opened a shop in Basingstoke. By 1870 the business had established a reputation for developing outdoor attire, and 1880 saw Thomas Burberry invent a gabardine fabric which was hardwearing and waterproof. The famous Burberry check was first used in 1924 as a lining for the company's trench coat. The check now holds 'iconic' fashion status, with associated products worn by Humphrey Bogart in '*Casablanca*' and Audrey Hepburn in '*Breakfast at Tiffany's*'.

Today the brand has a global presence, with outlets all over the world. It boasts an impressive range of merchandise including apparel, eyewear and golf-related products. Burberry views the brand as: '… *a luxury brand with distinctive British sensibility, strong international recognition and differentiated brand values that resonate across a multi-generational and dual-gender audience*'. (*Source*: www. burberryplc.com.)

Required

The success of Burberry, or any brand for that matter, depends on effectively transforming the brand vision into reality. Comment on actions the company has taken to do this, the financial implications of such actions and provide an outline of your recommendations for the future. Support your analysis by making reference to two relevant academic journal articles.

■ References

Bligh, J., Problem-based learning in medicine, *Post-Graduate Medical Journal*, **71**(8), 1995, 323–326.

Bould, D. and Feletti, G., *The Challenge of Problem-Based Learning*, 2nd edn, Kogan Page, London, 1997.

Duch, B., *The Power of Problem-Based Learning*, Stylus Publishing, Sterling, VA, 2001.

Samford University, www.samford.edu/pbl, 2003.

Savin-Baden, M., *Problem-Based Learning in Higher Education*, Open University Press, Buckingham, 2000.

Sherwood, A. L., Problem-based learning in management education: a framework for designing context, *Journal of Management Education*, **28**(5), 2004, 237–557.

Smith, G. F., Problem-based learning: can it improve managerial thinking? *Journal of Management Education*, **29**(2), 2005, 357–378.

Index